# Robespierre

# PROFILES IN **POWER**

*General Editor: Keith Robbins*

# Robespierre

John Hardman

Longman

*An imprint of* **Pearson Education**

Harlow, England · London · New York · Reading, Massachusetts · San Francisco
Toronto · Don Mills, Ontario · Sydney · Tokyo · Singapore · Hong Kong · Seoul
Taipei · Cape Town · Madrid · Mexico City · Amsterdam · Munich · Paris · Milan

**Pearson Education Limited**
Edinburgh Gate
Harlow
Essex CM20 2JE
England

and Associated Companies around the world

*Visit us on the World Wide Web at:*
*www.pearsoneduc.com*

First published 1999

ISBN 0 582 43755 5

*British Library Cataloguing-in-Publication Data*
A catalogue record for this book can be obtained from the British Library

*Library of Congress Cataloging-in-Publication Data*
A catalog record for this book can be obtained from the Library of
Congress

10 9 8 7 6 5 4 3 2 1
04 03 02 01

Produced by Pearson Education Asia Pte Ltd.,
Printed in Singapore

. . . . .

# FIGURE AND MAPS

# PREFACE

This book is a rather unconventional treatment of Robespierre, at least in Part Two, dealing with Robespierre's brief – one year to the day – period in government. The focus is on Robespierre at his desk rather than Robespierre at the rostrum. The conventional approach is to look at Robespierre's set-piece speeches, but apart from the fact that they are highly allusive and almost incomprehensible (in places), even to the expert, it is also very difficult to demonstrate how a two-hour speech about republican virtue translated into action. Robespierre made a speech and a hundred heads fell? No. What happened was that Robespierre issued directives to arrest people, through his police bureau and through his protégé Herman, effectively the head of the civil service. Also, there was no great oratory in Robespierre's last year because parliament was itself terrified. If you want oratory, turn to the early period of the Revolution. Unfortunately Robespierre was a minor character then, whose speeches were mocked for their inordinate length and jargon, as they would have been in 1793/94 if people hadn't been so scared of him. After all, would he have been allowed to finish his appallingly self-indulgent two-hour last speech if his audience had not been craning their necks to discover if they were on his proscription list?

Moreover, during his period in power Robespierre was little in the public gaze, finally becoming almost a total recluse, addressing the Convention only once in the last two months of his life. Robespierre's power was mediated through a faction which he built up *pari passu* with the increase in his patronage. This being the case, I have devoted considerable sections to the constituents of this faction. Herman, Payan who governed

Paris, Hanriot who controlled its armed forces, the circle of Maurice Duplay, with whom he lodged, a group of Lyon ex-patriots. Such men were Robespierre's arms and legs, eyes and ears.

During this period there was very little constructive legislation and government consisted almost exclusively in repression. Robespierre was a police boss and France a police state. Much of what he did was trivial (except to those arrested): deciding, for example, whether a man who cut down a tree of liberty was doing it for the timber or to bring about the counter-revolution. This book concentrates on close-ups more than the big picture because he did; and because in doing so he made mistakes which contributed to his fall. There was also a price to pay for having a faction, for these men developed their own agenda: the Lyon group, for example, involved him in a fatal struggle with Fouché, who was to become a far greater policeman than he; Payan involved him in an armed insurrection against parliament.

Nearly every surviving piece that Robespierre wrote has been published, the exception being his directives to the police bureau which are in the Archives Nationales. I have therefore decided to minimize footnotes by referring to the two main published collections of material within round brackets in the text. These are the ten volumes of his *Oeuvres*, published by the Société des Études robespierristes, 1912–67, and the three volumes of *Papiers inédits trouvés chez Robespierre, Saint-Just, Payan etc.*, 1828. To distinguish between the two collections, the volumes of the *Oeuvres* will be given in Arabic numerals followed by the page, for example (10, 42), and the volumes of the *Papiers inédits* will be given in Roman numerals, for example (II, 288). In addition, references to Robespierre's police directives will be given by date in the text, since they all have the same code: Archives Nationales F7 4437. I have also employed throughout the text the conventional abbreviations of the *Comité de salut public* and the *Comité de sécurité général* to CSP and CSG respectively.

I have adopted as my guide through the maze of Revolutionary politics an early historian of the Revolution, John Wilson Croker, whose essay on Robespierre first appeared in the *Quarterly Review* in 1835. Croker was an arch-Tory junior minister (villified as Rigby in Disraeli's *Coningsby*). He was an arch-reactionary who compared the massacre of the Champ de Mars to the Peterloo riots and approved of both. Yet he is fair to Robespierre, his prejudice being dissolved by his saturation in the printed primary sources, and he lays claim to being the first 'scientific' historian of the Revolution. His work still possesses an arresting freshness and originality.

The more or less 'contemporary' painting by Tassaert of the fall of
Robespierre, reproduced on the cover of this book, was inevitably
painted after the event. Though dramatic, it has limited authority
as a historical record of the session of the Convention on 9th
Thermidor (27 July 1794) that ended so violently. The pen-and-ink
sketch of Robespierre reproduced here, however, was drawn from
life (by P. Grandmaison) in the chamber on 9th Thermidor itself,
only a little while before Robespierre's arrest. He was executed the
following day.

# PART ONE

# OPPOSITION

# Chapter 1

# THE FIRST THIRTY YEARS

. . .

## SITUATION OF FRANCE AT ROBESPIERRE'S BIRTH

Maximilien François Marie Isidore de Robespierre was born in Arras, the capital of the northern province of Artois, on 6 May 1758, into a modest and declining legal family. Shortly before his birth, in November 1757, at the battle of Rossbach, a French army had been destroyed by Frederick the Great of Prussia. The defeat was the worst for France since Agincourt and led to decades of military reform which only served to lower morale. In 1759, a year after Robespierre's birth, France suffered defeats still greater overseas at the hands of Frederick's ally and France's competitor for empire, Britain. France's losses included India, Canada, and some immensely profitable West Indian sugar islands. 1759 was Britain's *annus mirabilis* but France's *annus horribilis.* The sense of national decline under Louis XV was intensified in 1772 when Russia, Prussia and Austria seized territory from one of France's oldest allies in the first partition of Poland. Russia and Prussia and indeed Britain had recently acceded to the ranks of the Great Powers, to the obvious disadvantage of France and Austria, who in consequence replaced their centuries-old enmity in 1756 with an uneasy alliance.

Louis XVI succeeded his grandfather in 1774 and temporarily reversed the decline by assisting Britain's American colonies to win their independence, which they did in 1782. But it was at enormous financial cost and when Prussia and Britain invaded Holland in 1787 and ousted the pro-French government, Louis did not have the funds to stop them. Frenchmen have always cared about *gloire* but foreign policy was the essential *métier* of a king and the failures of the later Bourbons in this field played a part in the collapse of their regime.

France was a rich country but the period of economic expansion under Louis XV, when the population had increased from 20 to 26 million, was coming to an end when Robespierre was born. France still had far greater resources than Britain but her political system did not allow her to mobilize them. France was an 'absolute' monarchy; that is to say that her national representative institution, the Estates-General, was in abeyance, having last been summoned in 1614. (The meeting of the Estates-General in 1789 marked the start of the French Revolution.) The king proclaimed his legislative self-sufficiency but, for reasons of propaganda, registered his edicts in 13 appeal courts called *parlements* (the one in Artois, before which Robespierre would plead, was called the Conseil d'Artois). But, again at about the time of Robespierre's birth, the *parlements* began refusing to register the king's edicts, particularly financial ones.

Unlike the British Parliament, in which the mercantile interest was strong, the *parlements*, consisting of landowning, noble judges, had no interest in paying for an overseas war to benefit the merchants of Bordeaux. And it was noble landowners who were being asked to foot the bill: it was accepted that the peasants could not pay any more and it was administratively difficult to tax the towns. But the noble riposte was increasingly that of France's American allies: 'no taxation without representation', via the Estates-General. And Louis XVI himself may have come to realize that with the Estates, though he would cease to be an absolute monarch, at least he would have the money to conduct a foreign policy which, as I have said, was his main function.

Before that happened, however, in 1771, Louis XV brutally suppressed the main *parlement*, the Parlement de Paris, exiled its members to remote areas and replaced it with a puppet body, dubbed the 'Parlement Maupeou' after Chancellor Maupeou the architect of the coup, or as it was called at the time the 'revolution of 1771'. The ease with which the old king had destroyed the Parlement led many Frenchmen to consider they were ruled not by a Christian king but by an oriental or at least Russian-style despot. They expected troops to help in the collection of taxes, believed to be the hallmark of such regimes. A stable system which had endured for hundreds of years (it was believed) had been knocked down like a house of cards. The king died detested, of small pox; it was said he had contracted it from a prostitute. A society with lax morals, at least in its upper reaches, hypocritically censured his sexual excesses. A canon of Notre Dame relates that when Louis had been ill in 1744 6,000 candles had been lit for his recovery, which they had achieved. In 1774 there were only three candles and they had no effect.

Louis XVI recalled the exiled Parlement because, as he said, he 'wanted to be popular'. But this only gave the regime the worst of both worlds. Maupeou's 'revolution' had created a feeling of impermanence but it had allowed the king's ministers to start reforming the abuses of the regime – making the nobility pay a fairer share of taxation (though they were still exempt from the main peasant tax, the *taille*), making justice cheaper and swifter. Maupeou's secretary, Lebrun, was working on a codification of French law which 30 years later, when Bonaparte was first and Lebrun second consul, became the Code Napoléon. The restored Parlement blocked most of Louis XVI's reforms but its recall did little to alleviate the sense of instability.

.   .   .

## ROBESPIERRE'S ANCESTRY AND FAMILY

Robespierre, then, was born into a declining family in a declining country. The Robespierres' finances were as precarious as the king's. Maximilien was the eldest child of another Maximilien, a barrister, who had married Jacqueline Carraut four months before his son's birth. Jacqueline was the daughter of a brewer and the Robespierres considered the match something of a *mésalliance* – in England the disapproval would have come from the other side. The Robespierre family had enjoyed centuries of respectable bourgeois obscurity but had made no further progress since emerging from the ranks of the peasantry in the fifteenth century. Robespierre's great-great uncle had registered a coat of arms in 1696,[1] but whereas in Britain this would have signalled the entry of the family into the gentry, in France it had little legal significance; as did the use of the particle 'de', which anyone could use.

The thing that mattered in the *ancien régime* was entry into the nobility, a legal category which conferred prestige and fiscal privilege. There were some 250,000 nobles in France, which made them akin to the British gentry rather than the peerage. However, unlike in Britain, the border between the upper bourgeoisie and the gentry was not fluid but legally defined and difficult (and increasingly difficult) to cross. The resentment caused by this difficulty was one of the main causes of the Revolution. 'Living nobly', that is like a gentleman, which the Robespierres probably and Maximilien certainly did, was not sufficient; the gulf between them and those, otherwise indistinguishable, who had crossed the technical frontier into the *noblesse* was vast. And yet the gulf could be leapt and many leapt it; and many were in mid-flight when the Revolution broke out in 1789 and nobility was abolished in 1790.

There were two main methods of entering the nobility, the quick way and the slow way. The quick way was to buy the sinecure office of *secrétaire du roi* for the equivalent of £10,000. The slow way was via an ascending ladder of legal offices which culminated in the desired object of *noblesse*. Many of those Robespierre would encounter in the Revolution had travelled some way on this journey, for example Danton and Joseph Payan, whom Robespierre, at the height of his power, had appointed 'minister for propaganda'. In 1787 Danton bought the office of *avocat aux Conseils du roi* for the equivalent of £3,500;[2] this did not confer nobility but preparing cases for the Conseil d'État was prestigious and was only one step away from the offices that did – such as that of *conseiller* in the Chambre des Comptes of Grenoble which Joseph Payan acquired.

In contrast with the Dantons and the Payans, the Robespierres were stagnating and Robespierre's own legal career did nothing to reverse the process. The law was *the* way to attain nobility in the *ancien régime*, but it had to be used as a ladder of ascent. And it is also worth making the distinction between those who, like Danton and Payan, would have arrived anyway with or without the help of the Revolution, and those like Robespierre who would not. Robespierre himself came to believe that those to whom the Revolution had given most must give it back most.

In 1760 Maximilien was joined by a sister, Charlotte, who survived to provide 'ghosted' memoirs of her brother, and in 1763 by Augustin, who through the influence of his elder brother became an 'MP' in 1793. In 1765 their mother died after giving birth to a stillborn child; shortly afterwards their father absconded, though he returned at intervals before dying in 1777 at Munich.[3] Robespierre and Augustin were brought up by their grandfather, the brewer. At eight Maximilien went to the well-endowed Collège d'Arras and at eleven he won one of the Collège's four scholarships to the Collège Louis-le-Grand in Paris.

. . .

## LOUIS-LE-GRAND

Louis-le-Grand was the equivalent of a modern secondary school and university rolled into one. So Robespierre spent seven years of general studies before specializing in law for the last three. He went home for the vacations. Louis-le-Grand was one of the most prestigious educational establishments in France, the French Eton, where scholarship boys such as Maximilien rubbed shoulders with the sons of dukes and ministers. Unlike Eton there was no sense of equality between all those privileged to be there. But there were plenty of '*roturiers*' (commoners) like Robespierre, including future colleagues Camille Desmoulins and Fréron. Fréron was later to depict Robespierre as a moody, misanthropic loner. But he developed a deep friendship with Camille Desmoulins, a boy with a stutter, two years younger than Maximilien.

Robespierre worked hard at his studies and with success – most years he won a prize for classics, though it was usually a second prize. Latin was his forte and he was known as the 'Roman'. In 1775 he was chosen to read a Latin oration to Louis XVI on his return from the coronation at Rheims. Louis and Marie-Antoinette did not get out of their carriage but Louis, a keen Latinist himself, would have understood the oration. It is hard to overemphasize the influence of classical, and especially Roman history on the course of the Revolution. It was the staple of secondary education and it provided the only parallel of a republican regime in a large country.

In July 1780 Robespierre graduated as a Bachelor of Law and in the following May received his licence to practice. In June 1781 Louis-le-Grand awarded him 600 livres (£25) as recompense for 'twelve years' good conduct... [and] good results in philosophy and law exams'.[4] In addition the college transferred his scholarship to his brother Augustin, who was to lead a more dissolute life. On graduation Maximilien faced a choice of whether to practise in Paris or return to Arras. For an ambitious man the likely decision would have been in favour of the former course of action – many who were to play a part in the Revolution, such as Danton and Desmoulins, did just that. But it was also risky and for many future leaders the gamble did not pay off. At all events Maximilien returned to Arras and set up home with his sister Charlotte.

.  .  .

## PROVINCIAL BARRISTER

In 1781 Robespierre was enrolled as a barrister pleading before the Conseil d'Artois and in 1782 he became a judge in the ecclesiastical court, an unexpected honour for one still only 24. Also in 1782 Robespierre gained a brief national celebrity in defending a man who had installed a lightning-conductor: his neighbour had sought a prohibition on the grounds that it would endanger his life. The case drew the attention of Condorcet and Franklin, the American ambassador, and Robespierre's client paid for the publication of Robespierre's presentation. The case caught the public mood as Robespierre was able to present his client as the champion of enlightened thinking and the victim of provincial obscurantism. Many of his cases no doubt were workaday ones, indeed Robespierre acquired something of a reputation as a poor man's lawyer, but the more celebrated ones illustrated a theme of national interest, turned on an abuse of the regime, and were invariably directed by Robespierre from the particular to the general. He sought to win (and he generally did win) by eloquence rather than legal niceties;[5] his abhorrence for the latter was to influence his attitude to legal procedure in the Revolution.

As a diversion from his legal pursuits, Robespierre joined two literary societies, the Rosati Club, which wrote poetry in praise of the rose, and the more serious Académie d'Arras, to which Robespierre was elected in 1783. His inaugural paper was the *Discours sur les peines infamantes*, a discussion of the prevalent notion that a criminal's shame must be shared by his family. He submitted this for the prize medal of the Metz Academy and came second, using the prize money to pay for publication of the work. Publication was to be of immense importance to Robespierre throughout his career.

Robespierre's legal and social career, then, began promisingly enough, though he never had many cases: his best year was 1787, with 25. 1787 proved to be a turning-point both in

Robespierre's own career and in national life, and the two impacted on each other. In 1788 he had only ten cases, the lowest number of his career. So in early 1789 he put in for another salaried job, that of *procureur du roi* in the *maréchaussée* court to add to his position in the ecclesiastical court. There was also some ill-feeling between Robespierre and the Academy, of which he was director in 1787. It is said that he was mortally offended when the Academy, in response to a two-hour paper from Robespierre in 1786, cut the length for future efforts to half an hour. For whatever reason, Robespierre told the Academy in 1787 that his 'business and health' did not permit him to give a paper.[6]

.   .   .

## NATIONAL AND PROVINCIAL POLITICS

In February 1787 the finance minister, Calonne, shocked the country by announcing to a specially convoked Assembly of Notables that there was a recurrent annual deficit of over 100,000,000 livres. He proposed to cover it by ending the fiscal privileges of the nobility and clergy. Calonne had been forced to turn to the Notables because relations had broken down between the crown and the *parlements*. The Notables were nominated by the king but from fixed categories (for example two from each *parlement*). Nearly all belonged to the nobility and clergy and, faced with the end of their tax exemptions, they demanded a say in how the money was to be spent; Lafayette, who had served with Washington during the American war, called for the Estates-General. Calonne fell in April, but not before he had secured the appointment of Lamoignon as Keeper of the Seals. Calonne was succeeded by Loménie de Brienne, who was forced to concede the meeting of the Estates-General for 1792.

Meanwhile it was known that Lamoignon was planning radical changes to the legal code, particularly to the criminal code, which had been his life's work. In response to these developments Brois de Beaumetz, the head of the Conseil d'Artois, convoked a series of meetings with the leading lawyers of Arras to discuss the changes which should be made to the customary law of Artois. One barrister, probably Robespierre, complained of his exclusion from this discussion group in a pamphlet signed only M.R., entitled *Lettre adressée par un avocat au Conseil d'Artois à son ami, avocat au Parlement de Douai*. The pamphlet contains some of Robespierre's hallmarks, notably that of looking for conspiracies everywhere. The author complains of being 'black-balled' and of the 'secret machinations to bring about his ruin'. He also complains that 'the extreme slowness with which one advances in one's career had dashed the bright hopes with which he had embarked upon it'.[7]

In 1788 Lamoignon introduced his May Edicts. Their salient features were: the introduction of his reform to the criminal code, the virtual abolition of the private courts of the lords of the manor, the ending of the *parlements*' legislative function and the provision for general legislation for the whole country without the king's having to deal with each province separately. Lamoignon's measures, like Calonne's, were radical but authoritarian and deeply unpopular – at least in towns with a *parlement* and backward provinces such as Brittany, where the government lost control. They prompted Robespierre's first political act: on 21 June he signed the Arras bishop's court's refusal to register the May Edicts.[8] This was a stock reaction, particularly in a town such as Arras with an appeal court; the legal fraternity drew attention to 'ministerial despotism' rather than to the threat to their own privileges and the reforms which the May Edicts embodied and enabled. Robespierre's distinctive contribution to the debate was to present the minister's action as a 'frightful conspiracy' against the king – a routine approach, compared with, say, that of Mirabeau and Sieyès.

The Abbé Sieyès, in a famous pamphlet published in 1788, *Qu'est-ce que le tiers état*, argued that the struggle between the king and the nobility and clergy (the first two orders or estates) was a sideshow and that the commons, the 'third estate', should seize legislative power from both. The Comte de Mirabeau, professional intriguer, pamphleteer, member of Calonne's 'think tank' before turning against the minister, perennial ministerial aspirant, saw through the *parlements* and considered that 'the attack they are now preparing against the government was a conspiracy against the nation' – a conspiracy again but this time against the royal revolution which Mirabeau never ceased to advocate. When Lamoignon fell in September, Mirabeau offered to defend him if he were impeached by the Parlement de Paris.[9]

Robespierre followed the routine line of trusting all to the good king Louis, who had 'escaped from the frightful conspiracy' by replacing Brienne and Lamoignon with Necker, a brilliant self-publicist and former finance minister, who had achieved popularity by financing the American war with loans rather than increased taxes. For eight months Necker became Robespierre's and the nation's idol. The Parlement de Paris lost its popularity on its restoration when it announced that the forthcoming Estates-General must have the same organization as in 1614. In 1614 the third estate had had just over a third of the seats: in view of the vast increase of wealth of the 'commons' since 1614, their champions, such as Sieyès, now claimed half the seats, that is as many as those of the first estate (the clergy) and the second (the nobility) combined. They also claimed that votes should be counted individually ('by head') rather than by order, otherwise they would be in a permanent minority of 2:1 despite the increase of seats. The Parlement's ruling seemed to reject both these claims. In December 1788 in the *résultat du conseil*, the king granted double representation to the third estate but left the question of voting undecided – a big mistake as he still had enough prestige to impose his will on both these issues.

.   .   .

## ELECTIONS TO THE ESTATES-GENERAL

The first four months of 1789 witnessed an electoral campaign of great vigour up and down the country to choose deputies to the Estates. There was virtual manhood suffrage and the government abstained from all interference: such conditions were not to be repeated for over a century. Thwarted in the development of his legal career, Robespierre determined to seize this unexpected opportunity to widen his horizons by seeking election to the Estates-General, scheduled to meet at Versailles in May. This meant mastering and exploiting the politics of Artois. These were complex in the extreme, even by the standards of the *ancien régime*. As a province only recently incorporated into France (it was ceded by Spain in 1659), Artois retained its own provincial Estates, divided into the traditional three orders of clergy, nobility and third estate, and these claimed the right to co-opt the province's deputies to the Estates-General.

The Estates of Artois were very unrepresentative: only those with six generations of nobility could represent the nobility and for the third estate it was worse; they were represented *ex officio* by the 32 town councillors of Arras and the other towns in the province. And to make matters worse the town councillors themselves were no longer elected but were appointed by the crown. Robespierre stood no chance of election to the Estates-General under this system. He therefore attacked the organization of the local Estates in an anonymous pamphlet: *À la nation Artésienne, sur la nécessité de réformer les États d'Artois*, published at the beginning of 1789. In it Robespierre advanced the radical doctrine that 'election [is] the only source of a mandate'.[10]

Robespierre attacked both the local Estates' organization and their claim to co-opt the province's delegates to the Estates-General. He found an ally in the royal *baillage* court of Arras, which claimed that Artois should choose its deputies through the electoral unit of the *baillage*, as in most of France. On 19 February the king ruled in the *baillage*'s favour and ordered the elections to proceed on this basis. This was the most important of a series of rulings which the government made: on 7 January, for example, Puységur, the war minister who had responsibility for Artois as a frontier province, ruled that all nobles were eligible to sit in the local Estates.[11] So at this stage, although the government was divided, with Necker (liberal), Puységur (neutral) and the reactionaries Barentin, keeper of the seals, and Laurent de Villedeuil, minister for the household (interior), all involved in Artesian politics, nevertheless it felt able to make decisions. These decisions moreover were (under some protest) accepted in the province. None of this was to happen when the Estates-General met.

For Robespierre, the royal decision meant that he could stand as a candidate for the third estate to the Estates-General. The third estate of Artois was to send eight deputies to Versailles, the clergy and nobility four each, in accordance with the king's ruling in the *résultat du conseil* of 27 December doubling the representation of the third estate. Robespierre came fifth on the list after a three-tier electoral process, Arras sending delegates to the *baillage* which sent delegates to the provincial college which chose the eight. The whole process took several weeks and there is evidence, though from hostile sources, that Robespierre campaigned aggressively, sending his brother Augustin into the villages to lobby for him and instructing his agents to hand out slips of paper with his name on at the end of a speech to the provincial college.[12]

He also produced two more pamphlets which, though their perspective is local, contain passages which would not have been out of place at the height of the Terror in 1794. The first, entitled *Les ennemis de la patrie démasqués par le récit de ce qui s'est passé dans les assemblées du Tiers État de la Ville d'Arras*, contains the passage:

> Citizens the nation is in danger! Domestic enemies, more dangerous than foreign armies, are secretly plotting its ruin . . . What does it matter to me that . . . they are already considering the martyrdom of all the defenders of the people?[13]

France was not at war and Robespierre's life was not remotely threatened.

The other pamphlet bears the less dramatic title *Au peuple de l'Artois par un habitant de la province* (March 1789), but it contains an extraordinary passage couched in Robespierre's full-blown rhetoric of 1794:

> Distrust new-minted patriots, those who go around proclaiming their mercenary devotion [to the people], and hypocrites who despised you yesterday and who flatter you today to betray you tomorrow. Question the past conduct of candidates: it must stand guarantee for their future conduct. To serve one's province worthily one must be without reproach.[14]

This short passage contains three characteristic Robespierre themes: beware new patriots, beware traitors, and construct a political biography of politicians. There is also the germ of a fourth: the need for purges. These ideas are born fully armed rather than growing out of the experience of the Revolution. Moreover, they seem more typical of the last phase of Robespierre's Revolutionary career than the earlier ones.

An explanation may be that the incestuous and claustrophobic life of a small provincial capital resembled the equally introspective world, equally small in numbers, of Jacobin politics in 1794. The Jacobin Club and the Arras Academy must have had a similar atmosphere. Robespierre talks about betrayal: no one had betrayed the Revolution at the beginning of 1789, but Robespierre's long allocution to the Arras Academy had invited the same sort of secret ridicule that his equally long speeches to the Revolutionary assemblies were to do.

## INTELLECTUAL INFLUENCES:
## ROUSSEAU AND JANSENISM

The fully armed birth of Robespierre's ideas in 1789 has been noticed by N. Hampson in a related context, his 'conversion' to Rousseau, which took place at this time and is first evidenced in his defence of Dupond, his last case.[15] From this point on Robespierre lards his diction with references to the Supreme Being, immortality of the soul, all couched in a tearful rhetoric. Two passages from Rousseau's 1762 political treatise *Du contrat social* seem to have particularly influenced Robespierre. They both concern the expression of the will of the people (the 'general will') through voting. The first extract, from the section 'Of voting', runs:

> The citizen consents to all the laws, even to those which are passed despite him . . . when someone proposes a law in the assembly of the people, what is being asked of them is not exactly whether they approve the proposition or reject it, but whether or not it is in conformity with the general will, which is theirs: Every man in casting his vote gives his opinion on the above question and from a combination of the votes is extracted the declaration of the general will. *So when the opinion contrary to my own carries the day, that proves only that I was wrong, and that what I took to be the general will was not.* If my particular opinion had carried the day, I would have acted against my true wishes; and then I would not have been free. [My italics.][16]

This is a very dangerous doctrine: democratic politics should be about what the people *actually* want (even if they are wrong); the introduction of the notion of what they *really* want (but don't realize) leads to false messiahs proclaiming that they can interpret the general will, without the objective correlative of counting numbers, and Robespierre was open to this seduction.

The second Rousseau text comes from the chapter entitled 'Whether the general will can err?'. Rousseau answers his own question by saying only if there are political parties:

> If when the people deliberates . . . there are intrigues [*brigues*], partial associations at the expense of the main one, the will of each of these associations becomes general in relation to its own members and particular in relation to the State: one can say then that there are no longer as many voters as men but only as many as there are

parties. The differences become less numerous and give a result which is less general.[17]

This idea was to have a profound influence on the course of the Revolution when political parties were equated with factions, run by what Robespierre called 'intriguers'. The notion of a 'loyal opposition' was completely alien to the Revolution and the search for an impossible unity led to a constant supply of 'traitors'.

Besides Rousseau there is another or rather parallel source for Robespierre's political ideas, Jansenism. The Jansenists were a Catholic sect which believed in predestination and was condemned as heretical by the Pope in 1711 but continued to enjoy strong support in the Parlement. Camille Desmoulins later called Robespierre a 'republican Jansenist'.[18] There is no suggestion that Robespierre was a practising Jansenist during the Revolution: he wasn't even a practicing Christian and said that earlier he had been a 'pretty bad Catholic' (10, 197). But in many ways he has the Jansenist mind-set.

I am thinking particularly of the idea that the general will is represented by a persecuted minority, a faithful remnant; whereas the mere numerical majority has what Van Kley calls an 'egotistical amour propre'.[19] Robespierre's lament that 'virtue has always been in a minority on earth' is pure Jansenism. His aggressive and crude use of paradox is similar to the Jansenists', who claimed that they were more royalist than the king, more catholic than the Pope. Such a device, as with the general will, conveniently dispenses with the need to count numbers. Finally in their last months the Robespierristes appeared less as an embodiment of Rousseau's general will (however interpreted) than as an elect, a persecuted and persecuting minority.

The Jansenist model provided Robespierre with a political dynamic which the reclusive Rousseau could not. The political wing of the Jansenists was located in the Parlement of Paris. Peter Campbell has shown how the Jansenist faction, a tiny minority in that body, managed to hijack the agenda of the Parlement as a whole by presenting their sectional concerns – the Church's enforcing the Bull *Unigenitus* – as threatening the jurisdiction of the Parlement. By cleverly intervening when their aims happened to coincide with the Parlement's, the Jansenist tail could often wag the parlementaire dog.[20] This was precisely the only way in which Robespierre could have any influence on the decisions of the Constituent Assembly of 1789–91, and it was the method he adopted. Robespierre's reception of Rousseau was mediated by Jansenism. As Van Kley has observed (without however making the connection between Robespierre and Jansensim), 'Rousseau himself confessedly lived through a Jansenist phase' when he read all their texts.[21]

Robespierre continued to praise the Parlement months after the more radical members of the third estate turned against it. In his last case, he goes to quite extraordinary lengths to praise the Parlement and chastises those who seek to destroy patriotic unity by criticizing it. The Parlement's resistance to the Lamoignon coup, 'one of the most formidable conspiracies ever perpetrated against the safety of a great people', was unrivalled in the fasts of antiquity. The Dupond case turned on the abuse of a *lettre de cachet*, that is imprisonment without trial on the king's sealed instructions, one of the most infamous features of the *ancien régime*. It enabled Robespierre to castigate the government for imprisoning parlementaire opponents, notably Duval d'Eprémesnil, who gets a ten-line encomium. Rhetorically, Robespierre asks, 'Is it necessary to the royal authority for theological quarrels to become the reason for imprisoning 80,000 citizens by arbitrary orders?'. In a footnote Robespierre gives the following explanation of the 80,000 prisoners: 'The number of state prisoners in Jansenist affairs is put at 80,000'.[22] These events happened 50 years previously, why hark back to them? But he does so again, this time praising the parlementaires for 'banishing from our midst . . . the absurd usurpations of the ultramontane despotism', presumably a reference to the expulsion of the Jansenists' opponents, the Jesuits, in 1764.[23]

Without labouring the Jansenist theme further (research into whether any of Robespierre's teachers at Louis-le-Grand were Jansenists would be desirable), it does provide a working hypothesis which helps us to understand both Robespierre's mind-set and his *modus operandi*.

·   ·   ·

## ROBESPIERRE SOWS DISCORD

An episode towards the end of the electoral process may serve as a bridge between the provincial and the national stage. At a meeting of the three orders in the cathedral of Arras, the Bishop solemnly renounced the clergy's fiscal privileges and the nobility followed suit. When the third estate had retired to its own chamber, it was proposed to send the first two orders a vote of thanks. Robespierre objected and, as he later recounted, 'engaged [the meeting] to declare, as its only reply to the noblesse of Artois, that no one had the right to make a present to the people of what already belonged to it' (6, 19). The Duc de Guines, the governor of Artois who was presiding, informed the government that,

> a barrister [Robespierre] had got up and said that one owed no thanks to people who had done no more than renounce abuses. This motion was adopted by the majority. This order [the third] being in general badly composed, one presumes that it will present obstacles to the desired union and that the assembly will last a long time.[24]

On 9 January Robespierre had welcomed Guines to the Arras Academy, citing the 'superior virtues and talents of a citizen-governor'.[25] These qualities were merely those of a participant of the noble revolt against the king of 1787–88, which passed for 'citizenship' then. By April Robespierre had moved from this conventional position. When he reached the capital he would update his information and attitudes and apply his conspiracy theories to them.

. . .

## NOTES

1. E. Hamel, *Histoire de Robespierre*, 3 vols (1865–67), I, p. 10.
2. N. Hampson, *Danton* (1978), p. 22.
3. N. Hampson, *The Life and Opinions of Maximilien Robespierre* (1974), p. 2.
4. G. Walter, *Robespierre* (1946), p. 28.
5. J.M. Thompson, *Robespierre* (1988), p. 40.
6. Walter, *Robespierre*, p. 53; J.-A. Paris, *La jeunesse de Robespierre et la convocation des États-Généraux en Artois* (1870), p. 146.
7. For a discussion of the authorship see Thompson, *Robespierre*, p. 58; Walter, *Robespierre*, p. 55; Hampson, *Robespierre*, p. 20.
8. Thompson, *Robespierre*, p. 39.
9. J. Hardman, *The French Revolution* (1981), p. 71.
10. Paris, *Jeunesse*, p. 238.

11. Hampson, *Robespierre*, p. 35.
12. Le Blond de Neuveglise, *La vie et les crimes de Maximilien Robespierre* (1795), pp. 72–4.
13. Cited by Hampson, *Robespierre*, p. 42.
14. Cited in Hamel, *Robespierre*, I, p. 77.
15. Hampson, *Robespierre*, pp. 29–32.
16. J.-J. Rousseau, *Du contrat social*, ed. C.E. Vaughan (1918), pp. 93–4.
17. Rousseau, *Contrat social*, p. 24.
18. C. Desmoulins, *Le Vieux Cordelier*, ed. H. Calvet (1926), pp. 201–2.
19. D. Van Kley, *The Religious Origins of the French Revolution, 1560–1791* (1996), p. 178.
20. P. Campbell, *Power and Politics in Old Regime France, 1720–1745* (1996), pp. 193–295.
21. Van Kley, *Religious Origins*, p. 296.
22. *Oeuvres complètes de Maximilien Robespierre*, ed. V. Barbier and C. Vellay (1910), I, p. 665.
23. *Oeuvres*, ed. Barbier and Vellay, I, p. 681.
24. Guines to Villedeuil, 20 April, Archives Nationales B. II 7, cited in Hamel, *Robespierre*, I, p. 84.
25. Walter, *Robespierre*, p. 653.

# Chapter 2

# ROBESPIERRE IN THE CONSTITUENT ASSEMBLY, MAY 1789–SEPTEMBER 1791

The Estates-General, or at least the third estate, changed their name three times in the two months following their opening by the king on 5 May. These changes marked the transformation of a semi-medieval body into a modern assembly which would remodel French government and society from top to bottom. First the third estate started calling themselves the 'commons' – an allusion to the dominant role played by their counterparts in the British Parliament. They then demanded that the clergy and nobility should join them in their chamber where voting should take place 'by head'. When these orders refused, in the knowledge that some 50 liberal nobles and 150 parish priests would vote on the same side as the third estate if voting were by head, the commons declared themselves the National Assembly on 17 June and on 20 June the National Constituent Assembly, arrogating to themselves the sole right to draft a new constitution for France.

This brought them into conflict with the king, who always insisted that, in accordance with the mandates or *cahiers de doléances*, drawn up by the electoral colleges, the constitution (and all legislation) should be enacted by the king and the Estates in conjunction (as in Britain). His intervention in the *séance royale* of 23 June was ignored, and his summoning of troop reinforcements to the Paris region and dismissal of the popular Necker led to the storming of the Bastille on 14 July. On 26 August the Assembly issued its preamble to the constitution, the Declaration of the Rights of Man, based not on the traditions and needs of France but on revolutionary dogma. When Louis refused to accept this, on 5 October Versailles was invaded by a Paris mob which attempted the murder of

Marie-Antoinette. On the 6th the royal family was dragged back to Paris and installed in the Tuileries, under virtual house arrest. On the night of 20/21 June 1791, as the drafting of the constitution neared completion, Louis and his family escaped from Paris, making for Montmédy in Lorraine in the hope that as a free agent Louis could negotiate articles of the constitution, but he was recaptured at Varennes, sent back to Paris and suspended from the throne. Though he was restored in September, on his acceptance of a constitution slightly modified in accordance with the manifesto he had left behind on his flight, his last remaining credibility was destroyed.

The destruction of the monarchy can be derived from the early writings of Sieyès (if not those of Robespierre) but the revolutionary leaders were not following a blueprint. The theory followed the practice. So it was with the remodelling of France's social institutions. The transformation of France between 1789 and 1791 did not reflect the *cahiers*. But as the collapse of monarchical power led to the development of a new theory of popular sovereignty, this in turn led to new institutions. 'Election is the only mandate', Robespierre had said, and it became the criterion for most appointments except those in the government and the diplomatic service. The king appointed his ministers but they had no power because their departments were virtually superceded by parallel parliamentary committees; he appointed ambassadors but was deprived of the prerogative of making peace and war.

There was even election of the clergy under the Civil Constitution of the Clergy, voted in July 1790. This measure also assimilated the 135 bishoprics with the 83 *départements* which replaced the historic provinces. According to canon law, the new bishops needed papal institution, which the Pope would not give and which the Civil Constitution would not let him give. Schism was established when half the clergy refused an oath to uphold the Civil Constitution. This was the third crack in the 'magic unity of 1789': the first had been the emigration of die-hard nobles after the fall of the Bastille, and the second the alienation of the king.

Although election was established for most offices – municipal, judicial, clerical – the National Assembly showed that it was merely replacing one ruling elite with another by imposing property qualifications for voting. The Abbé Sieyès, whose clerical mind had come up with 'national assembly' and the 'dictatorship of constituent power', now devised the distinction between 'active citizens' who had the vote and 'passive citizens' who didn't: all citizens were equal but some were more equal than others. Robespierre exposed the hypocrisy of this. Distrust of the king made these *haute bourgeois* and liberal noble deputies more radical than they wanted to be. When in the summer of 1789 the peasants fired the chateaux to destroy the charters recording their feudal obligations, the Assembly, unwilling to allow the royal army to suppress the disturbances lest it suppress the Assembly too, instead 'abolished the feudal regime entirely' on the famous night of 4 August. This they had not intended since many non-nobles owned feudal rights and in fact provision was made for compensation.

Fear of the king also led the revolutionary leaders into an always uneasy alliance with the new popular politics which developed in the electoral wards or *sections*, of which there were 60 in Paris, subsequently reduced to 48. These in turn elected the municipal government of Paris, the Commune. Strictly speaking only 'active citizens' took part in these operations or were eligible for the military wing of the *section*, the bourgeois militia known as the National Guard, but those who stormed the Bastille or invaded Versailles on 5 October were not restricted to respectable men or, in the latter case, to men at all, since they included many market women. Eventually, in July 1792, the legal straitjacket of citizenship distinctions was removed and Robespierre was as responsible as anyone for bringing it about.

The other countries of Europe watched these events unfolding, with interest but not at first hostility. Most people in Britain thought that France was establishing a parliamentary system like the British one: '1789' emulated the Glorious Revolution of 1688. Despite the suspicions of the Revolutionary authorities, the British government had no intention of taking advantage of France's preoccupations to seize her remaining colonies. Leopold II, Marie-Antoinette's brother, from 1790 Archduke of Austria, King of Bohemia and Hungary and Holy Roman Emperor, thought Louis XVI should make a go of being a constitutional monarch. Earlier, as Grand Duke of Tuscany, he had introduced a liberal constitution. Only quixotic rulers such as Gustavus III of Sweden (who lacked the money for it) and Catherine II of Russia (who was only posing) talked of intervention. There were problems, such as the feudal rights of imperial subjects in territories previously ceded to France, such as Alsace and Lorraine. Also the Austrian Netherlands (modern Belgium), which had witnessed a noble revolt (similar to the one against Louis XVI) against the Emperor, was now threatened with radical contagion from France. But not until the failure of the flight to Varennes was intervention in France even discussed. Austria, Russia and Prussia had more than half an eye on Poland, which underwent a second partition in 1792.

Robespierre arrived at Versailles just in time for the opening of the Estates, putting up at The Fox in the town together with two more Artesien deputies. He adjusted very quickly to national politics and made a sharp analysis of the situation opening before his eyes. On 24 May he told his friend Buissart back at Arras that there was no point negotiating with the nobility over voting arrangements because neither side could make concessions. If the third estate conceded voting by 'order', the doubling of their representation would have been, in Robespierre's word, 'illusory' (6, 89). If on the other hand voting was to be by head, the nobility and clergy, minus liberal defectors, would be in a permanent minority. Robespierre quickly became disillusioned with his former heroes the parlementaires, saying that the 'parlementaire party' in the Estates was prepared 'to immolate the whole human race to preserve the power of the parlements' (3, 36–42). Throughout his career he was to reserve his special wrath for fallen idols.

He realized immediately that the storming of the Bastille, 'a revolution as marvellous as it was unexpected' (6, 89), changed the situation: consent by the Assembly to taxation proposed by the king was no longer enough; that was 'before the nation had recaptured the legislative power' (6, 65). But in a letter to Buissart he added an original postcript, almost a throwaway line, on the lynching of the junior minister Foulon, whose mouth had been stuffed full of grass for (allegedly) saying 'let them eat grass': 'M. Foulon was hanged yesterday by a decree of the people' (3, 30). Barnave, the radical young deputy from Grenoble, had shocked some sensibilities by asking just 'how pure the blood' had been of the royal agents killed in the recent disturbances? But Robespierre gives a theoretical, legal basis for the people's action: decree (*arrêt*) was a precise legal term being used by a lawyer.

Robespierre was quick to detect hypocrisy. Though the Assembly decided that it would ignore the deputies' mandates which gave the king a say in drafting the constitution, it wanted to draw what was termed a 'religious veil' over this usurpation by giving him the right merely to 'sanction' the finished job. Robespierre objected: 'Does the nation', he asked rhetorically, 'need any other will than its own to frame a constitution?' And concluded, 'we must rend the religious veil with which you have desired to cover these primitive rights of the nation' (6, 83 and 100).

Robespierre's clarity of vision seems to have won him an early celebrity for on 9 July he was chosen as one of the 24 deputies to ask the king to withdraw his troops from the Paris region (6, 37). Nevertheless Robespierre was only one of 1,200 members of the Estates-General, which included 600 'commons'. He was remembered for the lightning-conductor case (6, 25) but his style was prolix, pedantic, formulaic, allusive, wilfully obscure and given to crude paradox; in addition he had a weak speaking-voice, an unattractive northern accent and a funny name which it took journalists nearly two years to get right – the following versions appear: Robetspierre (6, 196); Roberspierre (6, 200); Roberts-Pierre, used by Mirabeau (6, 200); Robess-Pierre and Robetspierre (6, 214 and 541); and Robertz-Pierre (6, 541). (These phonetic spellings serve to re-mind English speakers that 'Robespierre' is pronounced with four syllables.) Desmoulins noted that 'journalists affect to call him Robertspierre, apparently finding this latter name more noble and softer'.

Despite labouring under distinct disadvantages, by the time the Constituent Assembly finished its labours, in September 1791, Robespierre was a household name throughout France. At the end of the Constituent's last session, the crowd presented him and his fellow radical Pétion with garlands of oak leaves and dragged them to their lodgings in carriages. What remains to be explained is how he achieved this and what if anything this meant in terms of power or even influence?

Robespierre adopted three methods to maximize his effectiveness. First his interventions in the Assembly were consistently radical, tending to the literal application of the principles expounded in the Declaration of the Rights of Man. Secondly he concluded *ad hoc* alliances with the Right Wing in the Assembly who were pursuing a *politique du pire*: they were prepared to wreck the constitutional monarchy in the hopes of a return to the *ancien régime*. Robespierre's third ploy was to maximize his influence outside parliament by that tireless self-publicity he had employed in Arras. This involved relentlessly circularizing the incipient national network of Jacobin clubs and getting his speeches reported in the radical press. Robespierre's influence always depended on his position at the intersection of two circles, one the parliamentary and the other radical opinion outside parliament, which he depicted as the voice of the people.

Robespierre believed that since the Declaration of the Rights of Man was the preamble to the constitution, all the constitutional articles should be derived from it. In his speech on the *marc d'argent* (the property qualification for deputies), Robespierre himself highlights those articles of the Declaration which were of particular relevance:

'All men are born and remain free and equal in rights' [Article I].

'Sovereignty resides essentially in the nation' [Article III].

'The law is the expression of the general will. Every citizen has the right to participate in its formulation, either in person or through freely elected representatives . . . All citizens are eligible for all public employments, without any distinction save their virtues and talents' [Article VI]. (6, 160)

Obviously these criteria could be applied to most situations: qualifications for voting, membership of the new patriotic militia, the National Guard, eligibility for local government and so on. By the same token the king derived his authority from the constitution, not hereditary right. During the debates about the king's prerogative of declaring war and making peace, Robespierre shocked his colleagues by calling the king a '*commis*'. But he was only being honest: the majority in the Assembly wanted to make use of the 'religious veil' to hide this fact and employed other obfuscations, like the distinction between 'active' and 'passive' citizens.

Deriving everything from first principles enabled Robespierre to intervene on matters where he had no expert knowledge. Indeed he believed that professionalism was at variance with patriotism. He sought to intervene in the debate on the status of the feudal rights of German princes with possessions in

France but was unable to catch the speaker's eye. As he sat down disconsolately,

> The ducs de Liancourt and de la Rochefoucauld told him how astonished they were that he was risking speaking on a matter of this nature without ever having read or learned anything on the subject. 'But you are at least familiar with the Treaty of Ryswick? – No. – Have you studied German public law? – No. Public law and treaties don't come into it, only the law of peoples.' (6, 231)

. . .

## TACTICAL ALLIANCE WITH THE RIGHT

Robespierre moved effortlessly from principle to expediency with his tactical alliance with the Right. The right-wing deputies, the *noirs* as they were called, some 250 in number, argued that all the Assembly's acts since 5 October 1789 lacked legitimacy because of the violence done to the king. That was not Robespierre's position but he always preferred frank opponents to those who wore the 'mask of hypocrisy'. He also understood the opposition of those who had lost everything in the Revolution, and by the same token reserved his greatest contempt for beneficiaries who had turned against it. Thus Robespierre opposed Mirabeau, a nobleman sitting for the third estate whose oratory earned him the sobriquet 'tribune of the people', when he proposed that Condé, a Prince of the Blood, should be declared a traitor for allegedly publishing a manifesto denouncing the Revolution. Why, he asked, make an example 'of a man who, attached by every possible link to every kind of abuse, has not found our principles to his liking?' (6, 489–50). Again in August 1790 he proclaimed,

> I blame those less who out of romantic enthusiasm justify their attachment to former principles they cannot abandon than those who cover their perfidious designs with the mask of patriotism and virtue. (6, 515–16)

In August 1790 the *Journal de Versailles* noted,

> A remarkable thing is that there were only seven or eight deputies against this decree [ratifying existing treaties], among whom were

MM. Maury and Robespierre, so much is it true that the two extremes are often ready to touch. (6, 525)

.   .   .

## THE JACOBIN CLUBS

The third string to Robespierre's bow was his influence in the Jacobin Club. The genesis of the Club was a reunion in a café in Versailles of Breton deputies to the Estates, who tended to be amongst the most radical because the nobility and clergy of Brittany had boycotted the Estates. Soon the Bretons were joined by such 'advanced' patriots as Mirabeau, Barnave, Lafayette, elected commander-in-chief of the Parisian National Guard, and Robespierre. Shortly after the National Assembly moved to Paris, the club rented a hall in a Dominican convent in the Rue Saint-Honoré. The Dominicans were familiarly known as the Jacobins and, though the Club styled itself the Society of the Friends of the Constitution, the shorter label was soon used by friend and foe alike (it was first coined by royalist pamphleteers).[1]

The purpose of the Club was to influence the National Assembly by giving a prior airing to matters which were to be debated there. Sieyès trailed his proposal for a National Assembly and d'Aiguillon his for the renunciations of privilege on 4 August. By the same token, however, it was a convention of the Club (consistently flouted by Robespierre) that once a measure had been decided by the Assembly, the Jacobins would bring no further pressure to bear.

Similar clubs sprang up all over France, some developing out of the sort of social club to which Robespierre had belonged at Arras, often with a bar as the principal attraction. They sought to influence the elections which, in 1789–90, were introduced into every aspect of national life, including the three tiers of local government, commune, district and department. The first elections in which the Jacobin network was able to make an impact were the municipal elections of November–December 1790, when they made great gains by adopting candidates for a Jacobin 'slate'. At Marseille, Grenoble, Toulon and Bourges Jacobin candidates swept the board. Adopting the tactics of the militant Jansenists in the *parlements*, they exploited general apathy by making sure their supporters turned out – at

Tours, which had 3,500 voters, the Jacobin candidate was elected mayor with only 171 votes.[2]

The effectiveness of the Jacobin clubs could be greatly amplified by association and this was the great discovery of 1790, the consequences of which were soon appreciated. In January 1790 the Strasbourg club suggested that each provincial club should correspond with the others and with the Paris club, which became known as the 'mother society'.[3] This practice rapidly spread and enabled the clubs to bring a national pressure on the Assembly in the form of petitions. The king believed that the practice was based on that of the provincial *parlements* under Louis XV, which claimed that the various *parlements* were but one and that a matter touching one of them concerned them all. The clubs also employed the *parlements'* tactic of seeking to prevent government agents from carrying out their orders.

Robespierre used the mechanism of the circular and the petition to buttress his slender structure in the National Assembly. Sometimes this happened spontaneously, sometimes Robespierre took the initiative in sending his speeches to key provincial clubs, such as Marseille. A good example is his speech inveighing against property qualifications for membership of the National Guard. Unable to deliver this in the Assembly, he gave it in the Jacobins on 6 December 1790, despite Mirabeau's objection that the Assembly had already voted on the matter. Robespierre then sent a copy to the Marseille club, which petitioned the Assembly and circularized all the clubs with their petition and a five-page précis of Robespierre's speech. Desmoulins published the petition in his journal. The affiliated clubs then discussed the Marseille circular (Lorient devoted four sessions to it); the Versailles club, with which Robespierre retained strong links after his removal to Paris, then implored the network to keep up its support for Robespierre.[4]

In the spring of 1791 Robespierre revived the question of manhood suffrage with a speech in the Assembly. It was not reported in the press, so Robespierre distributed it widely through the network. On 20 April he repeated the speech to the Cordelier Club, the political base of Danton and Desmoulins with a lower subscription rate than the Jacobins, and the Cordeliers had it reprinted and circularized. The result of all this activity was mass petitioning of the Assembly and numerous letters of congratulation to Robespierre, to which he replied in equally flattering terms.[5]

.   .   .

## THE SELF-DENYING ORDINANCE AND
## THE FLIGHT TO VARENNES

Robespierre's greatest parliamentary triumph in the Constituent Assembly occurred, with Right support, on 16 May 1791 when the Assembly accepted his motion that deputies be ineligible for membership of the next assembly and in any case (it was decided on the 18th) for two years. Opinion is divided about whether Robespierre's motives were disinterested, machiavellian or based on a miscalculation. Croker's analysis seems the most satisfactory. In the spring of 1791, 'The Revolution was said and even thought to be closed'. And, shortly after the self-denying ordinance was passed,

> the very three names most prominent in this supposed self-sacrifice – Robespierre, Pétion and Buzot – were nominated by the electoral body of Paris to the three highest judicial offices in the state: Pétion to be president; Buzot vice-president; and Robespierre to '*the safe and lucrative and most desirable office*', as he himself subsequently described it, of *Accusateur Public* or Attorney-General of the *Supreme Criminal Tribunal* created by the new Constitution. What higher, more lucrative, or more honourable result and reward of their two years' political service in the Assembly could these provincial lawyers have expected or even imagined?[6]

In his letter of acceptance, dated 11 June, Robespierre told the electors that his name had been put forward for this post 'without his knowledge' (3, 109). However, a letter written by his brother Augustin from the previous November makes it clear that Maximilien was already thinking along these lines: 'My brother could well be elected a Parisian judge, but not a word, no one knows' (3, 93). So his appointment was the fulfilment of a long-held ambition. The Revolution was over; likewise the heroic days of parliament; time to cash his chips.

Robespierre's calculations were overturned by the king's escape from Paris on the night of 20/21 June. The timing of Louis's flight was determined by two considerations: first to halt the elections to the successor Assembly, the Legislative, for which the 'primaries' were in progress, and secondly to force the Assembly to modify the constitution in line with the manifesto he left behind in Paris. Louis told the Duc de Choiseul, who organized the troop relays on the escape route, that, having renegotiated the constitution from a position of freedom and equality at Montmédy, he planned to take up residence at Compiègne, some 30 miles from Paris, and remain there until the constitution was bedded in.[7] In December 1790 a consignment of furniture arrived at Compiègne 'for the Estates'.[8]

In 1789 the king had adopted a *laissez-faire* attitude to the elections to the Estates; in 1791 he was following them closely and he was worried. His manifesto observed that:

> It can be seen from the dominant mentality of the [Jacobin] clubs and the way in which they are seizing control of the new primary assemblies what can be expected of them and if one can detect any disposition on their part to revise anything it is to destroy the remains of the monarchy and set up a metaphysical and doctrinaire form of government which would not work.[9]

Kennedy writes of the June primaries, 'Never before, even during the voting for bishops and priests, had Jacobin interference in the electoral process been so flagrant'. At Avallon all the members of the electoral college were Jacobins; the Lille club told the 'mother society' that nine-tenths of the electoral college were 'Jacobins, pure Jacobins'.[10]

Flushed with their successes in the primaries, the clubs girded up their loins for the election of deputies, due on 5 July: church halls were hired, 'slates' posted outside the clubs and the 'mother society' urged every elector to be at his post. As a result of the king's flight the elections did not take place until August, in a less favourable climate. Robespierre well understood the timing of the king's flight: four times he employs the rhetorical refrain 'why did he choose this precise moment' to go? And answers: 'he chose the moment' when the primary assemblies were in progress and with the prospect of a Legislative Assembly more radical than its predecessor and prepared to 'revoke a portion of its measures' (7, 518–23).

The patriot leaders of 1789, Barnave, Duport and Alexandre de Lameth (the 'triumvirs') and Lafayette, now wanted to end the Revolution before it degenerated into an attack on property. Robespierre believed they were in league with the king to achieve this; not only would they have exploited a successful escape by the king but they actually connived at it: 'The king fled with the consent of La Fayette' (8, 383). Robespierre had seen how the 'triumvirs', who had entered the committee charged with finalizing the constitution the previous September, had striven to revise it to strengthen the executive, and he had witnessed the measures they had taken to attack the Jacobins. At the beginning of March 1791 the king was given the right, in certain circumstances, to replace local officials – to the chagrin of the local Jacobins who had often been instrumental in their election.[11] On 11 May Le Chapelier introduced a law banning wall-posters and collective petitions, which as Robespierre's unsuccessful intervention made clear was aimed at the Jacobin clubs (7, 315).

No evidence has survived for Robespierre's belief that these men colluded in the king's flight, but in a sense it is not necessary: everyone knew that the king wanted to escape, because that is a characteristic ambition of prisoners. In any case the two possibilities were fused when Barnave, sent to escort the royal family back to Paris, struck the following deal with Marie-Antoinette: his party would induce the Assembly to revise the constitution in the light of the king's manifesto and in return the queen would get her brother Leopold, the Emperor, to renew the 1756 treaty of alliance with France and thus confer international legitimacy on the Revolution.[12] Robespierre guessed much of this; unlike most historians and many contemporaries, he did not think that the king's flight was meant to bring about the restoration of the *ancien régime.* Nor, Robespierre adds, 'could it have been upon Leopold and the King of Sweden and on the army [of *émigrés*] beyond the Rhine, that he placed his hopes'. No, Robespierre argued, something more dangerous because more insidious was afoot: the king intended to do a deal with the National Assembly which would enable the *émigrés* to return voluntarily to France. (Louis mentions this objective in his manifesto.) The triumvirs, according to Robespierre, would 'at first ask for very small sacrifices to bring about a general reconciliation'; and they would have little 'trouble in inducing a weary people to accept a deal, a half-way compromise'. 'You will have observed', he added 'how [the king] distinguishes between those things in the constitution which he finds offensive and those he deigns to find acceptable' (7, 518–23).

Robespierre could not believe that the 'liberal' nobles of 1789, men such as Duport and the Lameths, were capable of a disinterested sacrifice of their privileges. They expected a quid quo pro from the Revolution and his main fear was that in return for ministerial portfolios the 'triumvirs' were preparing to do a deal with the court. For Robespierre ministers were *ipso facto* bad: 'I will always get up to oppose every motion proposed by the ministers' (6, 445). He proposed in the Jacobins that ministers should be chosen by popular election. Then on 7 April he proposed in the Assembly that no deputy could become a minister for four years after he had left parliament – a motion which was carried almost unanimously, the Right hoping it would destabilize the new regime, the Left hoping it would weaken the executive, the Centre shamed into silence by Robespierre's accusation of self-interest (7, 201).

There was a process whereby those revolutionary leaders who came to appreciate the problems of government came also to understand the predicament of the king; but the same process also robbed them of their former authority in the Assembly and out of doors, for whatever the revisionist eddies, the undercurrent was still strongly radical. The king's touch which once had healed scrofula now turned everything to dross. Barnave, Duport and Lameth were submitting themselves to these processes as had Mirabeau, who died on 2 April. However, this political education passed Robespierre by – at least until the summer of 1793 when he entered government. Up until that point his stance was strictly oppositional; and so he kept his revolutionary authority intact.

The king's flight gave birth to the first serious expressions of republicanism and resulted in his suspension from the throne; but it also facilitated the revision of the constitution, as had been its purpose. Robespierre realized this: 'Faithful and on his throne, would he have obtained the advantages which [the "intriguers"] lavished on him after his defection and during the period of his apparent ban?' (7, 411). For Louis's manifesto, which as Robespierre realized was essentially a critique of the constitution, gave the work of revision a focus, just as his flight had given it the leisure to effect changes. Robespierre was engaged on both these fronts, the revision and the republican petition.

The constitutional committee would have liked to have given the king similar powers to those of the King of England, such as the initiative in legislation and the right of dissolution, but the Right, pursuing its *politique du pire*, refused to cooperate.

The committee managed merely to give the king a bodyguard of 1,800 men and to give ministers the right to address the Assembly (without however being members of it); in addition the Civil Constitution of the Clergy and the removal of the king's prerogative of mercy were reclassified as ordinary legislation subject to repeal. On 13 August Barnave told the Assembly that in view of the modesty of these gains the committee had considered resigning.

Robespierre, however, by means of palpable untruths, asserted that the king had been treated munificently. According to him, the king had a civil list of 40,000,000 livres, whereas everyone knew the figure was 25,000,000; and he also claimed that the king had the initiative in legislation which, again, everyone knew he hadn't. These factual errors recur throughout Robespierre's public career, as when in 1789 he had claimed that Louis XV had imprisoned 80,000 Jansensists, more than the whole of France contained. These figures were mobilized to prevent the king making further demands as the price of his acceptance. If the constitution were thus revised *twice*, he told the House, 'they would be left with no alternative but to resume their chains or their arms'; to which a member from the Centre called out: 'That's a bit of an exaggeration!' (6, 668). Nevertheless, the triumvirs did not defend themselves and if it had been their intention to trade the king's acceptance of the constitution in this way, they were now shamed into abandoning it.

.   .   .

## THE FEUILLANT SCHISM[13]

The prelude to the revision had been schism in the Jacobin Club and the Massacre of the Champ de Mars; that was how it must have seemed to Robespierre and how it probably was. On 16 July 1791 300 deputies and 25 of the 30 members of the crucial committee of correspondence (with the affiliated societies) seceded from the Jacobins and set up in another disused religious house, the Feuillants. They claimed that they were the 'true' Jacobins and asked for the archives from the tiny remnant which included only six deputies, headed by Robespierre and Pétion. The secessionists were protesting at the favour shown by the Jacobins towards a Cordelier petition against the restoration of the king to his functions. This petition was opposed by Robespierre as a premature and therefore aristocratic declaration of republicanism and he argued that so long as sovereignty lay with the people it did not matter whether the head of the executive power was hereditary or elective.

The following day national guards under orders from the 'revisionists' fired on a crowd which had gathered in the Champ de Mars to sign another variant of the Cordelier petition. It is therefore clear from the chronology that the schism was not caused by the petition (which Robespierre opposed) nor by the 'massacre' (which it preceded). In fact those who seceded on the 16th had ceased attendance at the Jacobins for some time. There were substantive differences between the Robespierristes and the future feuillants, notably on the question of political rights for freed slaves and coloureds in the French colonies, but the heart of the matter was Robespierre's attempts to get control of the vital correspondence committee, the key to the indoctrination of the provinces, and other crucial positions in the Club. Pétion (whose role Kennedy considers to have been equal to Robespierre's in saving the Club) argued with some justification that the schismatics had left not because of principles but because they had been worsted in this power struggle and hoped to recoup their position by capturing the provincial network.

It was clear by September that they had failed in this attempt and their efforts had served only to purge the society for Robespierre and leave him the undisputed master of it, which he had not been before. Robespierre also resolutely refused any reconciliation with the schismatics as a club, though many deputies who had defected to the feuillants were allowed back as individuals.

· · ·

## CHANGE OF ADDRESS

When the National Assembly moved to Paris in October 1789, Robespierre had taken furnished lodgings (two rooms and a kitchen) 'in the depths of the Marais', to use Mme Roland's condescending phrase. The Marais had been the fashionable quarter in the seventeenth century but was now somewhat seedy, though Robespierre's flat was in a new building. On the night following the affair of the Champ de Mars, rather than make this perilous two-mile journey, with hostile national guards patrolling the streets, Robespierre was prevailed upon by a fellow Jacobin, Maurice Duplay, to spend the night under his roof at no. 366 Rue Saint-Honoré, a few yards from the Club. In August Robespierre moved in permanently and no. 366 became his home for the rest of his life. Duplay was a fairly prosperous cabinet-maker of 55, living with his wife, three marriageable daughters and a son of 13. Robespierre was offered a small room whose one window overlooked the timber-yard.

Robespierre was idolized by his adoptive family; the walls were lined with portraits of Maximilien; terracotta busts stared out from the alcoves. His every wish was anticipated at table and care was taken to provide him with his favourite delicacies, such as white bread, fine jams and a pyramid of oranges, which, according to his schoolfriend Fréron, aided his digestion and which no one else was allowed to touch. At this tiny court access was regulated to Robespierre as strictly as it had been to the king at Versailles. Fréron wrote,

> It is perhaps to this change of domicile that one should attribute the development of [Robespierre's] ambition. Whilst he lived . . . [in the Marais] he was accessible to his friends and to any patriot. Once installed at the Duplays', little by little he became invisible. They sequestered him from society, adored, intoxicated, ruined him by exalting his pride. (I, 156–7)

It is partly just a question of the layout of buildings. When Robespierre lived in the Marais, he answered the door himself (he had a secretary and apparently a mistress but they did not lodge with him). At no. 366 the first floor, on which Robespierre had his bed-sitter, was approached either by an outside staircase or by narrow stairs, 'little better than a ladder', from the dining room.[14] One is reminded of the equally narrow staircase which led from Louis XVI's apartments to the quarters, hardly more commodious than Robespierre's, of his chief minister, Maurepas. Unless he took the outside route, any visitor to Robespierre had to be screened by Mme Duplay, just as Maurepas screened the king's contacts: only Saint-Just ever had the effrontery to go straight up.

Yet the Duplays were gregarious and entertained a wide circle of friends, indeed two circles, particularly on Thursday evenings when Duplay, who had apparently been taken up by Mme Geoffrin, held a somewhat less exalted salon than the fabled hostess of the *ancien régime*.[15] The first circle consisted of deputies to the successive Assemblies – Constituent, Legislative, National Convention – some of whom, including Dom Gerle, Anthoine, Couthon and Augustin Robespierre, at various times also lodged with Duplay.[16]

The second circle consisted of people nearer to Duplay's own social station, who also became Robespierre's friends. Some remained private friends: artists such as Gérard (for whom Robespierre sat), Prudhon (who painted Saint-Just), the sculptor Cietty and the musician Buonarotti. For others he found jobs as his patronage expanded when he entered government in 1793. Many of these, such as the wallpaper manufacturer Arthur, were active in popular politics and gave Robespierre an entrée into this political demi-monde.

. . .

## VACATION

On 30 September the Constituent Assembly finally dispersed. Robespierre had felt the strain of attending the Assembly from 10.00 till 4.00 and the Jacobins in the evening, snatching a hasty *diner* at 5.00. At the time of the king's escape he had suffered one of what would become periodic bouts of nervous fatigue, brought on by a combination of overwork and political crisis.

But now he was free. The Legislative Assembly began on 1 October; but Robespierre, thanks to his own self-denying ordinance, was not to be part of it. The important but, in these pre-Terror days, apolitical job of attorney-general in the Paris criminal tribunal awaited him but it would not be operational for six months. So he took a long holiday – a six-week progress through Artois which became a triumph.

The failing provincial lawyer had come a long way in two years, but his precise impact is hard to measure. In the Assembly it had been limited to putting a break on the monarchical revision of the constitution and to the self-denying ordinance. His main impact, however, had been on the development of the Jacobin network, which he saved after the feuillant schism. But it is difficult to speak with precision about the influence of the Jacobins. The network was a parallel power, almost a counter-power, one of opposition, both to the Assembly and to the king, as the latter said in his manifesto. The network was not mentioned in the constitution; it was not, as the phrase went, a 'constituted authority'. It was made up of a small minority of political activists but it was the most unified and uniform national organization there was, never entirely transcending local differences but doing so more completely than any other organization.

Above all it had a unified mentality and this was largely due to Robespierre in the sense that the fledgling organization was brought up on a diet of his speeches. With the clubbists his phrases became current coin, stamped out like the clichés that they were. Computer-assisted research could demonstrate this. But it could not demonstrate how it translated into power. It is unsatisfactory merely to assert that his writings sapped the foundations of the monarchy or prepared people for the re-public of virtue.

Through the network, Robespierre could orchestrate a national campaign, such as the one in favour of the imprisoned mutineers of a Swiss regiment in the service of France, the Chateauvieux, which ultimately (in 1792) bore fruit. Or he could take up cudgels in favour of Jacobins worsted in local power disputes with 'aristocratic' local authorities such as in the *département* of Jura, whom he called 'oppressed patriots'. (Like Homer, Robespierre consistently used 'stock epithets': patriots were always 'oppressed', hypocrites always 'wore a mask'. His patriots were never happy just as Homer's dawns were never haggard but always 'rosy-fingered'.) He had an extensive per-sonal correspondence with such men and when, from 1793, he had patronage at his disposal, they would be recipients: in the Terror a '*patriote opprimé*' from the Jura, for example, was to head the Revolutionary Tribunal which tried political crimes.

One of the main expressions of Jacobin power was in man-aging elections and we have seen that they enjoyed consider-able success at local level. The first general election since 1789 was that for the Legislative Assembly, which was deferred from July to August 1791 because of the king's flight. But because of his own self-denying ordinance Robespierre was not a candid-ate and there is no direct evidence of his trying to influence these elections (though he thought the primary elections were going well in June): this is in marked contrast to his conduct in the elections of 1792 when the Paris electoral college actu-ally sat in the Jacobins and Robespierre's candidates swept the board.

# NOTES

1. M. Kennedy, *The Jacobin Clubs in the French Revolution: The First Years* (1982), pp. 3–4.
2. Kennedy, *Jacobin Clubs*, p. 217.
3. Kennedy, *Jacobin Clubs*, p. 12.
4. Kennedy, *Jacobin Clubs*, pp. 253–5.
5. Kennedy, *Jacobin Clubs*, pp. 255–7.
6. J.W. Croker, *Essays on the Early Period of the French Revolution* (1857), p. 331.
7. Duc de Choiseul, *Relation du départ de Louis XVI le 20 Juin 1791* (1822), pp. 34–5.
8. I. Dunlop, *Marie-Antoinette* (1993), p. 246.
9. J. Hardman, *The French Revolution* (1981), p. 133.
10. Kennedy, *Jacobin Clubs*, pp. 220–2.
11. Kennedy, *Jacobin Clubs*, p. 27.
12. Marie-Antoinette et Barnave, *Correspondance secrète*, ed. A. Soderhjelm (1934), p. 42.
13. Unless otherwise stated the information in this section is taken from Kennedy, *Jacobin Clubs*, Chapter 15, pp. 281–96.
14. J.M. Thompson, *Robespierre*, (1988), p. 178.
15. E. Hamel, *Histoire de Robespierre*, 3 vols (1865–67), I, p. 518.
16. Hamel, *Robespierre*, pp. 297–8; Thompson, *Robespierre*, pp. 184–5.

# Chapter 3

# OUT OF PARLIAMENT,
# SEPTEMBER 1791–SEPTEMBER 1792

September 1791 to September 1792: the 805th and last year of the Capetian monarchy; the first and last year of the operation of the constitution of 1791 and of the Legislative Assembly; the year in which France embarked on a war with Austria and Prussia (and shortly after with most of Europe) which would last for a generation; the year in which Robespierre's political career almost died but rose like a phoenix from the ashes of the monarchy so that for six weeks in August and September 1792 he was the dictator of Paris. Since Robespierre was politically *hors de combat* for most of this period – he did not return from Arras until the end of November and was due to take up his legal post in the spring – it will be briefly summarized.

The constitutional monarchy fell because no one believed in it and because it was unbelievable. Also because foreign policy, leading to war, became a mere extension of domestic politics. After Varennes the king abandoned his attempt to modify the constitution by his direct action, but as he told a trusted minister: 'my opinion is that the literal execution of the Constitution is the best way of making the nation see the alterations to which it is susceptible'. It was a kind of *politique du pire* and as such highly irresponsible. Marie-Antoinette sought to have the constitution modified by an 'armed congress' of the foreign powers, 'not war but the threat of war' as she put it.[1]

The politicians can be divided for convenience into four groupings. The strongest group on paper were the feuillants. The Feuillant Club, as we have seen, had lost the battle for provincial membership but on arrival in Paris many deputies, even on Jacobin 'slates', opted to join the more moderate club. On 4 December 161 deputies joined the Feuillant Club, bringing its complement of deputies to 264. The number of Jacobin deputies dwindled to 52.[2] However, the fragility of feuillant strength was underlined when the Legislative Assembly, itself with a feuillant majority, felt obliged to close down the Feuillant Club, following a Jacobin-inspired riot outside its headquarters at the end of 1791. It was a reminder that the parliamentary system did not operate in a vacuum.

The feuillants, or at least their leaders, aimed to strengthen the constitutional monarchy by such measures as repealing the Civil Constitution of the Clergy, giving the king the initiative in legislation and closing down the Jacobin Club – the last policy being specially associated with Lafayette, who in consequence became the special bugbear of Robespierre. But there was division between the feuillants as to how to achieve this end. For the triumvirs, and especially Barnave, no longer in parliament because of the self-denying ordinance, but privately advising the queen, peace abroad was essential to the preservation of the constitutional monarchy. He was right but in December he retired to his native Dauphiné, convinced of the queen's bad faith. That left the way clear for Narbonne, the illegitimate son of Louis XV and minister for war, and Lafayette to attempt to strengthen the monarchy through a short war aimed at the Elector of Trier on the pretext that the small *émigré* army of 4,000 men under the Prince de Condé was based in his territories. After this military promenade through the Rhineland, the glorious victors would shut down the Jacobin Club.

A shared bellicosity brought about an alliance of convenience between Narbonne and a third group of politicians, subseqently called the Girondins. At the time they were usually called 'Brissotins' after their parliamentary leader Jean-Pierre Brissot, the editor of the influential *Patriote française*, but for convenience we shall call them by the name by which they have gone down in history. This derives from the name of the Gironde *département* centred on Bordeaux which supplied many of their leaders, such as Guadet, Gensonné and Vergniaud. The alliance between Narbonne and the Girondins was one of convenience because whereas Narbonne sought victory, the main objective of the Girondins was to smoke the king out – hence the infamous words Brissot uttered on 30 December:

Either we will win ... or we will be beaten and the traitors will finally be convicted and punished. I have only one fear; it is that we won't be betrayed. We need great treasons, our salvation lies there, because there are still strong doses of poison in France and strong emetics are needed to expel them. (7, 74)

Their war policy was just part of the Girondins' general policy of wrecking the constitutional monarchy by making life impossible for anyone who was not a passionate believer in the Revolution. Under Girondin pressure, feebly resisted by the numerically superior feuillant deputies, the Legislative Assembly devoted the first two of the eleven months of its existence to framing draconian legislation against the *émigrés* and those clergy who opposed the Civil Constitution of the Clergy. The Girondins' sole purpose in framing these measures was to force the king to 'de-popularize' himself by applying the suspensive veto (for two parliaments) which he had been given under the constitution. They knew he would apply the veto because he could hardly sanction decrees sentencing his two *émigré* brothers to death and harrying what he believed to be the true clergy of France. Nearly everyone by now acknowledged that the Civil Constitution was a disaster but the sheer hypocrisy of the Girondins is revealed by the fact that a week before they had the draconian measures against the non-jurors passed (29 November) Vergniaud and Gensonné actually voted for a proposal to abolish the Civil Constitution itself.[3]

The fourth and smallest group of politicians consisted of Robespierre's faction which will be called the montagnards, though this label was not applied to them until they occupied the high-banked seats, the 'mountain', to the left of the speaker in the next legislature, the National Convention. They included the comedy actor Collot d'Herbois and the lawyer and amateur dramatist Billaud-Varenne, neither in parliament but active in the Jacobins. Hitherto Robespierre had been friends of those few Girondins who had sat in the Constituent Assembly; in particular he had been inseparable from Pétion, who now became mayor of Paris. But he quarrelled with them over one issue, war or peace, and upon that quarrel was erected a lofty superstructure of hatred.

. . .

## DECLARATION OF WAR

Robespierre's attitude towards the war was complicated. He was not a pacifist and on his return from his vacation in Arras on 28 November for a while he swam with the bellicose tide, but he feared militarism and dictatorship by a successful general (Lafayette). Billaud-Varenne also argued in the Jacobins that the king could not be trusted with an army (as in 1789) and if war broke out should be forced to abdicate.[4] The alliance of Narbonne with the Girondins first raised Robespierre's suspicions, for he held it as axiomatic that all ministers were bad: 'those who have tasted despotism', he told the Jacobins on 12 December, 'can never be at home with equality' (7, 40). By the end of the year he had come out unequivocally against war.

Yet events moved rapidly in the opposite direction. In January the pacific Louis XVI's special envoy, Bigot de Sainte-Croix, prevailed on the Elector of Trier to disperse the *émigré* army, which he was glad to do since, as Bigot told the pacific de Lessart, the foreign secretary, 'the French *émigrés* are now masters of the electorate'.[5] But the Emperor Leopold followed this by provocatively guaranteeing the Elector's territories from French attack. In the Legislative Assembly the Girondin Gensonné questioned whether the Emperor's declaration was compatible with the 1756 treaty of alliance and on 25 January 1792 the Assembly asked Leopold to clarify this point before 1 March on pain of war: distrust between France and Austria was so deep-seated that neutrality was impossible; it was either alliance or war. Leopold's position had hardened because his position was strengthened by a secret alliance with Prussia, concluded on 7 February. This did not mean he was preparing for war; but it meant that he couldn't be pushed around. It also meant that if war came to France it would be with the formidable military machine of Prussia as well as the softer Austrian target. The incompetent Girondins were confident they would not have to fight Prussia.

The crisis was hastened by two events: the sudden death of Leopold in March and the replacement of the feuillant ministry by one of Girondin complexion. On 26 March Robespierre once again revealed his pitiful grasp of foreign policy by arguing in the Jacobins that the need for war had been sensibly diminished by the 'providential' death of Leopold II (7, 230). In fact Leopold was far more pacific than his firebrand son Francis II.

De Lessart's diplomatic triumph also exacerbated a fault-line within the ministry dating from the *ancien régime*: tension between the grand seigneur Narbonne and the two ministers from the old administrative nobility, de Lessart and Bertrand de Molleville, the naval minister who was the particular recipient of Narbonne's spleen. Louis, who even before the Revolution regarded ministers from the administrative nobility as the only ones truly loyal to him, reacted by dismissing Narbonne for behaving as a prime minister. The Girondins sprang to the defence of Narbonne by having de Lessart impeached for the new crime of *lèse-nation* and sent for trial to the High Court at Orléans. The rest of the ministry resigned rather than share his fate.[6]

Louis responded by a bold but risky stroke (which Robespierre called 'desperate machiavellism' (1, 177)): the appointment of a Brissotin ministry. We know from a letter to the king by the agent who negotiated the entry of the new ministers that Louis wanted them to be openly identified with the Brissotins and so much was this the case that Robespierre asked, rhetorically (did he ever ask a non-rhetorical question?): 'Is it not a manifest violation of the prohibitory decrees that Brissot should fill with his private friends the places that he cannot hold himself?'[7] Louis's objective, however, was to make the Brissotins take full responsibility for war with Austria, declared on 20 April, which he did in spectacular fashion by making each minister sign his formal advice and publishing them through the Imprimerie Royale.[8] The appointment of the Girondin ministry led to a period of calm lasting three months. The Legislative Assembly, though far from possessing a Girondin majority, accepted the new ministers.[9]

Robespierre was in despair. All he could think of was to orchestrate a reception for the released mutineers from the Swiss Chateauvieux regiment, many of them murderers, who had been sent to the galleys at Brest. Despite constant pressure from 'patriots' in general and Robespierre in particular, who had campaigned on their behalf for two years, the government did not amnesty them because that would have violated the treaties with the Swiss Cantons. Eventually their pardon came through and they marched through Paris in triumph. Robespierre's protégé Collot d'Herbois proposed that they be invited to the Jacobins where Robespierre repeated his proposal that all mutineers should be reincorporated in the army as an elite corps, which was his solution to the dangers besetting the country. He also proposed that the national guards and *gardes françaises* should take part in the 'festival of liberty' of

15 April in honour of the Chateauvieux martyrs. Some 100,000 people, many armed with pikes, took part in the festival, which included sets designed by David, including as its centrepiece a giant galley built on the chassis used for the apotheosis of Voltaire in 1778. It is difficult to be sure whether Robespierre had any objective more precise than that of a demonstration against Lafayette, the immediate enemy, or stealing the limelight from the Girondins, the ultimate enemy. It was the first of many such synthetic fêtes that Robespierre sponsored.

.   .   .

## ROBESPIERRE LOSES CONTROL OF THE JACOBINS

The unpopularity of Robespierre's anti-war stance affected even his control of the Jacobins, where the Girondins gained control of the vital correspondence committee. In February 1792 Billaud-Varenne discovered that the correspondence committee was about to send the affiliated clubs a pro-war circular without consulting the mother society (7, 205–9). On 27 May Robespierre proposed that the Club should not admit any further affiliates 'until it had healed its internal divisions', that is as long as new recruits were likely to be of a Girondin complexion (7, 357). Again Robespierre opposed the Girondin minister Servan's proposal for an armed camp of provincials in Paris to overawe the king because 'if, as is entirely possible, the five men whom it is proposed to choose per canton were five aristocrats [sic, for Girondins], what would become of liberty?' (7, 366).

On 26 March he objected to yet another pro-war circular and proposed his own which argued that the need for war had been sensibly diminished by the 'providential' death of Leopold II. His invocation of Providence, 'which always looks after us much better than our own wisdom does', excited some ridicule, notably from the Girondin deputy Guadet, who asked him whether his words were to be taken literally. Instead of laughing this off, Robespierre proceeded to regale the Club with details of his personal beliefs. Despite boos and calls for 'next business', Robespierre told the members that religious belief was a 'sentiment of his heart, one which was necessary to him'. Only this ability to be 'alone with his soul' had enabled him to sustain all the abuse that had been hurled at him during the Constituent Assembly (7, 229–35).

Few were moved and on 30 March Robespierre withdrew the idea of his rival circular, hinting darkly that 'he had other means at his disposal to produce on public opinion the salutary effect he had expected from [his circular]' (7, 248); in other words he would launch a journal, *Le défenseur de la Constitution* to silence 'calumny'. The time needed for this task was the reason he gave for resigning his post of attorney-general of the Paris criminal court, which he had only just taken up. This was not the end of his travails: on 10 May he complained that he 'had had to fight for $^3/_4$ of an hour to obtain a hearing' (7, 346); and on 13 June, 'it is not possible for liberty to triumph in this place, when I am interrupted after every word' (7, 374). Brissot's *Patriote française* proclaimed that 'the Jacobins . . . have thrown off the yoke of Robespierre and it will be thus with his despotism as with all the others' (7, 376).

.  .  .

## DISMISSAL OF THE GIRONDIN MINISTRY

Providence, however, was watching over Robespierre; and one can see why he believed in it since the unexpected twists and turns of the Revolution seemed to play into his hands. Now, worsted by the Girondins on all fronts, Robespierre was saved by the inexplicable folly of his rivals, who decided to pick a quarrel with the king. In June they introduced three measures – the disbandment of Louis's constitutional guard, the creation of an armed camp of 20,000 provincial national guards in Paris to overawe him, and further measures against the nonjuring clergy – which forced Louis to dismiss them since he needed a ministerial counter-signature to his vetoes. Croker puts it thus: 'however natural it would have been to return to their role of *opposition* when they were *out*, there appears no motive for their taking violent opposition measures when they were *in* government'.[10] Robespierre rightly regarded the agitation they whipped up, which culminated in the occupation of the Tuileries on 20 June, as frivolous: 'overturning the state for so shameful a pretense – the dismissal of three ministers foresooth – as if the fate of the Revolution depended on their elevation or disgrace'.[11]

When the king faced down the rising on the 20th, standing in a window embrasure for hours surrounded by the mob, affable but defiant, refusing to withdraw his veto, his bravery caused a royalist backlash, in Paris as well as the provinces. Most dangerously Lafayette returned to Paris from his army with a view to closing down the Jacobins with the aid of the National Guard. This failed through lack of royal support but, to Robespierre's fury, the Legislative Assembly would not censure him. The military situation deteriorated further when on 3 July Prussia entered the war. The French offensive against Austria in Belgium had collapsed whenever it met with resistance but the Austrians had not embarked on a major counter-offensive. The Prussians, however, planned to march on Paris with a formidable army.

With the failure of their rising, the Girondins were left with no further resource, since, though many were doctrinaire republicans in a way that Robespierre was not, they (again inexplicably) were not prepared to bring down the monarchy. Vergniaud and Gensonné entered into secret negotiation with the court with a view to a return of the Girondin ministers or at least the addition of some 'patriot' ministers without portfolio to the council. They also asked Louis to make a personal intervention with the King of Prussia to halt the invasion. Louis gave a reply which, in the opinion of the intermediary, 'would not satisfy either a friend of liberty or a man of ambition – it is dry and negative': 'we owe the declaration of war entirely to the self-styled patriot ministers', who could get themselves out of their own mess.[12]

With the Girondins at an impasse, the initiative began to pass to Robespierre for the first time since his return from Arras. On 16 July he was elected vice-president of the Jacobins and on the 29th in a key-note speech he argued that not only was the dethronement of the king necessary but so also were guarantees that the Girondin-dominated Legislative Assembly would not simply annex his powers. To prevent this the Legislative Assembly must be replaced by a National Convention from which ex-members of the Constituent and Legislative Assemblies would alike be excluded (7, 416–20). That was the only way to 'keep away all the intriguers' (7, 424). Stung by this threat to their political future, the Girondins, like the feuillants before them and with even less success, seceded from the Jacobins, forming the little known Réunion Club. Here, on 30 July, Brissot and the inflammatory Isnard decided to have Robespierre impeached for his speech against the king.[13] Although there was little chance of their succeeding in this, there was no chance that Robespierre's proposals should find favour with the Assembly. That would take an insurrection as much against the Assembly as against the king.

.  .  .

## THE INSURRECTION OF 10 AUGUST

The insurrection was made possible by the arrival of provincial national guards (*fédérés*) in the capital and by the radicalization of the Paris *sections* and Commune. Robespierre had been apprehensive about the armed camp of 20,000 *fédérés* because he feared they would be composed of Girondins or even Fayettistes. But he quickly realized that the replacement measure accepted by the king – *fédérés* attending the Bastille day celebrations in Paris on their way to a camp at Soissons – could be turned to his advantage through the Jacobins. The Club was put at their disposal and from early July a coordinating committee of 43 *fédérés* operated from the quarters of the correspondence committee.[14] They formed a secret committee of five which prepared the insurrection. According to one account, it met at the Duplays' but not in the cautious Robespierre's presence.[15] Robespierre drafted the petition which the *fédérés* presented to the Legislative on 17 July calling for the king's dethronement (4, 287–94).

The *fédérés* stayed on in Paris after the anniversary celebrations on 14 July at the behest of the Jacobins and in defiance of the government and the Legislative, which naturally refused to fund their further stay in order to bring down the monarchy.[16] Robespierre proposed in the Jacobins that members 'welcome them into their homes, sharing their lodgings, their table and thus rendering their stay in the capital practicable' (7, 400). The most radical *fédérés*, the Marseillais, arrived on 30 July, marching to Rouget de Lisle's anthem to which they gave their name, and formed their own battalion. They had been recruited by the Marseille Jacobin Club, of which Robespierre had been patron since Mirabeau's death; in a private letter Robespierre called these men 'French Brutuses', that is regicides (3, 151).

The radicalization of Parisian politics meant the entry of 'passive citizens' into local institutions, including the National Guard, which lost its bourgeois and royalist character. The turning-point had been the Legislative's declaration on 11 July that 'the fatherland was in danger'. This proclamation called up for national service everyone capable of bearing arms. On the same day the Commune decreed that everyone with a pike could enter the National Guard. The '*patrie en danger*' decree also ordered the administrative authorities to be *en permanence*, that is to meet daily. On 25 July the Legislative, under pressure from the *sections*, decreed that the 'permanence' ruling applied to sectional meetings and that in this emergency 'passive' citizens could also take part. Thenceforth (until 9 September 1793) sectional assemblies were in permanent session, 48 little republics. When Robespierre had tirelessly campaigned for the abolition of the distinction between 'active' and 'passive' citizens he was well aware that it was not just a question of what he called 'principles' but of power: the *journée* of 10 August was made by 'passive citizens'.

On the night of 9 August delegates from the radicalized Paris *sections* overthrew the moderate municipal government and formed an 'insurrectionary Commune' which gave the orders to march on the Tuileries the next day. Louis and his family fled to the adjoining Legislative Assembly but his Swiss guards continued to defend the palace until ordered to lay down their arms, whereupon 600 of them were massacred. Robespierre took no physical part in the rising (one would not have expected him to); but neither was he a member of the insurrectionary Commune. Instead, from the window of his bed-sitter he watched the events he had helped to prepare unfold. Robespierre himself denied both that the popular movement could be directed: 'Do not be deceived: when the people rises it is not because a scoundrel does all in his power to stir them up, it is because they are already that way inclined' (9, 119); and that he had directed the August rising: 'I was almost as much a stranger to that glorious event as you', he reminded Pétion, the mayor who had put himself under house arrest to avoid responsibility (8, 427).

. . .

## ROBESPIERRE AND THE COMMUNE

If Robespierre was ever a dictator, it was during the period of interregnum between the fall of the monarchy on 10 August and the meeting of the National Convention on 21 September. But if he was a dictator, his dictatorship was limited both in time and space. In space because it scarcely extended beyond Paris and because its objective, that of returning his allies to the National Convention, was only met in the capital. In time because it was akin to that of a Roman dictator under the republic, who exercised unlimited power for a limited period, generally six months. Roman history was 'the textbook of the Revolution',[17] and Robespierre, the prize-winning Latinist, was well aware of what a Roman dictator was: replying to accusations of dictatorship, he castigated his enemies for their 'terrible misuse . . . of [the name of] a Roman office' (10, 553).

Robespierre exercised his power through the Commune, the municipality of Paris elected by the 48 *sections*, and he exercised it against the Legislative Assembly. He had not been part of the insurrectionary Commune of 9/10 August but during the night of the 11th he got himself elected as a supplementary member of the insurrectionary general council by his own *section*, Place Vendôme, took up his seat on the 12th, and later that day harangued the Legislative at the head of a communard deputation. Robespierre entered the Commune because he disliked the measures the Legislative had passed on the 10th and the 11th, which he denounced in the last issue, no. 12, of his *Défenseur*. They included the suspension rather than straight dethronement of the king; the appointment of a governor for the Dauphin; and the ruling that elections to the Convention, though by manhood suffrage, were to be in two stages, the deputies being elected by an electoral college, which favoured wealthier candidates; also the waiving of the self-denying ordinance, though this allowed Robespierre to stand for the Convention. By the 12th it was also clear that the immediate beneficiaries of the insurrection were those, the Girondins, who had tried to call it off. Apart from the minister of justice, Danton, the new ministry was dominated by the Girondins, with Roland back as interior minister, Servan as minister for war and Clavière in charge of finances: the rising of 10 August had achieved for them what that of 20 June had not – an irony which would not have been lost on Robespierre. '10 August' also gave the Girondins an operational majority in the Legislative, by driving out some but not all of the feuillant deputies.

Before Robespierre entered it, relations between the Commune (in which the Girondin Louvet could find a place) and the Assembly were generally good. There was no necessary conflict between the Assembly and the Commune; indeed initially the montagnards in the Legislative were more hostile to the Commune than were the Girondins: it was Robespierre personally who envenomed the dispute.[18] This forced the Girondins to counter by using their new majority to try to muzzle the Commune. First they sought to resuscitate the *département* of Paris as an effective hierarchical superior to the Commune; Robespierre countered by saying that all departmental authorities were *ipso facto* counter-revolutionary and that the *département* of Paris should confine itself to collecting taxes: he even got the members of the newly elected departmental body to ask the Legislative to restrict them to that role. Secondly the Legislative sought to abolish the 'provisional' Commune by holding elections for a definitive one. After battles running throughout August Robespierre was able to defeat or turn both these attacks. On 13 August also the royal family was taken from the Legislative Assembly and imprisoned in the Temple, the grim medieval habitation of the former knights templar, guarded by officials of the Commune.

Robespierre's success was due to the greater degree both of power and of revolutionary legitimacy that the Commune possessed as against the Legislative Assembly. The revolutionary leaders, mostly lawyers, were great sticklers for legality, even if they honoured it more in the breach than the observance; but it was legitimacy rather than legality which mattered in absolutist regimes, whether royal or republican. The Commune, in Michelet's phrase, was 'King of Paris by the grace of 10 August'.[19] The seat of power was in the Commune; it had made the *dix-août* and could make another. That the Commune possessed greater legitimacy than the Assembly can be seen from comparing their relative democratic credentials in June 1791 (after Varennes) and in August 1792. In 1791 only active citizens could take part in sectional politics; the Constituent Assembly, however, as well as possessing the dictatorship of constituent power, had been elected by manhood suffrage. It had the authority to suppress the Champ de Mars assembly. In August 1792 these positions were reversed: since the 10th all citizens could participate in sectional politics whilst the Legislative Assembly had been elected on a restricted franchise; it was also a 'lame duck' body, 'elected under a fallen regime', as Robespierre put it. On 12 August Robespierre's fellow lodger at Duplay's, Anthoine, told the Jacobins, 'the people therefore must go in strength to the National Assembly, which it has deigned to conserve, and announce its pleasure': at least once a day for six weeks a communard deputation lectured parliament; on 12, 14, 15 and 22 August the deputation was led by Robespierre, wagging a bony and admonitory finger at the deputies.[20]

. . .

## THE SEPTEMBER MASSACRES AND ELECTIONS TO THE NATIONAL CONVENTION

It was not Robespierre's intention to remain in the Commune and indeed once it had served its purpose for him, he lost control of that power base, only recovering it in the spring of 1794. His purpose, that of his brief dictatorship, was to use it to manage the elections to the Convention or, as Robespierre would have put it, to secure the election of a patriot Convention in the teeth of the machinations of the '*intrigants*'. In the elections to the Convention, the montagnard slate captured all 24 of the Parisian seats. Robespierre, through the Commune, achieved this by naked terror and ruthless organization. As Michelet observed, during the Constituent Assembly Robespierre could win laurels by sticking to general principles, in the Jacobins by 'vague denunciations', but in this crisis 'for the first time in his life, he had to act and speak clearly or sink without trace'.[21] And at this time he displayed a brazenness, a ruthlessness (as clarity of purpose often appears) and a sureness of touch he was never to equal. It must have seemed to him that Providence, the tutelary genius of the Revolution, had created an unhoped for situation which it was his duty to exploit.

The Sorbonne was closed down as was the Imprimerie Royal. On 12 August, the day Robespierre entered the Commune, it closed down the entire royalist press, arrested its personnel and handed over its presses to radical journalists:[22] the need for press censorship was to be a leitmotiv of Robespierre's from this point to his dying day. Indeed according to Michelet it was as 'the most considerable member of the press', the proprietor of the *Patriote française*, rather than as leader of a faction in the Legislative, that Robespierre detested Brissot.[23] After all, it was the Girondin press campaign against Robespierre's anti-war policy which, more than anything, had poisoned his relations with them.

Other terrorist measures (this interregnum is sometimes called the First Terror) accompanied press censorship. The Commune installed the guillotine on a permanent basis.[24] 'Certificates of good citizenship' (*certificats de civisme*) were instituted, one being needed to get a job, or a passport or to plead a case; anyone stopped at night without a certificate was flung in prison. The prisons, emptied after 10 August, were by the end of the month brimful of 'suspects' of a different political hue.

The culmination of the process was the September massacres, when between the 2nd and 6th of that month some 1,300 political and common law prisoners were murdered. This is conventionally linked with the advance of the Prussian invasion: the fortress of Longwy fell to the Prussians on 23 August and on 1 September news reached Paris of the imminent fall of Verdun, the last fortress between the Prussians and Paris. The Prussian commander-in-chief, the Duke of Brunswick, had threatened Paris with destruction if any harm befell the royal family. The Jacobin thesis (advanced by Robespierre on 5 November 1792 and intoned by French historians ever since) considers that the massacres were caused by a sublimated cocktail of fear and vengeance (*volonté punitive*) imbibed by the people. The prisoners were massacred, it was said, because the people feared they would escape, slaughter the population and let the Prussians in. The minister Garat saw through this: 'they created new words with which to celebrate new crimes'.[25] Croker, writing in 1834, also castigates his contemporary, Thiers, for swallowing the Jacobin thesis:

> He attributes the massacres to the old hackneyed excuse of the terror occasioned by the advance of the Prussians, and endeavours, by what no doubt he thinks a philosophical reflection, to palliate these atrocities as the result of an accidental and not wholly irrational panic.[26]

Rather Croker convincingly explains the massacres in terms of the electoral imperatives of 'Robespierre and his partisans'. Croker draws a parallel between the September massacres and the riots in April 1789, when the premises of a wallpaper manufacturer called Réveillon were burnt to the ground. The latter had been designed to influence the Paris elections to the Estates-General. In September 1792 it once again 'became necessary' to apply the engine which had been found so effective in the case of Réveillon; and accordingly the massacres of 2d, 3d, and 4th of September filled Paris with consternation and horror; and the succeeding days saw elected *without opposition* that deputation of Paris, 'damned to everlasting fame'.[27]

Croker's interpretation of the electoral role of the massacres *ought* to be more acceptable to Frenchmen than the one provided by Robespierre and neo-Jacobin historians, namely the involvement of the whole of Paris in some hardly creditable panic killing. For Croker, Robespierre's greatest mistake and greatest regret had been the self-denying ordinance. This could only be repaired by his securing election to the National Convention. All other *ignes fatui*, such as the presidency of the new Revolutionary Tribunal (a political court designed to try the 'criminals' of 10 August), to which he was elected on 17 August, or membership of the surveillance committee of the Commune (which organized the massacres), must be eschewed. The insurrectionary Commune must be kept in existence until the meeting of the Convention,[28] the elections to which it would control. An immediate aim of the massacres was to force the Legislative to withdraw its decree of 30 August abolishing the insurrectionary Commune; otherwise it could not manage the elections. The decree was withdrawn on 2 September, at the height of the massacres.

On 26 August another synthetic festival (this time to bury the heroes of 10 August) was made to coincide with the opening of the primary assemblies to choose the electoral college which would in turn choose the deputies to the National Convention. According to the patriot journalist Prudhomme, it was not a great success: 'crêpe was on everyone's arms but mourning was decidedly absent from their faces'.[29] To make sure of the second stage of the elections Robespierre got his *section*, Place Vendôme, to pass a resolution that the electoral college should vote *viva voce* and in the presence of the 'people'. This should take place in the Jacobins, which had all the facilities. And just in case all these precautions failed, the results should be ratified by the primary assemblies. Robespierre then had these proposals accepted and placarded by the Commune, and the *sections* and 16 country cantons of the *département* were 'invited' (one of Robespierre's most menacing words) to adhere to this resolution (8, 443–4).

Nevertheless the electoral assembly opened on 2 September in the Évêché (where the deputies to the Legislative had been elected). A Robespierriste observed that the Évêché lacked public galleries and proposed that the corps should proceed to the Jacobins. Next day, 3 September, the electors, led by Robespierre and Collot d'Herbois, processed from the Évêché to the Jacobins, crossing over the Pont-au-Change where a mound of bodies was piled up, the fruit of the massacres in the Conciergerie and Châtelet prisons.

Duly installed, the electors were 'invited' by Collot d'Herbois to purge themselves of all ex-members of the feuillant and other anti-civic clubs and of all those who had signed the petitions of 20,000 and of 8,000, protesting against the invasion of the Tuileries on 20 June.[30] (Previously the Commune had obtained the manuscript of these petitions from the Legislative, printed it, and had the *sections* vet their residents.) The purge eliminated some 200 of the 990 electors. The Arcis *section* complained of this procedure but their complaint was rejected on the grounds 'that the complaint did not emanate from the *section* and was merely the result of the intrigues of a few signatories of anti-civic petitions'.[31] On 4 September Collot was elected president and Robespierre secretary of the college, which under his guidance acquired a corporate life.

The 24 deputies for Paris were chosen one at a time, Robespierre first on 5 September with 338 votes to Pétion's 136. Indignant, the mayor withdrew and had himself elected for Eure-et-Loir. Robespierre later said this was unnecessary since the plan was for him to be chosen unanimously on the second day. All went according to plan until 8 September when the Girondin Kersaint prevented Desmoulins from winning on the first ballot. Undaunted, Robespierre announced that each day proceedings should open with a discussion for at least an hour on the respective merits of candidates. That did for Kersaint. On another occasion Robespierre said that the electors should plump for patriots rather than intellectuals, butchers rather than scientists: taking the hint the British scientist, Priestley, withdrew his candidacy, leaving the field clear for the butcher, Legendre, whose occupation, alone of the candidates, was recorded in the minutes. All 24 of the Paris deputies to the Convention would sit with the Mountain; 16 of them were members of the Commune.

Robespierre never dominated a body so thoroughly as he did the electoral college; his was the power to include and to exclude. He got his brother Augustin elected and could have made his pet spaniel 'Brount' a deputy, had that sagacious animal not had better things to do. Ronsin unavailingly asked Robespierre to get him a seat in the Convention, 'less as a man of letters than as a revolutionary poet' (I, 215); and Tallien, a member of the Commune, was nevertheless rejected for foolishly boasting that 'he was neither Brissot nor Robespierre', though this was not the reason given by Robespierre in his denunciation. Rather, the college was told, Tallien lacked leadership qualities, 'blowing hot when the people blew hot and cold when it blew cold'; he had also 'not approved of the Chateauvieux festival' (8, 464). In Paris during the 'First Terror' Robespierre exercised neat power: he was the incarnation of the revolutionary word and the word was almost the deed – there seemed to be almost no need of a transmission mechanism.

. . .

## THE ELECTIONS IN THE PROVINCES

To appreciate Robespierre's success in Paris, it is instructive to compare these results with those in the neighbouring *département* of Seine-et-Oise. Five of the successful candidates there were local men. The others included Treilhard, who as president wrote Robespierre an ironic reply on his resignation from the criminal tribunal, implying that he had not put in a day's work (3, 144); Tallien, allowed in here; Kersaint, the unsuccessful rival of Desmoulins; the playwright Chénier; Gorsas, the Girondin editor of the *Courrier des départements*; Audouin; and Hérault de Séchelles.[32] Robespierre was to come to regard all of these as thorns in his side.

Robespierre's relative failure in the provinces was not for want of trying. From the first day of the new regime, he had realized that the Commune should attempt to extend its dictatorship beyond Paris. On 10 August he had told the Jacobins:

The Commune must take the important step of sending commissars to the 83 *départements* to inform them of our true situation; the *fédérés* must set the tone by writing, each and every one of them, to his respective *département*. (8, 427)

On 3 September the Commune's surveillance committee sent a circular to the provinces inviting them to emulate the Parisian massacres. The Paris Jacobins had tried to impose *viva voce* voting throughout France; the local clubs had 'invited' the local assemblies to adopt this procedure but had only succeeded in ten *départements*.[33]

The real problem in the provincial elections, however, was that although Robespierre could, through the Jacobins, prevent the election of constitutional monarchists, there was little machinery for distinguishing between the republican factions, all being at this stage Jacobins. On 22 August the mother society voted to print and circulate to the affiliates an analysis of the seven votes in the Legislative conducted by *appel nominal* (where the way individuals had voted was recorded) to indicate who should be re-elected. But this methodology did not distinguish between future montagnards and future Girondins. So although, as Kennedy concludes, 'the overwhelming majority of Conventionnels, at the time of their elections, were members of the Paris society or one of its affiliates', only a minority would vote with the Mountain when parliament met.[34] This dilemma perhaps explains the low profile of the Club in these weeks: Robespierre virtually ceased attendance and on 12 September a circular apologized to the affiliates for sending out no correspondence since 10 August.[35] (Another explanation is that the electoral college simply took over the Club, some of whose members had been reluctant to grant it this facility.)

Moreover the Legislative Assembly, though humiliated by the Commune, was nevertheless with the interior minister, Roland, able to impose on the provincial electoral assemblies a version of events which magnified, indeed distorted, its own role in the insurrection of 10 August and virtually wrote the Commune out of the script. The official propaganda expatiated on the crimes of the king and the vigorous measures taken by the Assembly but said little about the insurrectionary Commune, the *fédérés* and storming of the Tuileries in general. Though this was not intentional, only six departmental assemblies got to hear about either the September massacres or the news from the front which would have put the former in a patriotic context: when the new deputies came to assess the massacres in the Convention, the Prussians had retreated after the indecisive encounter at Valmy on 22 September.[36]

## ROBESPIERRE'S ABORTIVE COUP AGAINST THE GIRONDIN LEADERS

Robespierre's realization that the provincial elections might not go well may throw some light on a subsidiary thesis of Croker's concerning the September massacres:

> though they may have exceeded the intention of their instigators in *one direction* [the numbers killed] they fell short of it in *another*. There is strong reason to believe that in September it was intended to sacrifice some of the Girondin leaders.[37]

Everyone seems to have known at the end of August that the massacres were about to take place and that an arrest warrant was equivalent to a death warrant. They acted accordingly, whether to have friends released from prison or enemies incarcerated in time. Thus Panis, of the Commune's surveillance committee, declared that they had removed Villain d'Aubigny from prison 'on the eve of the people's vengeance'.[38] D'Aubigny was a protégé of Robespierre's. Sergent, of the same committee, also had the papal nuncio released, because of the international implications.[39] On 3 September the Legislative had the deputy Jouneau released from the Abbaye where he had been incarcerated for striking another deputy: the decree releasing him was pinned to his chest.[40] Finally either Robespierre or Desmoulins (or both) had the grand master of their alma mater, the Collège Louis-le-Grand, taken from the Carmes prison to the Commune on 2 September.[41]

On 2 September, the day of the Abbaye massacres, Robespierre and his ally Billaud-Varenne (who had witnessed them)[42] made inflammatory speeches in the Commune. They accused Brissot and the leading Girondins of plotting to make the Duke of Brunswick King of the French (8, 457–8). (Robespierre later told Pétion that he really believed this (8, 458 n.8) ). That night the Commune's surveillance committee issued warrants for the arrest of Brissot, Roland and up to 30 other leading Girondin deputies (accounts vary).[43] According to Michelet:

> The most influential member of the [Surveillance] Committee . . . Panis camped outside Robespierre's place; a hundred witnesses saw him go to Duplay's in the Rue Saint-Honoré every morning to take his orders.[44]

In the Convention the Girondins were to accuse Robespierre of all this. His denial was very limited, claiming weakly that 'to disarm a man [that is have him arrested] is not to have him assassinated'. He also claimed that he had ceased attending the Commune 'before that event [the Abbaye massacre]' (9, 90), whereas in fact he spoke in the Commune on 30 and 31 August and 1 and 2 September.[45]

If Robespierre had said that he ceased attending the Commune *after* 2 September, he would have been speaking no less than the truth. The electoral assembly opened on the 3rd and Robespierre devoted all his energy to managing that. Indeed he did not return to the Commune until 18 September and that was to defend himself against a pamphlet accusing him of election-rigging (8, 464–8). If he had said that he did not attend the Commune in the period *before* the massacres, that also would have been true since he spent the period 26–30 August managing the primary elections of his local *section* (9, 90 n.27). But in fact he interrupted his direct electoral pursuits to continue them by other means.

Robespierre deals with this period in the notes he furnished Saint-Just for Danton's trial in 1794. Having, rightly, accused Danton of intervening to save Duport and Charles Lameth, Robespierre continues the accusation:

> Danton imperiously rejected all my proposals to crush the conspiracy and to prevent Brissot from resuming his conspiracy on the pretext that it was necessary to concentrate exclusively on fighting the war.[46]

This is not just an admission that Robespierre tried to have Brissot murdered, it is, as he says, an attempt 'to *crush* the conspiracy' – in other words to remove the Gironde as a political force before the meeting of the Convention. That failing, he would be driven to the purging of parliament.

. . .

## NOTES

1. J. Hardman, *Louis XVI* (1993), pp. 203 and 208–10.
2. C.J. Mitchell, *The French Legislative Assembly of 1791* (1988), pp. 14–15.
3. Mitchel, *Legislative Assembly*, p. 53.

4. N. Hampson, *The Life and Opinions of Maximilien Robespierre* (1974), p. 98.
5. Hardman, *Louis XVI*, p. 213.
6. Hardman, *Louis XVI*, p. 214.
7. J.W. Croker, *Essays on the Early Period of the French Revolution* (1857), p. 339.
8. Hardman, *Louis XVI*, pp. 214–15.
9. Mitchel, *Legislative Assembly*, p. 172.
10. Croker, *Essays*, p. 175.
11. Speech to the Jacobins, 13 June 1792, cited and translated by Croker, *Essays*, p. 185.
12. Hardman, *Louis XVI*, p. 220.
13. Hampson, *Robespierre*, p. 114.
14. P.J.B. Buchez and P.C. Roux, *Histoire parlementaire de la Révolution française*, 40 vols (1834–38), XVI, p. 270.
15. Buchez and Roux, *Histoire parlementaire*, XVI, p. 271.
16. F. Braesch, *La Commune de Dix Aout, 1792* (1911), p. 113.
17. Croker, *Essays*, p. 355.
18. Braesch, *Commune*, pp. 396–9; Mitchell, *Legislative Assembly*, pp. 276–9.
19. J. Michelet, *Histoire de la Révolution française*, ed. G. Walter, 2 vols (1952), I, p. 1038.
20. Braesch, *Commune*, p. 387.
21. Michelet, *Histoire*, I, p. 1036.
22. F. Bluche, *Septembre 1792: Logiques d'un Massacre* (1986), p. 79.
23. Michelet, *Histoire*, I, pp. 1076–7.
24. Braesch, *Commune*, p. 361 n.3.
25. Buchez and Roux, *Histoire parlementaire*, XVIII, pp. 311–12.
26. Croker, *Essays*, p. 53.
27. J.W. Croker, 'Robespierre', *Quarterly Review* (September 1835), pp. 517–80, at p. 539. The Paris deputation consisted of Robespierre, Danton, Camille Desmoulins, David, Fabre d'Eglantine, Legendre, Panis, Sergent, Billaud-Varenne, Augustin Robespierre, Collot d'Herbois, Dusault, Fréron, Marat and Philippe Égalité – Croker's note.
28. Braesch, *Commune*, p. 452.
29. Buchez and Roux, *Histoire parlementaire*, XVII, pp. 209 et seq.
30. Unless otherwise stated the information on the elections is taken from Hampson, *Robespierre*, pp. 127–30, the best account of the proceedings.
31. M. Mortimer-Ternaux, *Histoire de la Terreur, 1792–1794*, 8 vols (1863), IV, p. 38 n.1; Braesch, *Commune*, p. 583.
32. Mortimer-Ternaux, *La Terreur*, IV, p. 58.
33. M. Kennedy, *The Jacobin Clubs in the French Revolution: The Middle Years* (1988).

34. Kennedy, *Jacobin Clubs*, p. 290.
35. M. Sydenham, *The French Revolution* (1965), p. 129 n.1.
36. A. Patrick, *The Men of the First French Republic* (1972), pp. 139–52.
37. Croker, 'Robespierre', p. 539.
38. Braesch, *Commune*, p. 553.
39. Bluche, *Massacre*, p. 171.
40. Mitchel, *Legislative Assembly*, p. 265 n.35.
41. Michelet, *Histoire*, I, pp. 1042 and 1493.
42. Bluche, *Massacre*, p. 159.
43. Mortimer, *Histoire*, III, p. 216; Braesch, *Commune*, p. 519.
44. J. Michelet, *Histoire de la Révolution française, edn définitive,* 7 vols (1868), IV, pp. 477–8.
45. Braesch, *Commune*, p. 520.
46. A. Mathiez, *Robespierre terroriste* (1921), pp. 136–7.

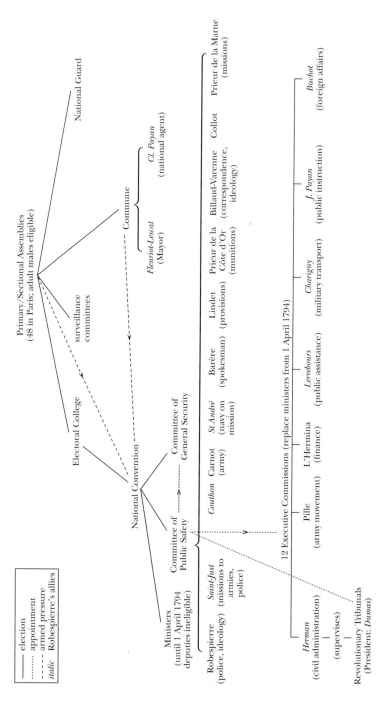

**Chains of command**

# Chapter 4

# THE NATURE OF POWER: THE INSTITUTIONS OF THE FIRST REPUBLIC, 1792–1794

Power flowed from the sovereign people, but how was it to be exercised? In the city states of ancient Greece, the people met in the *agora* to exercise their civic rights, but 28,000,000 Frenchmen could hardly fit into the Champ de Mars. (It could be managed today with television and the Internet.) The solution found by most populous democracies has been representative government. However, Rousseau had said that sovereignty could not be represented. Thus, he argued, the British were free only once every five years (at the time of parliamentary elections). Rousseau was followed by radical French politicians, notably by the *enragés*, who flourished in the summer of 1793. They argued that parliamentary deputies did not represent the French people but merely had a revocable mandate from them. Such a system is sometimes called 'direct democracy'. In token of this principle, the primary assemblies (*sections*, of which there were 48 in Paris) did not dissolve once they had performed their electoral duty but remained in being to chivy their 'mandatories' and assumed administrative tasks. So also did the body they elected to choose the deputies directly, the electoral college. Mainstream politicians, even Jacobins, did not accept this doctrine, but the Jacobin constitution of 1793 (never implemented) paid lip-service to it by providing for referenda on every legislative act if demanded by the people through their primary (electoral) assemblies.

Robespierre himself sometimes found it convenient to argue that whereas the temperature of the whole nation was difficult to take, a spot sampling of the people (say those who participated in a Parisian insurrection) could have a greater validity than the collectivity of its parliamentary representatives. The classic example was those Parisians and provincial *fédérés* (national guards) who overthrew the monarchy on 10 August 1792 in the face of a hostile Legislative Assembly. On that occasion, according to Robespierre, the insurrectionists 'stood proxy' for the people as a whole. Variants on this theme occurred on 31 May 1793 (when parliament was purged by the 'people') and on 9 thermidor/27 July 1794 when Robespierre (after some initial misgivings) declared that his supporters had greater legitimacy than parliament. The argument he employed on this latter occasion was derived from Rousseau's interpretation of the 'general will' (see above pp. 14–15). Nevertheless, as we shall see, mainstream Jacobin thinking in 1793/94 sought and, at some cost to popular morale, succeeded in integrating popular manifestations and institutions into the state structures.

Deputies, then, whether termed mandatories or representatives, were chosen by the people after the fall of the monarchy to sit in a national parliament, the National Convention. Only about one-tenth of the people, however, actually participated in the elections, despite the fact that they were held by manhood suffrage (women did not have the vote and the matter was not even discussed). There was apathy and intimidation: the Parisian elections were held at the time of the September massacres and Robespierrist candidates captured all 24 Parisian seats. This was not done by sleight of hand: Robespierre openly proclaimed that monarchists (defined as those who had signed certain monarchical petitions) should *ipso facto* be excluded and Saint-Just was soon to proclaim that such people in any case lay outside the 'sovereign' body. When there was a move to hold a referendum on the king's fate, Robespierre openly fretted that the terrorist conditions which had produced a good result in September 1792 could not be repeated.

The title Convention was derived from British and American precedents and denoted a constituent body. So the National Convention, like the National Constituent Assembly but unlike the Legislative Assembly which followed it, was designed to frame a constitution, this time a republican one, as well as to pass ordinary legislation. Unlike the Legislative Assembly it was not restrained by a royal veto. The Convention was to draft three constitutions: the first, so-called 'Girondin' constitution was rejected in February 1793; the second 'Jacobin' constitution, ratified by the people in August that year, was shelved; the third was voted, after Robespierre's fall, in 1795 and provided that two-thirds of the existing deputies must be returned to the next legislature. The Convention has acquired a deserved reputation of being a self-perpetuating oligarchy, rather like the 'rump' parliament which Cromwell finally dissolved. This reputation was reinforced when nearly 100 Girondin deputies were imprisoned in 1793.

How was this unicameral dictatorship to exercise its power? The problem was compounded by the current belief in the 'separation of powers', that is executive, legislative and judicial, based on American and a misreading of contemporary British practices and enshrined in the succession of French 'declarations of rights'. Under the constitutional monarchy the separation of powers was maintained by a law forbidding the king from choosing his ministers from the Assembly. This made them weak and their position was further undermined by the Assembly's practice of appointing committees from its own membership to shadow and supplement the ministries.

This device was the germ of the system the Convention devised to get round the inconvenient if hallowed doctrine of the separation of powers. After the fall of the monarchy, ministers were appointed by the Legislative Assembly and then the Convention but they came under the shadow of two parliamentary committees, the Committee of General Security (CSG), established in September 1792, and the Committee of Public Safety (CSP), established in April 1793. Finally the ministries were abolished in April 1794 and replaced by executive commissions which were subordinated to the two great committees, which were colloquially called the 'committees of government'. The creation of the CSP was essential, for, as Garat put it, the rising of 10 August had created 'a democracy which did not yet have a government'. Robespierre entered the CSP on 27 July 1793, following the purge of the Girondin deputies. Danton wanted to call the two committees officially the government, but Robespierre suspected a trap and they were left with the reality but not the trappings of power.

The CSG was concerned with police, that is to say, political police, which formed an increasingly large portion of the business of government. From December 1793 it was officially subordinated to the CSP, which was supposed to appoint its members, but it seems not to have exercised this right. The CSP was concerned primarily with diplomacy and warfare but increasingly it too descended to the details of police matters.

This was particularly true of Robespierre, who in the last months of his life lavished most of his attention on the police bureau which had been set up in the CSP in April 1794. This naturally led to jurisdictional disputes between the two committees of government and the conflict was to play a major part in Robespierre's fall.

The members of the CSP (12 at its height) were elected by the Convention from among its number every month. It is customary to distinguish between a 'first' CSP, dominated by Danton and favouring peace abroad and leniency towards political opponents at home (April–July 1793), and a second or 'great' CSP in which Robespierre served. The membership of this second CSP remained fairly static (four additions and one loss to the guillotine) during Robespierre's period in office but the Convention's theoretical right of appointment was never forgotten. Indeed on 26 July 1794 Robespierre asked the Convention to dismiss some of his opponents in the committee. However, on a day-to-day basis it would not be misleading to talk of the Convention's being dominated, even terrorized, by its own committee. The fall of Robespierre led to a renewal of the membership of the CSP: not just the necessary replacement of Robespierre and his adherents Couthon and Saint-Just (who had all been guillotined) but even of his opponents within the committee.

The individual members of the CSP had their own field of activity: Robespierre, police, justice, ideology; Carnot, military strategy and organization; Lindet, food supply; Barère, spokesman in the Convention etc. However, responsibility was collective; decrees of the committee, drafted by the specialist, needed a quorum of counter-signatures. There was and is debate about whether these were given on the nod. My conclusion is that they were, given that there were some 400 or 500 decrees to sign in a day, as long as harmony reigned in the government, but that in Robespierre's last months this was ceasing to be the case: we shall note resistance to Robespierre's directives from his police bureau.

The committee's measures were implemented by a variety of agencies. The ministries were subordinated to it. The only one with any independent power was the war ministry, which had a staggering (for the time) 600 employees. Under the minister J.-B. Bouchotte (April 1793–April 1794) the war ministry was filled with radicals and was the power-house of Robespierre's opponents to the left, the Hébertistes. After their execution in April 1794, the war ministry was split into seven commissions. The other ministries were also demoted – as a monarchical survival – to commissions. There were 12 of these. These mostly went to members of Robespierre's faction, notably Herman, who was put in charge of revolutionary justice and collaborated closely with Robespierre's police bureau. So for a period Robespierre controlled the terror through his police bureau and Herman's commission. But Herman increasingly took the initiative, particularly when Robespierre, having quarrelled with his colleagues, secretly seceded from the CSP in the last month of his life.

The CSP struggled to assert its authority over the country outside Paris. In the summer of 1793, following and anticipating the purge of the Girondins from the Convention, some 60 of the 83 departmental authorities refused to recognize the writ of the Convention. This was not as bad as it looked: the departmental authorities, the highest tier of local government, tended to be less radical than the second tier, the district, and the lowest, the commune. So it was often just the 'county council' that was in revolt. Nevertheless, major cities such as Lyon and Marseille were in rebellion and the great naval port of Toulon opened its gates to the British navy. The CSP gradually re-established its control by means of armies under deputies with roving commissions, the 'representatives-on-mission'. The CSP found, however, that these pro-consuls were too powerful and often pursued policies counter to those of the CSP – for example levying extraordinary taxation on the rich and raising private armies. So, when the rebellions had been suppressed, by December 1793, the 'representatives' were systematically replaced by sedentary officials called 'national agents' who were attached to the local constituted authorities and became the arms and eyes of the CSP. The Robespierristes Claude Payan and Achard became the national agents of Paris and Lyon, France's second city, respectively.

The national agents were set up by the law of 14 frimaire (in the revolutionary calendar introduced in October 1793) or 4 December 1793. This law is sometimes called 'the constitution of *gouvernement révolutionnaire*'. '*Gouvernement révolutionnaire*' was a technical term. On 10 October 1793 a decree of the Convention had proclaimed 'that the provisional government of France is *révolutionnaire* for the duration of the war'. What

this meant was that the implementation of the Jacobin constitution would be indefinitely suspended because of the wartime
emergency in favour of exceptional or 'revolutionary' measures, revolutionary in this special context meaning provisional,
emergency, extraordinary. Constitutional guarantees would be
suspended to deal with the crisis.

However, just because the measures were exceptional, they
did not have to be chaotic, hence the frimaire law. In fact this
is a very detailed and precise instrument integrating all power
in the country into a hierarchy culminating in the Convention's senior committee, the CSP. All the 'constituted authorities' – the key one being now not the disloyal *départements* but
the district – were thus subordinated and obliged to return
detailed questionnaires every *décade* (the new ten-day week).
The remit of the remaining 'representatives' was severely cur-
tailed – for example, they were expressly forbidden to levy
private armies. And, with two exceptions, from April 1794 all
'revolutionary', that is political justice was meted out in Paris
(which led to serious overcrowding in prisons, for which the
prisoners were blamed). This in turn led to swifter judicial
procedures, like the removal of defence witnesses, being introduced by the law of 22 prairial/10 June 1794, which was masterminded by Robespierre and railroaded by him through a
deeply unhappy Convention.

However, perhaps the most important and ambitious feature of the frimaire law was the integration of the parallel structures of popular power within the official hierarchy. The basic
unit of popular sovereignty, as we have seen, was the primary
assembly, also known as the sectional assembly. The primary
assemblies did not evaporate after an election but remained in
being to supervise the conduct of their 'mandatories'. They also
formed various executive sectional committees, the most important of which was the 'revolutionary' (in the above-mentioned
sense) or surveillance committees, which were responsible for
operating the law of suspects of 17 September 1793 and issuing
*certificats de civisme*, without which it was impossible to travel,
draw a pension, or find government employment.

In Paris, the 48 *sections* elected deputies to serve in the Commune of Paris, which in the interregnum between the fall of
the monarchy and the meeting of the Convention had dis-
puted power with the Legislative Assembly. Robespierre had
dominated the Commune at this time and the rationale behind

his dominance was that the Commune (which had made the insurrection of 10 August) possessed greater legitimacy than the Legislative Assembly (which had opposed the insurrection and would have liked to retain the monarchy). After Robespierre entered government he saw things in a different light: the popular demonstration before the Convention on 5 September 1793 was viewed with suspicion by the CSP. That had been the highwatermark of the popular movement and the alternative creed of 'direct democracy' with its parallel power structure. The frimaire law made the members of the surveillance committees in effect salaried public officials. Henceforth they were responsible not to the Commune, but to the committees of government.

The personnel of the Commune itself was renewed after the fall of the Hébertistes in spring 1794, under Robespierre's lieutenant, Claude Payan, the national agent of the Commune. Under Payan, the *sections* no longer elected their delegates to the Commune: they were appointed by the CSP on Payan's recommendation, often with no connection with the *section* they represented. Payan even abolished the very name 'primary assemblies' as an uncomfortable reminder of 'direct democracy'. So the primary assemblies, which had elected the members of the Convention, were now taken over by its committee, the CSP. The wheel had come full circle. However, Robespierre was fully capable of flipping back to the tenets of 'direct democracy' when it suited him to take an oppositional rather than a governmental stance; and this was what he did on 9/10 thermidor when the Commune launched an (unsuccessful) attack on the Convention.

The integration of the institutions of the popular movement into those of government was logical because both were parts of the democractic process, the *sections qua* primary assemblies elected the body which chose the deputies to the Convention. It was just a question of which had the superior legitimacy. Both were official, or rather constitutional parts of the electoral process. The network of Jacobin clubs – the 'mother society' in Paris and the provincial affiliates it directed through its voluminous correspondence – was a different kettle of fish. None of the constitutions even mentioned them. Indeed there was a feeling, expressed most forcibly by Louis XVI and by Le Chapelier, that they were actually *unconstitutional* because they recreated corporatism, that is states within states as the *parlements* had been, and corporatism had been abolished at the Revolution.

Robespierre, of course, did not take this line. He had nurtured the club through times of crisis and schism and it has given its name to the movement of which he was the foremost representative: Jacobinism. The Jacobin network was the only fully nationwide organization, because it fed on the same diet – notably Robespierre's speeches (Louvet had jibed that if the people were hungry they should eat Robespierre's speech on famine). The Jacobins performed two main functions: to influence elections (whether national or local or for officials) by providing 'slates' of officially approved candidates; and to spread Robespierre's ideology (ideology for most of the Revolution having suspended the operation of conventional politics). At work, for example at his police bureau, Robespierre issued ideological directives which were implemented by men who shared the same ideology and expressed it in their actions and words. So, 'looking with indifference at a tree of liberty' (or cutting one down for timber) was anti-patriotic and therefore treasonable. The officious zealotry of the local Jacobin clubs was a major factor in kindling civil war in the summer of 1793.

As Jacobinism moved from opposition to government (at the same time as Robespierre did, summer of 1793), so the clubs acted less as ginger groups and more as officials. They resembled the Communist Party in Soviet Russia. That is to say virtually every member of the Paris club (and the affiliates) became a public employee. And since they were a minority within a minority (most Frenchmen were monarchist at heart) there were not enough of them to go around and many had two or three jobs. That is why the Club, collectively, did not participate in the *journée* of 10 August 1792 or turn out for Robespierre's Commune on 9 thermidor: they were already there as individuals serving in more crucial capacities. At the same time, however, some people, and notably Saint-Just, thought that the soul had gone out of the Jacobins once they became bureaucrats instead of militants (for they may be said to have invented the militant tendency and displayed most of its characteristics). That may be what Saint-Just meant by his enigmatic, if graphic lament, 'the Revolution is frozen'.

The *ultima ratio* of government is armed force. Robespierre's abiding fear was that the army-of-the-line would intervene to change the course of the Revolution. His fears were proved right when Bonaparte seized power in 1799 but it did not happen in Robespierre's own time. That is not to say that Robespierre did not believe in armed force *per se* altering the course of the Revolution – it did on numerous occasions and with his backing – but that armed force should be a civilian force, that is one composed of part-time soldiers, in other words the National Guard. From September 1793 each of the Parisian *sections* had its own units of national guards, and became a miniature republic, though the artillery was organized separately.

Artillery was the key to military control of Paris, in particular the small four-pounder cannons firing grapeshot which were more effective in street fighting than the pikes carried by the bulk of the national guards. It was the gunners who operated the purging of parliament on 2 June 1793. (Their commander-in-chief, Hanriot, was an ardent Robespierriste, who turned out for him on 9 thermidor.) On 2 June there had been serious doubt as to whether the Convention could legally requisition troops for its own defence (just as there had been doubt as to whether the king could). Its attempts to countermand Hanriot's orders on 2 June failed miserably. However, on 9 thermidor its counter-summons to the national guard units (to turn out for it and to desert Robespierre, declared an outlaw) finally met with success.

# Chapter 5

# UNFINISHED BUSINESS, 20 SEPTEMBER 1792–2 JUNE 1793

. . .

## GIRONDINS AND MONTAGNARDS

The failure of Robespierre's coup against the Girondins in September and their return in strength to the Convention led to a period of acrimonious stalemate lasting until 2 June 1793 when parliament was purged by means of a further insurrection. Two diametrically opposed views of the parliamentary struggle have been advanced. The first, that of M.J. Sydenham,[1] considers that there was only one fully disciplined party in the National Convention, the 24-man Paris deputation, the Mountain, headed by Robespierre. These montagnards prepared their position in the Jacobins, voted as a block in parliament and their supporters used the public galleries to cheer them and heckle their opponents without mercy. This Paris deputation was opposed by virtually the rest of the Convention, so that its victory, with the help of the armed might of the Paris *sections*, was the defeat of parliamentary government itself. The more active part of the parliamentary majority was led by an inner group of some 60 deputies, known to history as the Girondins, with some 180 on the fringes. The voting discipline of this group was lax compared to that of the montagnards.

A. Patrick,[2] on the other hand, by adopting a different definition of 'montagnard' comes up with a different result. Granted that most deputies were hostile to Paris, this does not mean that they favoured the Gironde. There were many other issues – such as winning the war, defeating royalism, above all simply administering the republic and holding it together – where the Girondins were felt to fall short. This greater montagnard group, of some 200 deputies, was actually larger than the Girondin one. Moreover it took a much more active role in day-to-day administration, staffing the majority of the Convention's executive committees and, especially, providing the bulk of the representatives-on-mission to the provinces. Only in filling the offices of the Convention, the speaker and secretaries, essentially political positions, did the Girondins take the lead. Accordingly, what happened on 2 June was not so much a violent transfer of power as the insurrectionary legitimization of an already existing state of affairs.

There is truth contained in both these theses. Robespierre's group was the nearest to a party in the modern sense, which is ironic because he was loudest in his condemnation of party, which he equated with faction which, according to Rousseau, impaired the determination of the general will because it reduced the number of participants. Robespierre proclaimed:

> I do not recognize either a majority or a minority here. The majority is that of the good citizens; the majority is not permanent since it does not pertain to any party; it is recreated after every free vote. The general will does not form in shadowy cabals nor around ministerial tables. (9, 198)

The last sentence was aimed at the Girondins – *la faction brissotine* or simply *la faction* – but it described his own methods. Yet he was 'deeply shocked' when the minister Garat put it to him 'that he was no more than a party boss' and replied: 'One party pre-supposes a correlative; if there is one, there must be two of them at least. So where have you seen parties here? There have never been any; there is the Convention and a few conspirators.'[3] Precisely because it was a faction with a tight inner discipline the montagnard group had a disproportionately large influence.

As for the relative underlying strength of the two groups in parliament, the Girondins had the advantage for most of 1792 but lost it during the king's trial by the Convention (December–January): most of Patrick's examples of montagnard strength occur after that pivotal event. Patrick is right in saying that the relationship of the capital to the provinces was not the only issue (and right also to say that the Girondins were inept at and uninterested in administration) but it was easily the most important issue in 1793. And it enables us to answer

71

another hoary historiographical question: what distinguished the Girondins from the montagnards? Instead of saying that the former tended to be successful barristers, the latter unsuccessful ones, that one favoured free trade and the other was prepared to contemplate wartime regulation of the economy etc., we can say that the manner of the election of each group to the Convention constituted its essence.

So the montagnards represented not just Paris but the radical tendency there: they owed their electoral success to terror and relied on the same for its maintenance; they relied also on the sectional militants, the *sans-culottes*, and were prepared to propitiate them. This propitiation involved a return to the controlled economy of the *ancien régime* – price controls and rationing – for the *sans-culottes* were old-fashioned: their most authentic spokesman, the priest Jacques Roux of the group called the *enragés*, explicitly stated that the quality of life was better for the poor under the later Bourbons than under the Republic.[4] A controlled economy also helped with the war effort.

If Pétion and his colleagues had been returned for the capital things would have been very different. This is not a cynical observation: deputies were elected to represent the interests of their constituents. As it was the Girondins won the elections in the provinces. The very name of their party is derived from the *département* whose capital is the great mercantile city of Bordeaux, the rival of Bristol and Liverpool. Its values, and also those of cities like Marseille and Lyon, the great centre of silk manufacture, were those of the party. So the relationship between Paris and the provinces was at the heart of the problem, with the influence of the provinces on Paris almost as great as that of Paris on the provinces. It was a two-way process, with two-way travel of ideas and, above all, personnel from Paris to the provinces: one of Robespierre's partisans at Lyon called it a 'shuttle' (II, 226).

It was a case of Paris oppressing the provinces in the persons of their parliamentary spokesmen, and through the Commune's and then the Convention's agents in the *départements*. But it was also a case of an endless string of armed deputations of *fédérés* intervening or failing to intervene in the affairs of Paris. Sometimes, as with the Marseillais, that intervention accomplished an insurrection (on 10 August), sometimes, as with the Brest *fédérés* on 9–10 March 1793, it prevented one; sometimes they protected the Convention, sometimes threatened it. Yet in the final analysis, because of nearly a thousand years of centralization – temporarily reversed under the Constituent Assembly because of fear of the king but restored by the montagnards – what happened in Paris was decisive. If the king's head was cut off in Paris it could not be stuck on again in Avignon. War lords such as Lafayette, Dumouriez and Bonaparte had to seize Paris or fail; had, in an analogy they would have appreciated, to cross the Rubicon. Civil war was not really an option – there was no one to fight, with so many men of fighting age at the front. If you wanted to influence the outcome of the Revolution you had to lobby in Paris, if need be with the help of weapons.

The elections to the Convention also left a psychological mark on the protagonists. The Girondin leaders were well aware that Robespierre had tried to murder them. Mme Roland, the wife of the interior minister, wrote at the height of the September massacres: 'Robespierre has a knife to our throats'.[5] They wanted to avenge the humiliation of the Legislative by the Commune. But they were also conscious that the trial of the king would gravely damage them. The king was a valuable hostage as long as France was occupied by Prussian troops, but when Dumouriez checked them at Valmy on 20 September and negotiated their retreat, serious discussion of Louis's trial began. The fate of the king was a 'montagnard issue', one that the Girondins could not score off because their leaders had tried to save the throne (in January Vergniaud's letters to the king just before 10 August were produced and not disowned). As Croker put it, 'acquit him they [the Girondins] dare not; and, on the other hand, they were averse to his death. . . . Accordingly the Girondins had to delay the trial (which they did until December) and meanwhile use their parliamentary majority to cripple their opponents in advance'.[6]

This accounts for the frenetic quality of their activity. They flung everything at the montagnards but none of it was well directed. Louvet hoped to have Robespierre expelled from the Convention but his accusation of 'dictatorship' was too vague to convince the centre deputies (or 'plain') and Robespierre's defence on 5 November was well received. They also made the mistake of accusing Danton of peculation when he left the ministry to take up his seat in parliament. Not only was this ungrateful (Danton had saved their lives during the massacres) but it was foolish, for Danton, despite the violence of his language, was essentially a moderate, a *bon viveur*, the Mirabeau of the middle phase of the Revolution, 'the virtual leader of the "plain"'.[7] He probably had come by money illicitly at various stages of the Revolution and acquired loot in the sack of the Tuileries, but this made him a man of property and, as we have seen, he was already a man of position in 1788. Above all he had played a Churchillian role in national defence in September. Every French schoolboy knows his rousing cry: 'De l'audace, de l'audace et encore de l'audace et la patrie est sauvée!'. The Girondin attack on Danton failed.

So too did their proposal for a departmental guard for the Convention which was regarded as a needless provocation to Paris. Defeated in this, they fell back on the time-honoured custom of bringing up *fédéré* units from the south. However, Robespierre checked them here too by deploying his equally time-honoured tactic of getting the Jacobins to fraternize with them, and offering them 'a civic fête on the Place du Carrousel' on 16 January 1793 (9, 382). So the Girondins entered the king's trial weakened not strengthened.

.   .   .

## THE KING'S TRIAL

Robespierre's speech to the Convention of 3 December on this question is among his finest. He argued that Louis had been convicted by the people on 10 August and should merely be executed. On that day those who had stormed the Tuileries 'stood proxy for the whole of society' (9, 89). The legalistic Convention opted for a trial, though an unfair one since they were the prosecutors, judge and jury. Robespierre then insisted that Louis had no rights under the constitution he had violated and that when the safety of the state was at stake the legal safeguards possibly appropriate in cases between citizens could be waived. 'Louis must die that the country may live.' He must be cast out of the heavenly city and stoned (9, 311). Robespierre hoped he would be the last; he was the first of many. The doctrine which Robespierre enunciated in the king's trial was a milestone on the road to the charter of the Terror, the law of 22 prairial.

Louis was convicted unanimously (there were some abstentions) of his meaningless crimes, such as 'conspiring against liberty', and those who wanted to save his life proposed an appeal to the people through the primary assemblies. Robespierre made no bones about resisting this on the grounds that the terror which had produced a desirable result in September was no longer available:

> Would not this . . . be the surest means of rallying all the royalists, all the enemies of liberty whatsoever; of returning them to the primary assemblies which they deserted at the time of your nomination, that happy time of revolutionary crisis which restored some vigour to expiring liberty? (9, 189)

The motion was defeated by 424 votes to 287 and those who had voted for it were particularly vulnerable to reprisals. For the regicides had now burnt their bridges and were likely to be suspicious of the appellants, who could cross over theirs if there were a restoration of the monarchy.

The king's execution on 21 January was the turning-point in the struggle between Girondins and montagnards. Results were immediate. On 9 January the Girondins had forced some of their supporters on to the Convention's senior committee, the CSG, but on 21 January the Mountain staged a counter-purge in a deserted, late-night sitting of the Convention. The criterion applied had been provided by the king's trial: those who had not voted for the king's death and/or those who had voted for the appeal to the people were excluded. The next day Roland resigned as minister of the interior, to be replaced by Garat, a trimmer. Only two members of the Executive Council, Clavière (finances) and Lebrun (foreign affairs), were now Girondin sympathizers.

. . .

## THE EXTENSION OF THE WAR

The Prussian retreat enabled Dumouriez to concentrate his attention on the Austrians, whom he defeated in the battle of Jemappes on 6 November. The occupation of Belgium swiftly followed but led to errors of judgement by the Convention. On 19 November it declared that it would give armed assistance to any people wanting to throw off the yoke of their tyrants. This was ideological warfare but a more conventional motive was revealed on 15 December when Cambon proposed a novel way of shoring up the value of the *assignats*, the paper currency which was being printed to pay for the war. Collateral for the paper currency would be found by the confiscation of ecclesiastical, feudal and public property in occupied territories, including Belgium, the Rhineland and Savoy, the latter annexed on 27 November. The circulation of the *assignat* would also be enforced in these territories. Dumouriez protested in vain that it would alienate the Belgians and he was right: this policy produced rebellion in Belgium once the Austrians had knocked out the French garrison that General Dumouriez had left behind when he was ordered to invade Holland on 31 January.

The invasion was bound to lead to war with Britain (who had already withdrawn her ambassador on Louis XVI's death) since she could not allow a major continental Power to occupy the Low Countries with their ideal harbours for launching an invading fleet. So on 1 February France seized the initiative by declaring war on Britain too. Soon she was at war with all the Powers except Russia.

On 18 and 21 March Dumouriez was defeated by the Austrians at Neerwinden and Louvain. He then signed an armistice to allow him to march on Paris and proclaim Louis XVI's eight-year-old son king. Failing to carry his troops with him, he defected to the enemy on 5 April with his general staff. As late as 10 March Robespierre had expressed his confidence in Dumouriez, who 'was bound to the success of our arms by self-interest', that is his military reputation (9, 308). The Girondins on the other hand had quarrelled with him when he was foreign secretary during their first administration and they had no part in his treason. Nevertheless they had exploited his success and were blamed for his failure. Robespierre initiated the attack.

On top of this, between 10 and 15 March the *département* of La Vendée, in the Catholic west, rose for throne and altar. The occasion of the revolt was the levy of 300,000 men to serve at the front but to this was added deep resentment at the Civil Constitution of the Clergy and the king's execution. With a 50 per cent depreciation of the *assignat* there were serious food shortages in the capital and food riots on 23/24 February. Robespierre condemned these because sugar, the object of the rising, was not a fitting goal for a revolutionary *journée*. On 10 March news that the Austrians had taken Liège and crossed the river Meuse led to a still-mysterious popular *journée* in which Girondin printing presses were smashed. The rising fizzled out because it received no support from the Commune or the Jacobins, Robespierre arguing that it would harm relations with the provinces, and because it was resisted by *fédérés* from Brest.

The spring crisis also spawned a series of institutions which would be the mainstay of the Terror. On 10 March the Revolutionary Tribunal (briefly operational the previous August) was set up permanently to try political crimes – just three months after Robespierre had proclaimed that the king's would be the last such trial. Then on 21 March the 12-man 'revolutionary committees' were set up in each *section* to hunt for foreigners and later 'suspects'. Most important of all on 5 April the CSP was instituted. Danton was the moving force behind the creation of a strong government. Robespierre had supported him, arguing the need for 'unity of action', and had even briefly served in a prototype, the commission of public safety. But he had resigned from that body since it contained only six 'patriots' and, as he naively put it, 'these six members, of whom I was honoured to number myself, could not win a majority' (9, 368). The complexion of the first CSP, dominated by Danton, was also centrist, with such members as Barère, Lindet, Cambon and Treilhard. Robespierre preferred to stay in opposition, despite the fact that between 21 January and 2 June only two of the deputies who served either on the CSG or CSP had not voted for the king's death and both these had opposed the 'appeal'.[8] Robespierre was uncomfortable working with Danton, probably always distrusted him, but when Danton's wife died at this time Maximilien wrote him a warm letter: 'I love you as long as life lasts. At this moment I am you' (3, 160).

. . .

## THE FALL OF THE GIRONDINS

The CSP attempted to mediate between the Convention and the radical portion of the sectional movement which sought the expulsion of over 20 Girondin deputies and the execution of Roland. Robespierre's position was equally nuanced. He wanted the heads of his opponents (his personal hatred of them was at the centre of the matter) but he feared that a 'partial' insurrection would be made the excuse for a purge of the montagnards by departmental forces and even that the

Girondin leaders were trying to provoke one (9, 420). He wanted the Jacobin insurrection to be, as Garat put it, 'an apish imitation' of 10 August.[9] On 10 April Robespierre had a petition which the Halle-au-blé *section* intended to present to the Convention demanding the expulsion of the Girondin leaders rejected because of the 'terrible impression it would create in the *départements*'. He demanded that it be entirely re-cast and presented in the name of all 48 *sections*, specially convoked for the purpose. This was done and on 15 April it was presented to the Convention in the name of 35 of the *sections*. It demanded that a list of the culpable deputies should be communicated to the *départements* by 'special couriers' and that once the adherence of a majority of the *départements* had been ascertained, the deputies should voluntarily withdraw (9, 413–16). Needless to say the consultation exercise would be carried out by the local Jacobin clubs.[10] When the Girondins trumped the delegation's ace by calling for new elections, which they would have won, the idea was dropped.

Representatives-on-mission were sent to the provinces to prepare them for a coup. Anti-regicide and appellant deputies were largely excluded from the missions, only 8 per cent being sent compared to the 37 per cent of those who had voted for severity against the king.[11] But they often behaved tactlessly and the missions were counter-productive. It was a risky strategy for the montagnards: the absence of some 134 'patriot' deputies restored to the Girondins the majority they had lost in the king's trial. On 2 April Danton called for the return of the representatives in order to recreate the montagnard majority.[12]

Whilst Robespierre waited, the crisis was hastened by the Commune, which had passed out of Robespierre's control on his re-entry to parliament. A rising star was its deputy-procurator, Jacques René Hébert, who also edited *Le Père Duchesne*, a radical journal written in the popular idiom. Hébert aspired to be minister of the interior. Apart from pressing for immediate expulsion of the Girondin leaders, the Commune pressed on the Convention popular demands such as price controls. Alarmed at the situation developing in the capital, Garat, minister of the interior, proposed to the CSP abolishing the Commune and sending replacement deputies to Bourges where they would become the National Convention if anything happened to the one in Paris – in fact a Girondin policy. The CSP jibbed at this but it did set up a 'commission of 12', dominated by the Girondins, to investigate the Commune's proceedings. The Girondins had already sent Marat before the new Revolutionary Tribunal for inciting a purge of parliament, themselves setting the precedent for ignoring parliamentary inviolability: Marat was acquitted. Now the commission of 12 arrested Hébert and Dobsen, the president of the Cité *section*. It was this action which precipitated the *journée* of 31 May.

Much is still unknown about this *journée*. A radical committee meeting in the former bishop's palace (Évêché) seems to have contested planning of the insurrection with the Commune; a compromise was reached between the two bodies before the insurrection but this weakened the effectiveness of the *journée* of 31 May when the Convention consented only to dissolve the commission of 12. The Convention's defiance also stemmed from the fact that the popular movement was divided between montagnard and Girondin *sections* – Soboul reckoned there were some 20 with a natural 'moderate' majority.[13] On 31 May the *sections* Molière, La Fontaine, Pont-Neuf and Gardes-Françaises pledged their loyalty to the Convention, necessitating a second *journée* on 2 June.[14]

On that day, nothing was left to chance; a note among the papers of the Évêché committee dated 2 June explains:

> To prevent dangerous *sections* from deploying their cannons against the friends of the *patrie*, we must write to the commander-in-chief [Hanriot] to order the suspect *sections* to proceed to such and such a post with their cannons, etc. for the public safety, and there, surrounded by the other armed citizens of reliable *sections*, we will be safe from danger.[15]

So when the deputies left their chamber, perhaps trying to find the loyalist *sections*, they found themselves surrounded by hostile gunners whom Hanriot ordered to load their cannons. Browbeaten, the deputies returned to their chamber and ordered the house arrest of 29 Girondin members and two ministers. On 6 June 1773 Girondins signed a secret protest against the Jacobin *coup d'état*. Meanwhile some of the 29 broke their house arrest and sought to raise the provinces against the rump Convention.

As usual before an insurrection, Robespierre's trail goes cold. As usual before an insurrection he fell ill. He did not speak in the Convention between 5 and 27 May or in the Jacobins between 13 and 24 May. He told Garat, 'I am weary of the Revolution. I am ill'.[16] On 26 May he told the Convention: 'I cannot tell the people how to save itself. Worn out by four years of Revolution, that is beyond my strength' (IX, 537–8). He made just one intervention in the Convention between 31 May and 2 June: on 31 May he demanded that the Girondin deputies should not just be arrested but put on trial. For the moment he did not get his way. Nevertheless, his party was now in power and it was only a matter of time before he entered the government.

.  .  .

## THE SITUATION IN THE PROVINCES

Robespierre saw the rising of 31 May as pre-emptive, and given the strength of moderate *sections* there is something in this. The struggle was also mirrored in the provincial cities of France. The Jacobin lights were going out all over the Midi. Marseille fell on 28 April, Bordeaux gradually between April and June, and Lyon on 29 May. Toulon was the last city of importance to fall (on 12 July). News from it was cherished by the Paris Jacobin Club but seldom got through. Doubtless Toulon became a custodian of Jacobin as Granada had formerly been of Moorish civilization, as the elite refugees from fallen Jacobin citadels crowded in. Robespierre described the situation graphically to the Jacobin Club:

> from the north to the Midi, from sunset to dawn, the land is strewn with corpses and the blood of patriots drenches the whole of France; the Midi revolts and joins our enemies in the north to forge chains for us; Marseille, hitherto the rampart of liberty, is today its tomb. The same fate awaits us if we do not display energy and if Paris does not rise as one to crush the hydras which are whistling in our ears . . . (sighs, lamentations and groans). (9, 539)

In this sequence of *journées*, the Parisian one of 31 May comes towards the end, just after Lyon but before Toulon. Robespierre, with some justification, saw them all as part of a group, all closely contested, with the Jacobins winning out in Paris, but only at the second attempt on 2 June. At this time he wrote:

> The internal dangers come from the bourgeois; to defeat the bourgeois, it is necessary to rally the people. Everything was ready to

place the people under the yoke of the bourgeoisie and send the defenders of the Republic [*sic*, for Jacobins] to the scaffold. They have triumphed at Marseille, at Bordeaux and at Lyon; they would have triumphed at Paris but for the present insurrection. (II, 15–16)

There were two often distinct strands to what the Jacobins called 'federalism': local particularism and anti-Jacobinism. Sometimes even in strongly Jacobin areas there was resentment at the superior attitude taken by Parisian agents, a condition sometimes referred to as 'Jacobin federalism'. The Avignon Jacobins had been the beneficiaries of many speeches in their favour from Robespierre over the years and in the summer of 1793 the Avignon municipality was still dominated by the ultra-Jacobins and remained loyal, though shaken by events in Marseille. Nevertheless the 'representatives' Bayle and Boisset alienated them by calling their hinterland, the Comtat Venaissin, 'the homeland of anarchy'. True to their mentor, Robespierre, they replied that they had been 'calumniated'.[17] In a case such as this, Robespierre tended to side with the locals.

As W. Edmonds has shown, the towns which declared against the Convention tended to be those where the conflict between the local Jacobins and their 'moderate' opponents was unresolved. Where it was clearly resolved, even if the 'moderates' had won, they were able to 'apply the principles of *attentisme* and solidarity against outsiders, as did Rouen, Elbeuf and Bourges'.[18] There was no need for them to rebel for they were strong enough to ward off contagion from Paris. Where a battle raged, montagnard deputies were sent to tip the balance in favour of the local Jacobins but they generally behaved so ineptly that they tipped it the other way.

Many of the features of the provincial revolts are to be found in Lyon, the most serious of them. Some detail must be given since Lyon was to play an important part in the rest of Robespierre's story: the characters introduced here were to be key members of the faction he built up in government and played a part in his ultimate downfall. In Lyon, the second city of France, there was a vast gulf in wealth between the nobility and upper bourgeoisie, and the silk workers. In 1786 a weavers' strike had been violently suppressed and the city had been virtually out of control in both July 1790 and the autumn of 1792. In 1792 Joseph Chalier, a friend of Robespierre's who had first pointed out to him the depth of Roland's depravity (10, 525), had proceeded to Lyon and as 'an emissary of the Commune of Paris' invited Lyon to emulate the September massacres (III, 147). By these methods he had gained control of the municipality but control of the hierarchically superior *département* and of the National Guard remained in the hands of the moderates.

The Lyon Jacobins despatched two of their number, Gravier and Fillion, to Paris to lobby for reinforcements. They addressed the Convention and became friends of Robespierre's. On 3 March the reinforcements arrived at Lyon in the shape of three members of the CSG, Basire, Legendre and Rovère. Affecting impartiality, they upheld the election of Chalier's nominee as mayor but at the same time 'unmasked' his deputy 'for selling *certificats de civisme*'. Another characteristic act was the arrest of the anti-Jacobin editor of the *Journal de Lyon*. This was not enough for Chalier, who denounced their 'moderation'. They were also apparently reprimanded for moderation by Augustin Robespierre, on mission nearby.[19] Achard, a leading Robespierriste in Lyon, wrote to Gravier and Fillion, who had stayed on in Paris, that the 'representatives' were 'scoundrels who should be guillotined'; he asked his correspondents to denounce them in the Jacobins and burn his letter (II, 218–21). The deputies concerned were all mainstream montagnards. One of them later blamed Chalier 'for all the ills Lyon suffered in the Revolution' (III, 149).

Chalier maintained a 'regular correpondence' with Robespierre's intimate, the Lyon ex-patriot, violin merchant and juror on the Revolutionary Tribunal, Renaudin (III, 147). Chalier preached against a 'mercantile aristocracy' just as Robespierre claimed that 'the plan of our enemies is to reconstitute the aristocracy' out of the haute bourgeoisie and the remnants of the *noblesse*. Robespierre and Chalier were the earliest advocates of *armées révolutionnaires*, that is of *political*, civilian armies, similar to the Chinese Red Guard. Their role was to be, as R. Cobb put it in the case of Chalier's army, 'to preserve the fragile sans-culotte minority in the town'. In Paris and Lyon, when the armed struggle came, their respective 'armies' were incomplete. By 31 May the Parisian *armée révolutionnaire* was only embryonic, but among the papers of the Évêché committee, which organized the *journée*, is a list of 'the citizens who have enrolled for the *armée révolutionnaire* at the salary of forty sous per day'.[20] Fillion, back in Lyon, pointed on 28 May to a nucleus of 750 fully equipped men out of the intended total of 6,400.

However, the following day the 'moderates' abolished the Jacobin municipality at Lyon by force of arms before the Jacobin 'army' could be completed.[21] Chalier was executed, his head, as Robespierre told the Jacobins, being severed from his body only at the fourth attempt (10, 525). News of the fall of Lyon reached Paris on 1 June.

.  .  .

## NOTES

1.  M. Sydenham, *The French Revolution* (1965), p. 130.
2.  A. Patrick, *The Men of the First French Republic* (1972), *passim.*
3.  P.J.B. Buchez and P.C. Roux, *Histoire parlementaire de la Révolution française,* 40 vols, (1834–38), XVIII, p. 440.
4.  *Jacques Roux, Scripta et acta,* ed. W. Markov (1969), pp. 140–6.
5.  Mme Roland, *Lettres,* ed. C. Perroud, 2 vols (1900–2), I, pp. 434–5.
6.  J.W. Croker, *Essays on the Early Period of the French Revolution* (1857), pp. 355–6.
7.  A. Goodwin, *The French Revolution* (1966), p. 125.
8.  Patrick, *Men,* pp. 119–20.
9.  D.-J. Garat, *Mémoires* (1862), p. 377.
10. G. Walter, *Robespierre* (1946), pp. 367–8.
11. Patrick, *Men,* p. 116.
12. F. Bluche, *Danton* (1984), p. 322.
13. A. Soboul, *Les Sans-culottes Parisiens en l'an II* (1958), pp. 25–8.
14. P. Saint-Claire Deville, *La Commune de l'an II* (1946), p. 88.
15. Deville, *Commune,* p. 91 n.1.
16. Garat, *Mémoires,* p. 95.
17. H. Johnson, *The Midi in Revolution, 1789–1793* (1986), p. 232.
18. W. Edmonds, *Jacobinism and the Revolt of Lyon, 1789–1793* (1990), p. 41.
19. Edmonds, *Lyon,* pp. 168–9, 250–1.
20. Deville, *Commune,* p. 88.
21. R. Cobb, *The People's Armies,* trans. M. Elliot (1987), p. 23.

# PART TWO

# GOVERNMENT

# Chapter 6

# FROM ROBESPIERRE'S ENTRY TO THE CSP TO THE DEATH OF DANTON, JULY 1793–APRIL 1794

. . .

## THE FALL OF THE 'FIRST' CSP

The *journée* of 2 June brought Robespierre's party to power but he did not himself enter the CSP for another two months. The delay was because Robespierre could not serve in an administration headed by Danton and committed to peace at home and abroad. On 6 June Robespierre's intervention in the Convention caused the shelving of a series of recommendations, in the name of the CSP. The first was that the Convention should have the right to requisition armed force. On 2 June the Convention had tried and failed to requisition armed force and it was unclear whether it was legal/legitimate for parliament to resist the 'sovereign people'. Barère also asked that Hanriot should be replaced as commander of the National Guard and that an equal number of deputies to the arrested Girondins should be sent to their *départements* as hostages (9, 544–47).[1]

All these proposals implied criticism of the recent *journée*: the first two were designed to ensure that the Convention would never again be intimidated; the third underlined the government's intention to negotiate with the various provincial rebellions, which were spreading further in reaction to the recent insurrection. Garat, minister of the interior, sought to win back the revolted *départements* by offering fresh municipal elections, but was reprimanded by Robespierre:

> I see. You propose that we should dismiss a patriote Commune; it is against all true principles; the revolutionary government is here to maintain them and not to annihilate them.[2]

Danton also tried to calm international nerves by having the ideological and spoliatory legislation passed at the end of 1793 repealed on 15 April. He entered into discrete negotiations with the aim of detaching Britain and Prussia from Austria. Unfortunately his negotiating stance both at home and abroad was weakened by defeats. The one impacted on the other: the news that Saumur had fallen to the Vendéen rebels on 9 June, opening up the Loire valley to them, led to troops being sent there from Custine's army of the Rhine. Thus weakened, Custine was unable to prevent Condé, Valenciennes and Mainz falling to the Austrians. In addition the Kingdom of Sardinia and Spain entered the war, opening up two new fronts.

Robespierre equated defeat with treason, especially in a noble general like Custine, whom he harried remorselessly. Bouchotte, the radical war minister, attacked Danton. There was considerable hostility to Bouchotte from sections of the Convention, including Cambon and Carnot. They accused him of replacing talented generals with patriotic ones, such as the goldsmith Rossignol who was put in charge of the war in the Vendée. Twice the Convention voted to replace Bouchotte but the decisions were reversed by pressure from war office employees, ensconced in the popular movement. Robespierre assisted in the defence of Bouchotte and this was the issue on which he entered the CSP. Bouchotte's cause had been assisted from within the CSP by a new entrant, Saint-Just, who on 10 July was put in charge of military policy in the CSP leading to a time of 'ideological affinity' with the war ministry.[3]

Saint-Just, with four other deputies including Couthon, had been added to the CSP to draft what became the Jacobin constitution of 1793. Robespierre himself had a large input into this radical document, which included the legal right of insurrection and which was ratified by the primary assemblies by 1,800,000 votes to 12,000 in August. Garat admitted to spending heavily to secure a favourable outcome but even this was insufficient to achieve a decent turnout.[4] Despite all this effort, the constitution of 1793 was never implemented and probably never intended to be more than a propaganda exercise. It was hoped that it would allay fears of a Jacobin dictatorship since its implementation would have led to elections to a new assembly. Calling for the implementation of the constitution became a codeword for opposition.

The cripple Couthon had served in the Legislative Assembly and had got to know Robespierre through lodging with Duplay for a period. The beautiful, almost feminine Saint-Just had written Robespierre an admiring letter out of the blue in 1790 asking him to intervene to save the market of his local town, Blérancourt, in the general re-organization of the country (3, 87–8). In 1792, still aged only 25, he came to Paris and, legend has it, spent the night of 2 September, at the height of the massacres, together with Robespierre in a cellar. Robespierre procured his election to the Convention as part of the Paris delegation.

Saint-Just, Couthon and Saint-André (who was almost permanently on mission to naval towns) were to form the Robespierrist faction in the CSP but they did not slavishly imitate or obey him. For example, Saint-Just believed that the root of France's economic ills was the issuance of *assignats* without adequate collateral and that free trade should be maintained,[5] whereas Robespierre maintained that 'as much [produce] as is necessary to sustain life belongs to society, the residue only is a legitimate object of commerce' (9, 116). And on 28 June Robespierre ensured the defeat of Couthon's proposal, on behalf of the CSP, that the municipal officers of Toulouse should be provisionally reinstated, despite complaints from a deputation of '*patriotes opprimés*' who naturally found Robespierre's ear (9, 598–9).

Danton, Delacroix, and four others were voted off the CSP on 10 July. Robespierre entered the CSP on 27 July – a year to the day from his fall. On 14 August the composition of the CSP changed again, this time to Robespierre's disadvantage. In the belief that Robespierre's formula of 'punishing the guilty generals' was an insufficient military strategy, Barère called on two deputies who were also military experts to join the CSP, Carnot and Prieur (de la Côte d'Or). Carnot's appointment was predicated on acceptance by the committee of his strategy of an integrated front instead of the various armies acting separately. It also involved the eclipse and rivalry of Saint-Just, who had just set up a 'bureau militaire' in the CSP, and led to increasing friction with Bouchotte.[6] These quarrels would intensify over the next 12 months.

Robespierre too was displeased. He told the Jacobins that there were 'traitors' in the CSP and absented himself from the

CSP on the day of Carnot's entry and for the three succeeding days, he who had been so punctual in his attendance during his first fortnight.[7] Then he returned as if nothing had happened. Carnot was a natural conservative who had turned to the Revolution because he could not progress beyond the rank of artillery captain under the *ancien régime*. His enormous talent could not compensate for lack of noble birth. But he was a technician who detested ideology and though he joined the Jacobin Club he never attended. Carnot relied on good strategy, equipment and talent, Robespierre on patriotism.

Robespierre's accession to government was the signal for a redoubling of severity; the day after his entry to the CSP Saint-Just produced his report outlawing 16 Girondin deputies who had escaped from their house arrest and sending nine who hadn't before the Revolutionary Tribunal. Robespierre did, however, personally intervene to prevent the 73 Girondin backbenchers who had protested against the *coup d'état* of 2 June from being put on trial. On 1 August Barère, who was the committee's habitual spokesman in the Convention, proposed, among other things, that Marie-Antoinette be sent before the Tribunal, that the food given to the surviving members of the royal family should be cut down, and that on 10 August, the first anniversary of the storming of the Tuileries, the royal tombs at Saint-Denis should be smashed. The effect that Robespierre's entry to the CSP had on that body is most demonstrable in the treatment of the provincial rebellions, a policy of conciliation being replaced with one of repression.[8] Both Couthon and Barère changed from a soft to a hard line towards Lyon after Robespierre's entry to the CSP, and on 4 August, a week after that event, orders were given to march on the rebel city.[9]

. . .

## POPULAR POLITICS

Results, however, were not immediate, and on 2 September, the first anniversary of the massacres, news reached Paris that the rebels had handed the naval base of Toulon over to the British. There was also shortage of bread in the capital because a summer drought had made it impossible to operate the water mills. These were the immediate causes of another popular *journée*, 4–6 September. But to understand it we have to look at two factions to the Left of Robespierre, the *enragés* and the Hébertistes. On 13 July Marat had been assassinated by Charlotte Corday. Robespierre had never liked him but his sanguinary writing had provided a safe conduit for popular violence. His assassination left the way open for extra-parliamentary radicals, like the *enragés* who, to Robespierre's simulated disgust, claimed Marat's mantle and launched newspapers with the same titles as Marat's: *L'Ami du peuple* and *Le publiciste*.

Jacques Roux, the *enragé* leader, was a 'people's priest'. He was also the only leader of the popular movement who was able to articulate popular demands without distorting them. His power base was his *section*, Gravilliers, and, briefly, the Cordelier Club, which had been the stomping ground of Danton and was to become that of the Hébertistes. According to Robespierre, Roux was,

> known only by two dastardly actions, the first that of wanting [in a petition to the Convention] to have the merchants murdered because, according to him, they charged too much; the other that of wanting to make the people reject the constitution on the pretext that it was defective [for not banning hoarding of foodstuffs]. (9, 52–3)

Robespierre orchestrated a campaign of vilification against Roux, who was disowned by the Cordeliers and even by his own *section* and twice put in prison where he killed himself at the beginning of 1794.

That, however, only led to the popular mantle's being assumed by the Hébertistes. Yet they did not evolve naturally out of the popular movement and were not entirely identified with it. They possessed a power base in a hierarchy parallel to the one which was headed by the CSP. Hébertist mechanical power, so to speak, was based on the Cordelier Club, which supplied many of the personnel of the Hébertistes' other bastions, the war ministry and the Commune, of which Hébert was the deputy attorney-general; the faction's power of influence or reputation was based on Hébert's journal *Le Père Duchesne*, which was distributed by the war office to the army in large numbers.

Hébert was embittered because he felt he had not received recognition for his part in the *journée* of 2 June. His ambition was to be minister of the interior but in the elections to this post on Garat's resignation at the end of August Danton's friend Paré soundly beat him. Robespierre was well aware that the

Hébertistes were driven by ambition: 'They want our jobs', he told the Jacobins, 'let them have them' (10, 163). But Hébert expressed this in a coded way by calling for the implementation of the constitution. Behind this impeccably democratic demand there were ulterior motives which Robespierre was not slow to expose. Implementing the constitution meant the dissolution of the Convention (to which Hébert and his allies had failed to secure election, Ronsin being spurned by Robespierre) and the removal of the CSP's surveillance over the Hébertist bastion of the war ministry. Danton's friend Delacroix had also called for the implementation of the constitution and this may have planted in Robespierre the ripening suspicion that Danton and Hébert – the one too moderate, the other too radical – were conspiring together. He later gave the latter the Latin name *ultra* (too far) and the former *citra* (not far enough).

The September *journées* which climaxed on the 5th were not expressed in a constitutional rhetoric, still less in terms of ministerial ambitions, but in terms of long-standing popular demands: creation of an *armée révolutionnaire*, a law of suspects, price controls on a basket of 40 items of 'primary necessity' (law of the general maximum). Though the government was under pressure – Robespierre temporarily lost control even of the Jacobins – it managed to turn the popular demands to its own advantage. For example, the law of suspects became a cornerstone of a bureaucratic terror. The maximum law would also help the CSP to provision the army cheaply. Similarly Robespierre had been the first to propose an *armée révolutionnaire*. In the autumn he was still enthusiastic about one, witness the immortal entry in his notebook: 'complete the appointments to the *armée révolutionnaire* and then purge it'. And whilst the Cordelier Club was 'packed with officers from the *armée révolutionnaire*',[10] as Bouchotte reminded him, the list of its staff officers had been vetted by the Jacobins (II, 335).

Danton also, playing the elder statesman, came up with the double-edged proposal that a wage of 40 sous a day be paid to those attending sectional assemblies which, however, were reduced to two a week, thus ending their 'permanence' which had existed since July 1792. Varlet, a surviving *enragé*, protested against the measure and was imprisoned for his pains.

Another way in which the CSP turned popular pressure was by co-opting two radical deputies, Billaud-Varenne and Collot d'Herbois, the final additions to the 'great' CSP, after which it remained unchanged until the fall of Robespierre. Billaud and Collot are sometimes called Hébertistes. In fact they had long been close to Robespierre, though Billaud had recently given himself nuisance value by asking for a body (other than the CSP) to supervise the ministries. Billaud had been a loyal ally to Robespierre in the Jacobins during his conflicts with the Girondins and in the Commune during the September massacres. Collot also had worked closely with Robespierre, notably over the elections to the Convention. Billaud saw himself as a revolutionary theoretician, like Robespierre, and he was the architect of the law of 14 frimaire (see Chapter 4).

With hindsight the *journée* of 5 September marked the zenith of the popular movement, which after the law of 14 frimaire was increasingly integrated into the official bureaucratic structures. Militants became salaried officials. The *journée* also marked the zenith of the Hébertistes. True, Hébert followed up the *journée* by campaigning in the Jacobins, the Commune and in his journal for an end to the Convention's committees encroaching on the jurisdiction of the ministries.[11] On 19 brumaire/9 October Robespierre denounced this campaign in the Jacobins, proclaiming: 'They want our jobs' (10, 163). This silenced Hébert so effectively that he never mentioned the subject again.[12] Henceforth his faction was on the defensive.

.   .   .

## DANTON PLANS TO END THE TERROR

By the end of 1793, the Jacobin regime was victorious at home and abroad. Marseille, Bordeaux, Lyon and finally on 19 December Toulon were recaptured. The Vendéen army was slaughtered in the streets of Le Mans on 13–14 December, though a guerrilla war continued. With the departure of Admiral Hood's fleet from Toulon, there were no foreign armies on French soil, whether Austrians, Prussians, British, Spaniards or Sardinians. That, however, led to a new threat to the CSP: Danton's moderate policies, which had seemed inappropriate in the previous summer, now had a certain allure.

In September General Houchard had forced the Duke of York to raise the siege of Dunkirk but he had allowed the British army to retreat unscathed. Though he was a commoner, indeed common, he was arrested. In protest Thuriot, the last

Dantonist in the CSP, resigned and on 25 September attacked the popular and bureaucratic terror: 'we must check this torrent which is sweeping us back to barbarism'.[13] Shortly afterwards, Danton retired to Arcis-sur-Aube with his new wife. On 18 November he left Arcis to return to Paris. Why?

According to what he told Garat, Danton's objective was to end the reliance on '*sans-culotterie*' which had been forced on the montagnards by the intransigence of the Girondins and was leading to the 'barbarism' Thuriot had condemned. To this end all the proscribed deputies would be recalled; the constitution re-drafted and implemented to embody the rule of law; and peace be made abroad. As a first step Desmoulins would prepare public opinion for a relaxation of the terror with a new journal, *Le Vieux Cordelier*, and the Dantonistes would seek to renew the membership of the CSP and CSG, eliminating Saint-Just, Billaud and Collot but winning over Barère, by an appeal to 'such humanity as he was thought to possess', and Robespierre, 'by appealing to his known pride and his attachment to liberty'.[14]

There were also less altruistic reasons for Danton's return: he was sucked into the maelstrom by the activities of his friends, often pursuing single-issue politics, for as Bouchotte observed to Robespierre they were living 'in a time when points of contact are continuous' (II, 323). Philippeaux harried the war ministry and the CSP for its conduct of the war in the Vendée; Danton's friend (and secretary as minister of justice) Fabre was arrested on 12 January for receiving money to connive at the falsification of a decree winding up the India Company – other Dantonistes had been arrested in the Autumn. Bourdon de l'Oise sought the abolition of the ministries.

The Dantonistes' main fire was directed at the Hébertistes, who returned it; and this struggle dated back to the previous autumn, arising principally out of the conduct of the war in the Vendée.[15] The representatives-on-mission sent to the Vendée tended to espouse the cause of the generals to which they were attached and Philippeaux was no exception. The major dispute was between professional soldiers (whom Philippeaux supported) and war office patriots, such as Rossignol and Ronsin, the commander of the *armée révolutionnaire*, whom Robespierre tended to support. But it was not only a question of personalities, or of the rival merits of patriots and professionals. Philippeaux, who came from the region, objected to the scorched-earth policy advocated by his enemies, which amounted to genocide *avant la lettre* since hundreds of thousands perished there and in the *chouan* wars in Normandy.[16] The CSP had ordered the devastation of the Vendée and Phillipeaux did not mince his words.

The struggle between the factions reached a crescendo at the turn of 1793/94, dominating business both in the Jacobins (where a purge was instituted which lasted on and off for eight months) and the Convention. Vainly Robespierre tried to hold the line by diverting attention to a discussion of the crimes of the British government, the British premier William Pitt having been officially designated 'the enemy of the human race'. Why should he have bothered trying to keep the factions apart? Why not benefit from their mutual destruction? It is sometimes suggested that this was indeed his policy. But no, the failure to contain the rivalry between two factions represents an elementary failure of government, a failure which destabilizes government, rather as Shakespeare's Richard II failed to contain the rivalry between Mowbray and Bolingbroke and lost his throne in consequence. A government which cannot contain rivalry between factions is weak, as the last two Bourbon kings found to their cost.

At first Robespierre semed to favour the Dantonistes, being particularly alarmed at the de-christianizing policies of Hébert's superior Chaumette, the national agent of the Commune, and his ally Fouché, 'representative' in the Nivernais. The high-watermark of the de-christianizing movement was reached on 10 November 1793 when the Archbishop of Paris having been terrorized into resigning his see, a Festival of Reason was held in Notre Dame. Though Robespierre was no longer a Christian, he believed in a personal god and detested atheism, which he thought was immoral. Moreover he believed that the persecution of Christianity would alienate the peasantry and make it difficult to make alliances with the smaller European countries (his sole idea in foreign policy). An entry in Robespierre's notebook runs:

> Overturn the decree of the municipality which bans the saying of mass and vespers.
> It does not have the right.
> It is a source of trouble.

And overturned it was, by Chaumette himself, on 28 November.[17]

For similar reasons Robespierre had been hostile to the introduction of the republican calendar, introduced on 5 October and starting not with the birth of Christ but of the Republic: the date of its proclamation, 22 September 1792, became year 1 day 1. The names of months were taken from the weather and of the days from agriculture and nature. The months were divided into three *décades*, so that there were only three days of rest a month which did not coincide with Sunday. Robespierre wrote in his notebook: 'indefinite adjournment of the decree on the calendar'.[18] But the calendar went ahead.

Robespierre, who read the proofs of the first two issues of Desmoulins's *Le Vieux Cordelier*, at first supported the idea of a 'clemency committee' to investigate arrests under the law of suspects. It is said that Collot, returning from Lyon on 27 frimaire in the republican calendar (17 December old style), first alerted Robespierre to the dangers of such a policy. Reluctant to harm his old schoolfriend, Robespierre proposed to the Jacobins burning Desmoulins's paper to save the man. Even when Desmoulins retorted by quoting Rousseau – 'burning is not answering' – Robespierre saved him from expulsion from the Club.[19] Robespierre's flirtation with 'clemency' was finally ended by the revelation of Fabre's fraud on 15 nivôse/4 January, on which the CSP commissioned a report from him.

This report is almost exclusively directed against the Dantonistes. There is no mention of the Hébertistes. True, his brief was to have Fabre condemned, 'who best knows what springs to touch to impart a particular movement to the various political machines'. But the Dantonistes are criticized for attacking key revolutionary institutions which were largely in Hébertist hands – Bourdon having 'denounced in one fell swoop the Commune, the *armée révolutionnaire*, Bouchotte and all the bureaux of the war ministry'. His proscription list consists of ten deputies, including Danton, Desmoulins, Delacroix, Philippeaux, Bourdon de l'Oise, Dubois-Crancé and Lecointre. His heaviest criticism is reserved for Bourdon and Philippeaux. Danton is referred to indirectly as 'the indolent and proud patriot, enamoured of comfort and fame' and in terms, of being led astray, that suggest that perhaps his life was not sought (10, 326–42).

Robespierre never delivered this report. The strain of holding the Mountain together took its toll of him. He had been intermittently ill in January but from 22 pluviôse/10 February to 23 ventôse/13 March he did not stray beyond his lodgings.

Perhaps he fell ill before he could get round to sketching in the other part of the conspiracy, the Hébertistes; perhaps, as Hampson suggests, he realized that an attack on both factions at once would be suicidal.[20] We can never know precisely what was wrong with Robespierre but throughout his political career there seems to be a pattern of nervous illness before political crises and these seem to become more protracted. Whilst he lay ill he received numerous sycophantic wishes for a speedy recovery from individuals and constituted authorities, but only one political letter has survived, from Gravier, of the Lyon faction of 'friends of Chalier', informing him of the machinations of the Hébertistes, emboldened by Robespierre's absence (II, 194–6).

. . .

## THE FALL OF THE FACTIONS

On 14 ventôse/4 March in the Cordeliers Hébert seconded a motion of the deputy Carrier (responsible for drowning Vendéen prisoners in the Loire) to declare a state of insurrection. Symbolically, the Club's copy of the Declaration of Rights was draped in black. The insurrection was directed at the deputies Philippeaux, Fabre, Desmoulins and Bourdon (who had earlier featured on Robespierre's proscription list). But how they planned to carry it out is a mystery since the Commune and all but two *sections* remained aloof.[21] Perhaps it was, as they later claimed, merely a 'symbolic' insurrection. The short answer to the question, 'when is an insurrection not an insurrection?' is 'when the *tocsin* is not rung'. Only one person suggested ringing the bell and he was answered with '*violents murmures*'.[22]

Whatever the nature of the Hébertistes' 'insurrection', it was an act of weakness not strength, designed to prevent the further erosion of their power base in the war ministry. We have seen that the period of entente between the CSP and the war ministry had ended in August 1793 when Carnot entered the CSP and took over responsibility for military direction from Saint-Just. Carnot chipped away at the jurisdiction of the war ministry, inducing the Convention to set up commissions to deal with 'arms and powder' and 'subsistence and supply'. On 23 pluviôse/11 February 1794 he announced plans to dismember the war office altogether.[23]

Carnot's attack on the functions of the war ministry coincided with the Dantonistes' attack on its personnel, culminating in the arrest of Vincent, secretary-general of the war office, on 17 December. On that occasion, Villain d'Aubigny, a protégé of Robespierre's in the war office, successfully lobbied Robespierre for Vincent's release (14 pluviôse/2 February). Perhaps Robespierre was receptive to d'Aubigny's lobbying because the criteria Vincent applied in making appointments, patriotism before talents, were similar to his own.[24] But on the question of Vincent, the Robespierristes were divided. War office employees like d'Aubigny and Gatteau, Saint-Just's secretary who said he would eat his hat if Vincent were a traitor, supported the office's secretary-general, whereas Gravier, in a letter to Robespierre, referred scathingly to 'le sieur Vincent' – implying *ancien régime* airs and graces.[25]

The CSP could have ignored the weakened Hébertistes but not the provocation of their 'insurrection'. Robespierre returned to the CSP on 13 March, the day the arrest of the Hébertistes was decided. He could have had no part in making the decision. The inescapable conclusion is that his colleagues in the government roused him from his sick-bed to make him dip his hands in the blood. Robespierre had a certain sympathy with the ethos of the Hébertistes – patriotism before talent – and for some on the fringes of their 'conspiracy'. My guess is that Robespierre's colleagues in the CSP bought his acquiescence in the arrests with two concessions: first that his protégés would receive the lion's share of the Hébertist levers of power; secondly that friends of Robespierre's who were compromised would be spared. These were headed by François Hanriot, former customs clerk, present head of the Parisian National Guard: Robespierre wanted to take over this key institution, which had made the *journée* of 2 June, as a going concern. Moreover Hanriot's artillery, the key to military control of Paris, was strengthened by the disbanding of the *armée révolutionnaire* on 7 germinal/27 March following the execution of its general, Ronsin: its 24 artillery companies were kept intact and though they were supposed to have been sent to the front most were in fact attached to the Paris *sections* and put under the general command of Hanriot.[26] Robespierre also saved a general in the *armée révolutionnaire*, Servais-Baudouin Boulanger, despite the fact that he had goaded Hébert to declare his 'insurrection' in the Cordelier Club. Not only this, but Robespierre made him an agent in his police bureau.[27]

Robespierre also saved Pache and Bouchotte, whom Robespierre had in July 1793 given the joint accolade of 'fidèles enfants de la patrie' (9, 618). Pache had preceded Bouchotte as minister of war and had pioneered Robespierre's policy of placing patriots rather than technicians, an approach made easier by the abolition of entrance exams for some parts of the service on 11 September 1792.[28] Currently Pache was mayor of Paris. Fouquier-Tinville had come up with the story that Pache had been designated by the Hébertistes as *grand juge* or head of state: Fouquier was told to suppress all evidence of this nature.[29] Bouchotte was given 24 hours' warning to dismiss his secretary-general Vincent,[30] who together with Hébert, Ronsin and 17 others were guillotined on 4 germinal/4 March. On 24 germinal/13 April Chaumette followed them as an accomplice. I make one more assumption about Robespierre's return to duties: that it was dictated by the need to make decisions and not by the progress of his recovery. And indeed that he never fully recovered.

On the night of 9 germinal/30 March Danton, Desmoulins, Delacroix and Philippeaux were arrested, without prior notification to the Convention. They were put on trial together with Fabre (who sat on the *fauteuil* reserved for the conspirator-in-chief – his 'accomplices' surrounding him on ordinary benches) and a group of shady financiers. Billaud-Varenne later accused Robespierre of turning on him 'like a fury' when he, Billaud, had first denounced Danton.[31] Against that we have the evidence of the proscription list examined above and the fact that Robespierre certainly warmed to his task, briefing Saint-Just for his report. He also defeated Legendre's motion that the accused Dantonistes be heard in the Convention with the sinister threat, 'whoever trembles is guilty' (10, 412–18). A later retort of Robespierre's seems to suggest that he despised the Convention for not putting up a better fight for its own: 'So, you want to avenge Danton! Why then you wretched cowards did you not defend him?'[32]

Danton, who was still immensely popular both in Paris and the Convention, defended himself well. His booming voice attracted a crowd outside the courtroom. Herman, the president of the tribunal, passed Fouquier-Tinville a note: 'in half an hour I will suspend Danton's defence'. He told Danton he could resume the next day but then insisted on hearing the rest of the accused first.[33] The defendants demanded to call members of the Convention as witnesses. Fouquier wrote a note to the CSP passing on this request but Herman wrote a second draft emphasizing that in making this request the accused were disrupting the court. This gave Saint-Just the opportunity to get a decree from the Convention saying that prisoners who insulted the tribunal should be removed from the court. He made no mention of the request for witnesses. This was the turning-point in a difficult trial for Herman. Danton and his friends were condemned on 16 germinal/ 5 April and executed in the late afternoon, against the back-drop of a vivid sunset. 'Above all', Danton said to the executioner, 'don't forget to show my head to the people: it's worth seeing!'[34]

Rational explanations of the proscriptions risk banality. The Hébertistes were a declining force: their heyday was September 1793; their 'insurrection' was an attempt to resist the further erosion of their only serious power base, the war ministry. The popular movement they imperfectly represented was already in a decline which their fall precipitated. They could have been ignored. The execution of Danton and his friends seemed to mark the final eclipse of the National Convention and yet it was from it that the CSP derived its authority.

In this account of Robespierre's first eight months in government we have seen how his entry into the CSP led to a redoubling of severity, notably in the handling of the provincial revolts. But we have also encountered several examples of his failure to control key events: to prevent Carnot's entry to the CSP or the introduction of the Revolutionary calendar or the 'factions' from tearing each other apart and de-stabilizing the Republic.

.  .  .

## NOTES

1.  G. Walter, *Robespierre* (1946), pp. 373–4.
2.  D.-J. Garat, *Mémoires* (1862), p. 248.
3.  H. Brown, *War, Revolution and the Bureaucratic State: Politics and Army Administration in France, 1791–1799* (1995), pp. 74–6.
4.  P.J.B. Buchez and P.C. Roux, *Histoire parlementaire de la Révolution française*, 40 vols (1834–38), XVIII, p. 426.

5.  *Moniteur,* XIV, p. 604.
6.  M. Reinhard, *Lazare Carnot,* 2 vols (1952), II, pp. 55 and 64.
7.  Walter, *Robespierre,* p. 381.
8.  M. Mortimer-Ternaux, *Histoire de la Terreur, 1792–1794,* 8 vols (1863), VIII, pp. 397–400.
9.  P. Mansfield, 'The repression of Lyon, 1793–4: origins, responsibility and significance', *French History,* 2 (1988), pp. 74–101, at p. 82.
10. Brown, *War,* p. 94.
11. Brown, *War,* p. 79.
12. C. Macnamara, 'The Hébertists: study of a French revolutionary faction in the reign of Terror', Fordham University, Ph.D., 1974, p. 453.
13. M. Sydenham, *The French Revolution* (1965), pp. 180–1.
14. Buchez and Roux, *Histoire parlementaire,* XVIII, pp. 451–3.
15. This is the view of Macnamara, 'Hébertists', pp. 235–42.
16. F. Bluche, *September 1792: Logiques d'un Massacre* (1986), p. 252.
17. A. Mathiez, *Études sur Robespierre* (1958), p. 222.
18. Mathiez, *Etudes,* p. 220.
19. N. Hampson, *The Life and Opinions of Maximilien Robespierre* (1974), p. 244.
20. Hampson, *Robespierre,* p. 246.
21. Macnamara, 'Hébertists', p. 389.
22. Macnamara, 'Hébertists', p. 392, n. 101.
23. Brown, *War,* p. 115.
24. Brown, *War,* pp. 69–70 and 74.
25. Ch. Vellay, 'Un ami de Saint-Just: Pierre-Germain Gatteau', *Annales Révolutionnaires,* I, pp. 64–79 and 265–75; Gravier to Robespierre, 20 ventôse (II, 194–6).
26. R. Cobb, *The People's Armies,* trans. M. Elliot (1987), pp. 610–12.
27. Brown, *War,* p. 94; Cobb, *People's Armies,* p. 610.
28. Brown, *War,* p. 48.
29. M. Eude, 'La Commune Robespierriste', *Annales historiques de la Révolution française* XII, pp. 131–61, at pp. 139–40.
30. Macnamara, 'Hébertists', p. 386.
31. Buchez and Roux, *Histoire parlementaire,* XXXIV, p. 23.
32. Duval's version, cited by J. Croker, 'Robespierre', *Quarterly Review* (1835), pp. 517–80, at p. 577.
33. N. Hampson, *Danton* (1978), pp. 170–1.
34. Hampson, *Danton,* p. 174.

# Chapter 7

# THE FORMATION OF ROBESPIERRE'S FACTION, JULY 1793–APRIL 1794

. . .

## CHARACTERISTICS OF ROBESPIERRE'S FACTION

When Robespierre entered government he exercised power of a more conventional kind than he had in opposition and of a kind conventional in terms of eighteenth-century politics: he built up a faction and placed its members in the key institutions of the Republic. In this respect his faction was similar to one in contemporary Britain. But where emolument was the alpha and omega for members of a British faction, members of Robespierre's faction were financially incorruptible and were picked for their ideological affinity and this imbued all their decisions, at whatever level in the hierarchy they were placed. They were all 'patriots' and had all been 'oppressed patriots'. Patriot may seem a vague term – who would claim not to be one? – but a Robespierrist patriot possessed certain defined characteristics, a mind-set, which will be explored in this second part of the book. And people who possessed it were quick to recognize their own: this made it possible for Robespierre to build up a faction largely on personal recommendation, which was as well since he was unsociable: someone remarked that he had few enemies because he knew few people.

In government Robespierre acquired patronage and created a faction to absorb it. The two increased *pari passu*. In the autumn of 1793 he acquired control of the personnel of the Revolutionary Tribunal, which we will look at in this chapter. On the fall of the Hébertistes, an outcome he had not sought, he acquired most of their levers of power: the Commune, the National Guard and most of the ministries, the subject of the next chapter. This gave him control of the municipal government and armed force of Paris. His protégé Herman became in effect head of the home civil service. Men like Herman and Payan, the national agent of the Commune, were not ciphers; their influence on Robespierre was almost as great as his on them. He was not good at administration; he was increasingly reclusive: they were his arms and legs, eyes and ears. This flowed from Robespierre's belief that if you put a patriot, 'one of us' as Herman put it, in a job he could be relied on to make patriotic decisions. Indeed he did not have to think about his decisions, they were instinctive, intuitive, as Robespierre and Couthon explicitly said with reference to the 'patriotic' jurors on the Revolutionary Tribunal: that was why due legal process was not necessary.

Since Robespierre never fully recovered from his illness and in his last month became an almost total recluse, Herman and Payan were able to take major policy decisions: Herman dramatically escalating the numbers sent to the guillotine, Payan organizing an insurrection against the National Convention. This was also true at lower levels, for example the Lyon faction known as the 'friends of Chalier' encouraged Robespierre in a fatal confrontation with Fouché. So it is important to know who the members of Robespierre's faction were, their backgrounds, mind-set and *modus operandi.*

This approach involves a shift of focus from Robespierre at the rostrum to Robespierre and his lieutenants at their desks, and to the private communication between them, such as Robespierre's directives from the CSP's police bureau. This is a more rewarding approach than analysing Robespierre's set-piece speeches on virtue, the crimes of the British government etc., whose impact is not demonstrable.

.  .  .

## ROBESPIERRE'S ROLE IN GOVERNMENT

Robespierre acquired his patronage as a member of the government. But what was his role in that government? The individual members of the CSP developed their own field of activity: Carnot, military strategy and organization; Lindet, food supply; Barère, spokesman in the Convention etc. Robespierre's specialisms were political police, political justice, ideology. At certain times, generally in the evenings, those members of the CSP who were not on mission to the provinces would meet together in the green room in the Pavillon de Flore in the Tuileries to discuss the general affairs of government. The main fields allocated to the CSP by the Convention were the conduct of diplomacy, the war and internal coercion. In the first two Robespierre's ideas were rudimentary.

It will be remembered that when, in the Constituent Assembly, La Rochefoucauld had asked him whether he had read the Treaty of Ryswick, Robespierre had replied that all that was necessary for the formulation of foreign policy was 'principles', that is the Rights of Man. By 1793 he had not learned any more since he seriously believed that if Dumouriez had invaded Holland earlier, there would have been a revolution in Britain (9, 308). And why had such revolutions not occurred in other countries also? Well,

> I lay it down as a fact and I defy anyone to deny that there has been a scheme on the part of French diplomatic representatives abroad to reject the union of peoples which was about to happen. (9, 312)

Courtois, who edited his papers, said that 'an immense quantity' of unopened despatches relating to Constantinople and the vital Levantine trade was found among them (I, 110).

On 21 brumaire/11 November 1793 Robespierre delivered a report to the Convention on the general diplomatic situation of the Republic. In his 'Note essentielle' of June/July (II, 15–16) he had stressed the importance of good relations with neutral countries. Since Danton had been ousted for trying to conclude peace, this was by definition the only area left for diplomacy. Robespierre's lengthy report concluded that good relations should in particular be maintained with the United States and Switzerland. To convince the former of the utility of the French alliance he advanced perhaps the most extravagant of all his conspiracy theories. Britain's objective throughout had been to place the Duke of York on the French throne; in this they had been aided by the king's cousin Orléans; once in possession of Toulon, Dunkirk and the French colonies, Britain would seek to reconquer her former American colonies. The method chosen would be to seek to 'federalize' America as Britain had sought to federalize France and in the same way, that is by dividing it between north and south (10, 168–9). This ingenious explanation accounted for the loss of Toulon, the attack on Dunkirk and the federalist revolt. One wonders what Congress would have made of it all.

Robespierre's military notions were hardly more reassuring than his diplomatic ones, consisting as they did in little more than punishing 'treasonable' generals and the hawk-like observance of the rest. His 1793 notebook is peppered with denunciations of generals whilst the upshot of his grand report 'on the principles of *gouvernement révolutionnaire*' of 5 nivôse/25 December (theme: the Constitution would have to remain in 'dry dock' because of the mountainous seas surrounding it) is (article I) to send a string of generals before the Revolutionary Tribunal (10, 281). H. Wallon concluded that his policy 'was to suspend the guillotine over the whole *armée du Nord*'.[1] Simon Duplay, the nephew of his host and later head of a division in Robespierre's police bureau, declared: 'I know for a fact that Robespierre knew nothing about military science'.

However, diplomacy and military strategy were not Robespierre's chief concerns. Least of all was routine administration, for which he had no aptitude. Danton is supposed to have said that Robespierre 'couldn't even boil an egg'.[2] Merlin de Thionville said:

> He was never well-informed. He had forgotten all his sterile college studies and what he picked up during his legal practice. In working for the prize essays offered by provincial academies, he had acquired some ideas which were philanthropical rather than philosophical. That was the extent of his knowledge. He never had the faintest idea about government, administration and diplomacy.[3]

. . .

## IMPORTANCE OF PERSONNEL TO ROBESPIERRE

Rather, Robespierre's specialism was personnel. Shortly before entering government he told the Jacobins what business the CSP should be about: 'its first care must be the purging of all the bureaux' (9, 476). And he meant what he said. Near the begining of his notebook he writes: 'order the ministers to supply a list of their employees and their agents [in the provinces]' and later on 'purge the bureaux' and, possibly related, 'ask Bouchotte what he has done'.[4] In any civil service there is recruitment, promotion, retirement and dismissal. But Robespierre was not just an ordinary personnel manager. Dismissals were by purge and under chapter four of the law of suspects (17 September 1793) those dismissed were imprisoned as suspects. Since this law guided much of Robespierre's work for the remainder of his life, it is worth citing its provisions:

Article 1. Immediately after the publication of the present decree, all the suspects in the Republic who are still at liberty will be placed under arrest.

Article 2. Suspects are deemed to be:

1. Those who whether by their conduct, their liaisons, speech or writings have shown themselves to be adherents of tyranny, federalism, or enemies of liberty.

2. Those who cannot justify, in accordance with the law of the previous 21 March, their means of livelihood and the fulfilment of their civic duties.

3. Those who have been refused *certificats de civisme.*

4. Public functionaries suspended or dismissed from their jobs by the National Convention or by its commissioners and not reinstated, notably all those who have been or should have been dismissed in virtue of the law of the previous 14 August.

5. Those former nobles, including the husbands, wives, fathers, mothers, sons and daughters of *émigrés*, who have not constantly displayed their devotion to the Revolution.

6. Those who have emigrated in the period between 1 July 1789 and the publication of the law of 8 April 1792, even though they have returned to France within the time-limit stipulated by this law or previously.[5]

The information was collated by the surveillance committees of the *sections.*

Robespierre's principal instrument of government was the list. The negative list was for proscription, not just delinquent officials but generals and 'representatives-on-mission'. His notebook contains a list of 'Representatives' to recall: Bourault, Ferraud, Rovère; and another of 'Representatives to send elsewhere'; he also prompts himself to 'recall all the commissioners with the [Armies of] the Rhine and the Moselle'.[6] The positive lists, for preferment, chart the growth of his faction. He jotted down in his notebook:

Principal measure of public safety. It will be necessary to send through all the Republic a small number of strong commissioners, armed with good instructions and above all good principles, to reduce public opinion to unity and to republicanism [i.e. Jacobinism]

– the sole means of ending the Revolution to the profit of the people. These commissioners will above all concentrate on discovering and inventorying men who are worthy to serve the cause of liberty.

To purge the surveillance committees, we must produce a list of all their members, their names, occupations and addresses.

2 We must update the list of the leaders of the counter-revolution in each locality . . .

It should, he hoped, be possible to establish a shaded map indicating the 'degree of civism or anti-civism of the various departments'.[7] This again shows Robespierre's governmental priorities: he was a member of the CPS and the 'principal measure of public safety' was 'discovering and inventorying' patriots.

Were the 'strong' commissioners despatched and did they manage to 'discover and inventory' any patriots? The answer to both questions is 'yes', though the evidence is patchy. The notebook shows that Duplay was sent to Lille, but not the exact nature of his mission. Young Jullien reported from Le Havre, Saint-Malo, Vannes, Lorient and later Bordeaux, and there must have been others apart from the local correspondents such as Aigoin from Toulouse. But until Robespierre acquired the police bureau, for which this work can be seen as a preparation, it was not institutionalized. As Jullien's reports to Robespierre make clear, on arrival in a new place he made contact with the local Jacobins and took it from there (3, 245–50). And all the work did finally culminate in a grand list, the 'list of patriots with more or less talent' which he compiled in the spring of 1794 to cope with the vast addition to his patronage. Before then his patronage was patchy: his main sphere of patronage in the autumn of 1793 was over the personnel of the Revolutionary Tribunal.

·   ·   ·

## THE REVOLUTIONARY TRIBUNAL AND
## THE RISE OF HERMAN

Robespierre, whose pressure through the Commune had resulted in the institution of the prototype tribunal on 17 August 1792, was the leading advocate of a separate body to deal with political offences according to separate criteria and procedures, notably a lesser reliance on formal evidence and a greater on the instinct of the 'patriotic' juror. And he was keen to extend the jurisdiction of the Tribunal, particularly over the generals. As early as March 1793 Robespierre had insisted that 'principles dictated' that General Marceau, who had been defeated by the Vendéens, should be tried not by a court martial (as Barère proposed) but by the Revolutionary Tribunal (9, 332); and on 27 July, the day he entered the CSP, he thwarted General Custine's request to be tried by the military committee of the Convention rather than by the Revolutionary Tribunal.[8]

But 'what makes [the Revolutionary Tribunal] *revolutionary*?' Robespierre asked rhetorically, and answered his own question: 'It is the character of the men chosen' (9, 304). The personnel of the Revolutionary Tribunal underwent two major modifications. In virtue of the decree of 5 September 1793 its numbers were expanded and in virtue of that of 22 prairial year 11/10 May 1794 they were contracted – there were not enough patriotic jurors available so their numbers had to be decreased and procedure 'simplified'. On both measures the influence of Robespierre was paramount. The first entry in his notebook is 'Nomination of the members of the Revolutionary Tribunal' (there are five further references to the Tribunal including 'Tribunal révolutionnaire va mal').[9]

In Robespierre's papers there is a draft list of members, dating from August, which contains the key names which appear on the final one (II, 12–13). The list is headed by Herman, currently, Robespierre notes, 'president of the criminal tribunal of the Pas-de-Calais', but designated as president of the Revolutionary Tribunal. Armand Martial Joseph Herman (sometimes spelt Hermann, the 'n' is sounded) was born at Saint-Pol, in what was to become the Pas-de-Calais *département*. His father was the registrar of the Estates of Artois. Saint-Pol is near Arras and Robespiere had known Herman from childhood. He was a year younger than Robespierre, 34 in 1793. They both practiced law at Arras: before the Revolution Herman was deputy public prosecutor of the Council of Artois, before which Robespierre pleaded. After Robespierre launched himself into national politics, Herman continued his provincial career, ultimately becoming president of the departmental administration as well as of the criminal tribunal.[10]

Herman headed Robespierre's 1794 list of patriots, where he is described as 'an enlightened and honest man capable of the highest employment'. An early indication that Herman would show initiative and severity occurred in November when he reminded Robespierre that the CSP had not responded to his request to substitute a sentence of death for one of banishment which 'in grave error' had been already passed (1, 280). Other men from Artois were drafted into the Revolutionary Tribunal. In November Herman suggested that Robespierre replace a sick judge on the Tribunal with a colleague from the Arras criminal tribunal: 'I propose one Carron for your consideration . . . he is a good *sans-culotte* republican, whom I consider to be one of us [que je crois propre à être avec nous]: he has no idea that I have mentioned him to you' (I, 280). Another Artésien was Lanne, the public prosecutor of Saint-Pol, who became a judge prior to becoming Herman's deputy when he became the head of the home civil service the following spring.

The case of Lanne illustrates the intimate cat's cradle of relationships between the Robespierristes. In addition to his relationship with Herman, Lanne was also intimate with Lebas, one of only two Robespierristes in the CSG (the other was the painter David). Lebas went on several missions to the frontier provinces with Saint-Just. Lanne was Lebas's best man when he married one of the Duplay girls. With another, Eléonore, Robespierre pursued a 'platonic courtship'. Lanne used a favourite codeword with Robespierre's faction, 'au courant', to signify being abreast with the latest orthodoxy.[11]

Embattled provincial Jacobins (*patriotes opprimés*) formed an important category of Robespierre's recruits to the Revolutionary Tribunal. Apart from his own region of Artois, which Robespierre considered to be priest-ridden and a hundred years behind the rest of France, Robespierre recruited from the Jura and the Midi. Many a speech he had made on behalf of the '*patriotes opprimés*' of the Jura, whose departmental authorities had been the first to raise the federalist flag with the decision to send its substitute deputies to Bourges under armed escort to form a parallel Convention,[12] and Robespierre puts down for a judge in the Tribunal René-François Dumas, whom he describes as 'a lawyer from Lons-le-Saunier, a patriot proscribed by the counter-revolutionaries of the Jura'. In fact Dumas did better than judge, becoming first vice-president and then succeeding Herman as head of the Tribunal when the latter received his promotion. Robespierre characterizes Dumas as 'energetic', a slightly disturbing epithet in view of his formidable functions (II, 11). Another Jura patriot, also from Lons, was Ragmey, who was made a judge.

The southern contingent included as judge Subleyras, from the Gard; Fauvetty, from Uzez; Gravier, described as a 'vinegar merchant from Lyon' who was also an agent and frequent correspondent of Robespierre's; Meyère, a member of the departmental administration of the Gard; Aigoin, Robespierre's correspondent from Montpellier; Gillibert from Toulouse and Claude Payan from Valence.[13]

Another large category of Robespierristes in the Tribunal came from the overlapping circles of the Duplay acquaintances and Parisian sectional politics. They included the judge Coffinhal, Fleuriot-Lescot, later to be Robespierrist mayor of Paris, as deputy public prosecutor, who may have helped Robespierre compile the list;[14] the Duplay acquaintances included as jurors Duplay himself, Gravier, Nicolas, Robespierre's printer, Gérard, Girard the goldsmith, Souberbielle the Duplay family doctor, and Lohier, their grocer. Others included Vilate, Picard, who was to supply Robespierre with a project for national defence (3, 285), and Lumière, Desboisseaux and Renard, who were to be guillotined as members of the Robespierrist Commune. Each of these men was, in Herman's phrase, 'one of us'.

Fouquier-Tinville, who had been public prosecutor of the Tribunal since its inception, was not a personal adherent of Robespierre's. He regarded his first loyalty to the police committee, the CSG, which originally had jurisdiction over the Revolutionary Tribunal, and after the law of 14 frimaire subordinated the CSG to the CSP, Robespierre reprimanded him for not reporting to the CSP regularly.[15]

.  .  .

## THE FALL OF LYON AND THE RISE OF THE 'FRIENDS OF CHALIER' FACTION

Lyon was to be Robespierre's nemesis. It involved him in a fight to the death with two powerful proconsuls he had recalled, Dubois-Crancé and Fouché. Also from the beginning of 1794 Robespierre allowed himself to be captured by a local Lyon faction, the self-styled 'friends of Chalier', who were able to influence him through two expatriots living in Paris and forming part of the Duplay circle, Leopold Renaudin, aged 46, a violin-maker, and especially Claude Gravier, a distiller. As we have seen, Robespierre had made both, as well as Duplay, jurors in the Revolutionary Tribunal. Gravier recommended his own protégés to Robespierre as 'revolutionary in the fullest sense of the word'. When the Tribunal was modified in June 1794 Gravier and Renaudin were joined by some of these: Masson (a cobbler), Emery (a hat merchant) and Fillion (a manufacturer). Didier Fillion and Louis Emery lodged next door to Robespierre at no. 365 Rue Saint-Honoré.[16] The presence of so many Robespierristes living in the Rue Saint-Honoré (Gravier lodged at no. 355) gave rise to the idea that a bodyguard escorted Maximilien home from the Jacobins: in fact they were just going in his direction.

Gravier told Robespierre that Achard, the national agent of the commune of Lyon and leader of the 'friends of Chalier', was too useful in his present job to be moved. The leitmotiv of the friends of Chalier was that, once it had been recaptured from the rebels, there were enough local patriots left in Lyon to run the city without interference from Paris. Achard's letters to the Lyon exiles in Paris reveal the familial nature of the link with Robespierre, one ending, typically, 'greetings to Gravier, to the Duplay family, to Robespierre, Couthon, Renaudin and all the friends of the Republic' (II, 224).

Robespierre's was the guiding hand in the repressive policy pursued by the CSP towards Lyon. On 4 August, a week after Robespierre's entry to the CSP, orders were given to march on the city.[17] However, the 'representative' Dubois-Crancé, who conducted operations, chose on humanitarian grounds a protracted siege of the rebel city rather than the frontal assault preferred by Robespierre. Lyon fell on 6 October, vindicating Dubois's approach but on the 1st the CSP had recalled him, not informing the Convention until five days later. Dubois, however, had a spy in the committee's bureaux who also informed him when on 12 October the CSP, again without informing the Convention, ordered his arrest. Forewarned, Dubois raced back to Paris and successfully appealed to the Convention to have the decree against him repealed[18] – another example of the limits to Robespierre's power in 1793.

On 12 October the CSP also issued its infamous decree for the destruction of Lyon. A five-man commission was to be appointed to oversee 'military' executions; the buildings were to be destroyed, saving only the houses of the poor and the factories which gave them a living; finally Lyon was to be re-named 'Ville-Affranchie'. Collot congratulated Robespierre on devising the slogan 'Lyon n'est plus' (Lyon is no more) (I, 320). There were some 1,800 executions, including the infamous '*mitraillades*' – killing by cannon loaded with grapeshot. The Lyon Jacobins, the 'friends of Chalier', took a frenzied pleasure in the killings. The postmaster-general of Lyon, Pilot, rejoiced in a letter to Gravier, that

> the guillotining and shootings are not going badly; sixty, eighty, two hundred at a time are shot; and we take infinite care to arrest an equal number so as not to leave gaps in the prisons. (II, 211)

And Achard, the national agent, told Gravier,

> More heads, and every day they fall! What exquisite pleasure you would have experienced the day before yesterday if you had seen this national justice being exercised on 209 scoundrels. What majesty! Such an imposing tone! It is all so edifying. (II, 233)

Clearly these men had no objection to the killings. However, they found distasteful the view, first advanced by Couthon, who replaced Dubois-Crancé, that *all* Lyonnais were to an extent incorrigible. In a bizarre application of Montesquieu's theory of climate, Couthon told Saint-Just, 'I think that people here are temperamentally stupid and that the mists of the Rhône and the Saône bring a vapour into the atmosphere which similarly clouds their ideas'.[19] So Couthon planned to resettle in small numbers over the rest of France those Lyonnais who had not been executed. In the other 'liberated' towns, a handful of Parisians was thought sufficient to guide the local Jacobins, but in Lyon it was considered that the locals could not be trusted with anything. Lyon, 'this foreign land', would have to be *colonized* (such was the expression) by Parisians.[20] The Parisian attitude was summed up by one representative-on-mission: 'This would be a good town if it were rebuilt from scratch and given other inhabitants'.[21] The Lyon Jacobins objected to this philosophy, both as a matter of local pride and on grounds of expense – 40,000 livres a *décade* – to the physical destruction of their city (II, 232).

Couthon flinched from the detailed application of his ideas, was reprimanded by Robespierre for his soft-heartedness – 'you seem to have been taken in by a people which flatters its conquerors' – and asked to be transferred.[22] Robespierre personally asked Collot to replace him (I, 318) and he was joined by Fouché. They implemented the two-pronged attack: stepping up the killings and colonization, but the resettlement, ethnic cleansing *avant la lettre*, did not take place, despite Collot's enthusiasm for the scheme, which he raised in the Convention. The main obstacle would seem to have been Robespierre: Collot told Couthon that it was 'up to him' to convince Robespierre (he, Collot, having already done his best) that

> There are 60,000 individuals who will never make republicans. We must concentrate on seeing them off, carefully distributing them over the surface of the Republic ... even the generations born of them would never be entirely pure because the spirit of slavery and the absence of energy would be hereditary unless education remedied it ... once the population is dispersed it will be easy to demolish the town, so we can truly say 'Lyon is no more'. (I, 323–4)

The colonization took the form of infiltrating the local revolutionary institutions, such as the surveillance committees, with Parisian Jacobins and members of the *armée révolutionnaire* and placing them under a 'Temporary Commission' as a preliminary to their abolition. It was missionary work, the Paris Jacobins reporting back that 'they had neglected nothing in spreading instruction'.[23] This bureaucratic expansion led to an acute shortage of personnel, as Collot explained to Robespierre, the CSP's expert in the field. He appreciated that none of the original members of the Jacobin Club could be spared, 'being nearly all functionaries, they are needed at Paris'; and yet without them 'all the [administrative] details will fall on us and swallow us up'. Not being acquainted with the newer Jacobin recruits, Collot asked Robespierre to send him a list (I, 321–2). Perhaps Robespierre did not pay sufficient attention to constructing this particular list for the Jacobins sent to Lyon were won over by Fouché and remained loyal to him when they returned to Paris, leading to a civil war in the Paris Jacobins between Fouché's faction and Robespierre's in the summer of 1794.

On 3 nivôse/23 December 1793 Collot returned to Paris for good to counter the revived clemency campaign inaugurated by the Dantonistes, which exploited *inter alia* a revulsion against the *mitraillades*. Curiously Collot, and Couthon before him, seem to have carried the affection of the local 'patriots', the 'friends of Chalier', with them. Fouché, who remained behind, became the focus for their hatred. That was probably because only after Collot's departure did the 'colonists' attack the emoluments of the natives as well as their pride. On 5 pluviôse year II/24 January 1794 the 32 local surveillance committees were suppressed.[24] This meant not only a loss of power for the local Jacobins but a loss of income as well, since membership of such committees carried a salary of 2,000 livres a year and this at a time when alternative employment scarcely existed, the local economy having collapsed. So bad were things that Pilot, the postmaster-general, found it difficult to procure silk stockings for Robespierre, though he did manage to send Gravier two hams and a large sausage (II, 212). Many who lost their positions in the surveillance committees found employment at the lower level of guarding sequestred property at the indigence rate of 40 sous per day. They were guarding property which they considered should have been handed over to them as compensation for their 'oppression' and many were suspected of helping themselves in any case.

The representative-on-mission Reverchon told Couthon that these guards, some 2,000 of them earning five livres a day, were the nucleus of a party of some 3,000 so-called friends of Chalier, whose aim was to drive out the Parisians, including the 'representatives', and corner the wealth of Lyon as compensation for their 'oppression'. What made them dangerous was their lobbying of the CSP and the Paris Jacobins, though Reverchon could not tell Couthon that it was their friendship with Robespierre that made this possible.[25] Their leaders, Reverchon added, were in Paris, men such as Gravier, but they were joined by reinforcements from Lyon. Indeed there was a veritable counter-settlement and the Convention ordered the *sections* to carry out a census of all the Lyonnais domiciled in Paris.[26] The climax of this process came in ventôse when Achard himself gave up his job as national agent to lobby directly in Paris, even though this meant that he was replaced by a member of the hated Temporary Commission (III, 61–70).[27]

The appeal of the Lyonnais to Robespierre was twofold: their leaders were his friends, their ideas percolated through to him with his domestic coffee. This intimacy is caught by Achard's taking up (and doing to death) Robespierre's heavy pun that Philippeaux wrote not 'philippics' but 'philippotins' against the mismanagers of the Vendéen war (II, 230). Secondly, though their motive was local patriotism and local greed, they could plausibly present themselves as the champions of centralized orthodoxy, as embodied in the law of 14 frimaire, against 'anarchic terrorism' as embodied in the 'representatives'. After all Achard *was* the national agent for Lyon and should have displaced the 'representatives' as was happening all over France. Again their bugbears the Temporary Commission and the *armée révolutionnaire* were themselves outdated symbols of anarchic terrorism so it is hardly surprising that they were able to obtain the abolition of both.

However, the main objective of the 'friends of Chalier' was the recall of Fouché. Fouché played into their hands by seizing the papers of the Lyon Jacobin Club and announcing that it would be dissolved for slandering the Paris Jacobins and sending defamatory notes to Paris.[28] This forced Robespierre to intervene: two decrees of the CSP, in his hand dated 7 germinal/27 March, recalled Fouché and forebade further action against the 'friends of Chalier'.[29] The Jacobin Club was restored and given corresponding rights with the mother society prior to full affiliation.[30] Later we shall see the 'friends of Chalier' attempt to have Fouché brought to trial in a Revolutionary Tribunal packed against him.

The abolition of the hated Temporary Commission followed. But the fate of Parein, its president, reveals a struggle within the various groups in Robespierre's entourage. Parein's survival is remarkable, given his links with Ronsin and his conflict with Robespierre's intimates, the 'friends of Chalier'. However, he was protected by Claude Payan, whom he told to 'see Nicolas . . . tell him to speak on my behalf to the virtuous Robespierre'.[31] Nicolas, it will be remembered, was Robespierre's printer and former secretary. So successful was this intervention that Parein was not only saved from the Hébertist holocaust but placed on Robespierre's 'list of patriots.'

. . .

## THE RISE OF THE BROTHERS PAYAN

Courtois wrote in the introduction to his report on Robespierre's papers:

> Linked to Payan, a perfidious man, a more thorough and dangerous scoundrel than himself, he [Robespierre] followed the advice of this conspirator on more than one occasion. (I, 34)

115

For once Courtois was not exaggerating.

Claude-François Payan came from an old family from Dauphiné which had climbed the foot-hills of the mountainous ascent to nobility.[32] For several generations the head of the family had been *vibailli* of Saint-Paul-Trois-Châteaux, near Valence. *Baillis* let alone *vibaillis* had lost their duties several hundred years ago and the post was antiquated even by the standards of the *ancien régime*. Joseph-François Payan du Moulin, who became commissioner for public instruction, was the son of François Payan, the current *vibailli*. Before the Revolution Joseph was a *conseiller* in the Chambre des Comptes of Grenoble, an office which conferred personal nobility. The Payans, unlike Robespierre, did not need the Revolution. Nevertheless Joseph Payan and his father opted wholeheartedly for the Revolution. François became president of the *département* of the Drôme, based in Valence, in which Joseph, who has been described as 'the leading Jacobin of Valence', joined him. His youngest brother Claude, who started his career as an artillery officer, also joined the administration in 1791.[33]

However, the Revolution also divided the Payan family. Two of Claude's brothers had become priests; one took the oath to the Civil Constitution and later unfrocked himself and married, the other was deported as a non-juror. Worse, his eldest sister married an army officer, d'Audiffret, who took part in the Camp de Jalès (August 1790 – February 1791) which united counter-revolutionary elements from the Drôme and the two neighbouring *départements*. D'Audiffret, who had assumed the family office of *vibailli* of Saint-Paul-Trois-Châteaux, not only saw his office abolished but saw the name of his town changed because it contained four politically incorrect elements, a saint and *three* châteaux. After removing the sacerdotal and feudal elements, the town was renamed Paul-Les-Fontaines. Claude was undoubtedly influenced by the fact that his own family was deeply divided by the Revolution as was his locality. From a Parisian perspective there was no justification for a continuance of the Terror into 1794 but the Midi was still simmering and the Midi mafia had a big influence on Robespierre.

The Payans came to national prominence during the provincial rebellions against the Convention in 1793 (the 'federalist' revolt). Though their colleagues in the Drôme administration were far less radical than the Payans, Joseph Payan managed to persuade his colleagues to back the Convention, playing on

Valence's jealousy of Marseille to the south and Lyon to the north and arguing that civil war would lead to the very anarchy they so feared. On 4 July his colleagues finally and reluctantly refused adherence to the Marseille rebellion.[34]

The Payans also organized a federation of the Jacobin clubs of the Rhône valley which, by preventing a junction between the rebellious cities of Marseille and Lyon, contributed in no small measure to the ultimate victory of the Convention. (They also persuaded a dithering Grenoble to stay loyal to the Convention.) The clubbists dubbed Joseph Payan 'the Saviour of the Midi'.[35] The representatives-on-mission in the Midi, and in particular Jullien (de la Drôme), asked Claude Payan to report to the CSP on the situation. Jullien (and in particular his 18-year-old son Jullien (de Paris) ) was close to Robespierre who on 21 August had Claude Payan appointed head of the committee's bureau for correspondence with local government. At the time of his appointment Payan was 27, more of an age with Saint-Just than with Robespierre. A letter back to his brother Joseph shows his growing influence with Robespierre. He mentioned a decree being 'repealed, in line with the observations of Robespierre to whom I spoke on the matter in the morning. I see him often, also Barère . . .' (II, 438).

In September, whilst continuing his work at the correspondence bureau and his work on the Midi, Payan together with young Jullien set up a journal, whose title, the *Antifédéraliste*, addressed the needs of the times. The *Antifédéraliste* became the official organ of the CSP which subsidized it until 30 nivôse/ 19 January 1794 when it folded. Payan gives as a reason lack of contributors and the fact that 'we were suddenly abandoned by our workmen' (II, 351). Propaganda was of central importance to Payan. There is a draft decree in his hand dated 9 November 1793 providing for just one subsidized national journal, a daily newsheet and a weekly summary of the major measures of the Convention which would be sent regularly to the municipalities and the armies (II, 347–8). Presumably he tried this idea out on Robespierre and Barère, who found it too strong at this stage.

In September 1793 Payan also became a juror in the Revolutionary Tribunal. He tells his brother that Barère was 'very pleased' with the way the tribunal was operating (Payan kept its minutes and gave Barère a digest). Payan took part in the great show trials of the autumn: the king's radical cousin

Orléans, Marie-Antoinette and the Girondins. Concerning the execution of Orléans he makes some chilling but refreshingly honest comments,

> Philippe had to die. He was a rogue; even if he was innocent, . . . it was expedient that he should die. He was definitely not an accomplice of Brissot. He defended himself well on that one; no witnesses against him. Nevertheless we must spread it about that he was guilty to put a stop to these counter-revolutionary calumnies. Bailly and Roland will go the same way.

Robespierre never admitted even to himself that innocent people were condemned.

At the end of his letter to his brother, Payan complains that his administrative duties are crowding out his political life: 'For three weeks I have not been to the Convention or to the Jacobins. Will I be an administrator forever?' This is a curious distinction. One might be forgiven for thinking that his roles as juror on the Revolutionary Tribunal, as editor of a propagandist journal and chivvying local government through his bureau de correspondance were sufficiently political in themselves. He concludes his letter by asking his brother to get some 'temporary mission' out of one of the local 'representatives' as an excuse to come to Paris – the way to arrive (II, 348–9).

.   .   .

## NOTES

1. H. Wallon, *Histoire du Tribunal révolutionnaire de Paris*, 8 vols (1880–82), II, p. 272.
2. J. Michelet, *Histoire de la Révolution française*, ed. G. Walter, 2 vols (1952), II, p. 643.
3. L. Jacob, *Robespierre vu par ses contemporains* (1938), p. 188.
4. A. Mathiez, *Études sur Robespierre* (1958), pp. 218 and 225.
5. Wallon, *Tribunal*, I, p. 288.
6. Mathiez, *Études*, pp. 224 and 226.
7. Mathiez, *Études*, pp. 229–30.
8. J.M. Thompson, *Robespierre* (1988), p. 395.
9. Mathiez, *Études*, pp. 217–33.
10. A. Mathiez, *The Fall of Robespierre* (1927), p. 133.
11. Thompson, *Robespierre*, p. 29; E. Campardon, *Histoire du tribunal révolutionnaire de Paris*, 2 vols (1975), II, pp. 332–50.
12. M. Sydenham, 'The Republican revolt of 1793: a plea for less localized studies', *French Historical Studies*, 12 (1981), pp. 120–38, at p. 126.

13. For the complete list of the members of the Tribunal see Wallon, *Tribunal*, I, pp. 291–5.

14. Wallon, *Tribunal*, I, p. 295.

15. Thompson, *Robespierre*, p. 516.

16. J. Thompson, *Robespierre*, p. 185, erroneously gives Didier as his surname and locksmith as his profession; E. Herriot, *Lyon n'est plus*, 4 vols (1939), IV, pp. 173 and 198.

17. P. Mansfield, 'The repression of Lyon, 1793–4: origins, responsibility and significance', *French History*, 2 (1988), pp. 74–101, at p. 82.

18. Th. Yung, *Dubois-Crancé*, 2 vols (1884), II, pp. 31–42.

19. Cited in Heriot, *Lyon*, III, p. 40.

20. F.-A. Aulard, ed., *Recueil des actes du Comité de Salut Public*, 21 vols (1889–1911), V, p. 465.

21. Mansfield, 'Repression', p. 90, n. 109.

22. Mansfield, 'Repression', p. 85.

23. Heriot, *Lyon*, III, p. 275.

24. W. Edmonds, *Jacobinism and the Revolt of Lyon, 1789–1793* (1990), p. 292. Heriot, *Lyon*, III, pp. 318–22.

25. Aulard, *Actes*, VI, pp. 4 et seq.

26. Heriot, *Lyon*, III, p. 248.

27. Heriot, *Lyon*, III, p. 466.

28. Heriot, *Lyon*, III, p. 494.

29. Aulard, *Actes*, XII, pp. 217 et seq.

30. Heriot, *Lyon*, IV, p. 198.

31. R. Cobb, *The People's Armies*, trans. M. Elliot (1987), p. 577.

32. The following details about Payan's family are taken from M. Eude, 'La Commune Robespierriste', *Annales historiques de la Révolution française*, XII (1936), pp. 146–7.

33. H. Johnson, *The Midi in Revolution, 1789–1793* (1986), pp. 241–3.

34. Johnson, *Midi*.

35. A.M. Duport, 'Les Congrès de sociétés populaires de Valence en juin et septembre 1793', *Annales historiques de la Révolution française*, 58 (1986), pp. 529–33, at p. 532.

# Chapter 8

# THE DAILY EXERCISE OF POWER I: ROBESPIERRE AND PAYAN

*Section I: The general situation from the execution of
Danton to the law of 22 prairial: 5 April–10 June*

. . .

## THE CONCENTRATION OF POWER IN THE CSP

The fall of the Hébertist and Dantonist factions led to further
concentration of power in the CSP at the expense of the six
ministries (replaced by 12 downgraded 'commissions'), the
Commune and the popular movement (unfairly considered to
be tainted with 'Hébertism') and the Convention itself, which
had not protected its own. Robespierre, personally, was the
recipient of much of this additional power. However, these
measures, and the destruction of the 'factions' which made
them possible, led to widespread resentment and apathy and
sowed the seeds for the collapse of the terrorist regime.

When, on Danton's proposal, the Convention had reduced
meetings of sectional assemblies to two salaried sessions a week,
*sans-culotte* activists had tried to get round the measure by forming 'popular societies' to meet on the other days. The CSP had
been forced to tolerate this, but after the fall of the Hébertistes
it pressurized them into dissolving themselves: some 40 disappeared. Popular politics seemed dead: the *sans-culottes* confined their attention to digging (saltpetre) for victory, clubbing
together to equip a cavalryman (*cavalier jacobin*) and sending
sycophantic addresses to a sycophantic Convention.

Free from the threat of a popular insurrection, the CSP felt
able to loosen the economic regulations which it had conceded to popular pressure. Anti-hoarding agents were dismissed,

the *armée révolutionnaire*, which had pressurized reluctant peasants into releasing food supplies, was disbanded. The *assignat* fell to 36 per cent of its nominal value.

The Convention too was cowed, sullen and resentful. Robespierre and Carnot seldom bothered to come to the Convention; Saint-Just was at the front. The CSP's spokesman was Barère, honey-tongued, time-serving (a terrorist now, he had once belonged to the monarchist feuillant club). His lack of real belief underlined parliament's subservience. As one deputy put it, after Barère sat down, 'if anyone spoke after him it was merely to re-emphasise what he had said and his proposals were always adopted, tacitly rather than by a proper vote'.[1] Robespierre welcomed this last tendency, thought it showed patriotism (10, 486), and despised the deputies even more.

What was this unprecedented power concentrated in the hands of the CSP for? A naive question perhaps and one answered in different ways by the members of the committee. For Carnot, uncluttered with ideological baggage, the answer was simple: in order to win the war or rather to continue to fight it successfully.

.   .   .

## FRENCH VICTORIES

The Republic's arms were everywhere successful in the summer of 1794, entering Piedmont in April, Catalonia in May and occupying the Palatinate in July. On 18 May the British forces in Belgium under the Duke of York were routed at Tourcoing and on 26 June General Jourdan won the decisive victory of Fleurus against the Austrians. The reconquest of Belgium swiftly followed, Brussels being occupied on 10 July. At sea the great fleet built up at Brest by Jeanbon Saint-André was defeated by Admiral Howe on 1 June but its manoeuvres had achieved its main objective: to enable a vast food convoy from America to slip through the British blockade.

The victories also had negative repercussions on domestic politics which will later be explored at some length. They led to quarrels between Robespierre and Carnot. After Fleurus, Carnot raised his sights to achieving France's natural frontiers and beyond – a state of continuous warfare. Robespierre detected a creeping militarization of national life, with armies staffed by professionals rather than enthusiastic volunteers, and the ever-present threat of a military dictatorship. The victories also led to a coded call for the end of emergency government, since it had been declared only 'for the duration' and for the implementation of the constitution of 1793. This would have involved the end of the Convention and its principal committee, the CSP.

. . .

## AIMS OF THE ROBESPIERRISTES

Robespierre would never have admitted that he enjoyed exercising power for its own sake. His aim was to achieve the republic of virtue. This process had positive and negative aspects. The positive side centred on propaganda and especially the Rousseauesque state religion which Robespierre outlined to the Convention on 7 May and inaugurated with the Festival of the Supreme Being on 8 June. Saint-Just pinned his faith on 'republican institutions' to rear a new generation untainted by the *ancien régime*. The negative side involved the elimination of the unrighteous, repression. Whereas Carnot and the technocrats in the CSP were not afflicted with doubts, because they scarcely had beliefs, Saint-Just was aware that the Revolution had lost its way and become 'frozen'. He probably meant by 'frozen' bureaucratized – he specifically attacked his governmental colleagues for becoming bureaucrats – but there is also a sense that the Revolution had lost its soul. The progressive removal of the *sans-culottes* from politics (September 1793 – March 1794) had had the blessing of all the members of the committee but it is possible that Robespierre and Saint-Just were worried that by muzzling the shock-troops of the Revolution its momentum could be lost, the torrent 'frozen'.[2] Thus to compensate the *sans-culottes* for their loss of political activity and keep their interest in the Revolution alive, Saint-Just sought to cater for their material needs by confiscating the property of suspects and giving the proceeds to needy patriots by the laws of ventôse. To minister to their spiritual needs, Robespierre instituted a state religion, as proposed by Rousseau. It would rekindle the vital spark of the Revolution which seemed to have been extinguished with the germinal trials and re-establish a common belief.

.　.　.

## THE FESTIVAL OF THE SUPREME BEING,
### 20 PRAIRIAL/8 JUNE

The Festival of the Supreme Being was the happiest day of Robespierre's life. As speaker of the Convention for the fortnight on which it fell, Robespierre presided over the elaborate proceedings, with sets by David, under a clear blue sky. Blue too was Robespierre's coat: all the deputies were clad in their new official costume – cornflower blue coat, tricolour sash, sword and plumed hat. But there is dispute about whether Robespierre wore this light blue coat or a special dark blue version. Vilate, a juror in the Revolutionary Tribunal with whom Robespierre took a light luncheon before proceedings started, insists that he wore the regulation dress.[3] Be this as it may, he certainly held a larger nosegay than his colleagues and an additional one in his hat, both lovingly constructed of wheat ears and flowers by the Duplay girls.

The first part of the ceremony was held in the Tuileries gardens where Robespierre, having addressed the assembled dignitaries and representatives of the 48 *sections*, set fire to an allegorical representation of Atheism. From this conflagration emerged miraculously, if slightly singed, a figure of wisdom. Robespierre in a second speech drew the appropriate conclusion before leading the deputies in procession to the Champ de Mars, where 500,000 people, almost the entire population of Paris, were assembled. For their delectation a huge mound had been raised, topped by a tree of liberty, to represent the Mountain. From this vantage Robespierre and his colleagues participated in the singing of patriotic hymns.

To the casual observer Robespierre appeared at the festival as a head of state, with the two bouquets and possibly the darker coat. Such distinctions would not have been out of place at the court of Versailles. Outside France many believed that Robespierre was planning to replace emergency government with a personal dictatorship; and furthermore that it might be possible to do business with this more conventional regime. Stress was placed on the state religion, which they mistook for a step towards the restoration of Catholicism as the state religion, especially as 8 June coincided with Pentecost.[4] The peasantry also drew this conclusion: they crowded into Avignon for the local fête, 'delighted to see there was still a God'.[5]

Reaction in the cities was less favourable and if the festival marked Robespierre's zenith it also, with no resting place at the top, marked the start of his decline. For even as he processed, deputies behind mocked and taunted him within earshot. Robespierre, according to Vilate, replied to his tormentors: 'it's as if the pygmies were re-opening the conspiracy against the tyrants [*sic* for Titans]'.[6] Croker rightly observes that the festival was 'the *first* and *last* scene in which Robespierre, contrary to the cautious reserve of his whole life, exhibited himself as the solitary depositary of the public authority'.[7] He appeared both as a dictator and a pontiff. And apart from appearances, the content of Robespierre's religious policy was hated by many deputies and members of the governing committees and found little resonance among the *sans-culottes*.[8] Many people found the new religion embarrassing, to say the least.

The inaugural festival was supposed to be followed by 40 a year: no more were celebrated. Billaud-Varenne told Saint-Just that the other committee members wanted quietly to drop the state religion.[9] They had also quietly dropped the laws of ventôse. Many deputies were atheist and saw no need to exchange one Pope for another; the festival was an affront to their republican sensibilities and must have seemed as blasphemous to them as to devout Catholics. Such feeling was especially strong in the CSG, which contained Voltairean sceptics such as Amar and Vadier who, with personal and jurisdictional scores to settle with Robespierre, sought to weaken him by ridiculing his religion. The jurisdictional conflict arose from competition to control the main governmental activity in the summer of 1794: repression.

. . .

## ROBESPIERRE AND REPRESSION

Since the laws of ventôse and the state religion met with passive resistance from the rest of the committee members, it was repression, the negative side of the establishment of the republic of virtue, which occupied most of Robespierre's energies in the space of just over three months separating the death of Danton from his own. The late Richard Cobb liked to call this period 'Robespierre's red summer'. The summer was Robespierre's because his partisans acquired most of the Hébertistes' levers of power: the Commune, the National Guard and the lion's share of the ministries. It was red because this power was turned almost exclusively to repression. In the Middle Ages Frenchmen saw the king as a judge; in the Bourbon period as a taxman; in the period under consideration the government was viewed as a policeman, in that sense of political police with which the French are so conversant. The great legislation, the remodelling of France, had been achieved by the Constituent Assembly. Saint-Just lamented the fact that the Convention no longer legislated. Diplomacy was discredited with Danton and equated with defeatism. Apart from fighting the war, which involved its own kinds of repression, there was nothing else for government to do.

Since repression was now the main medium of government, it was logical that it should be directed by the senior committee of the Convention, the CSP. And to this end Saint-Just set up a police bureau in that committee on 4 floréal/23 April which Robespierre took over on 14 floréal/3 May when Saint-Just left to supervise the Armée du Nord. Since this is the only regular administrative work Robespierre ever did, we shall later be looking at it in some detail. The increase of the CSP's police work naturally led to friction with the CSG. The CSG had been set up as a police committee as early as September 1792; it had the right to issue arrest warrants which the CSP did not acquire until 28 July 1793, significantly the day after Robespierre entered government.

The CSG had been weakened in the autumn of 1793 when several of its members had been implicated in financial scandals and these had been replaced by the CSP. The CSP, not the CSG, had handled the arrest of Danton. Nevertheless, as the elder committee, its agents were entrenched in the bureaucracy and in the sectional movement and its tentacles were hard to dislodge.

During the 'federalist' revolt repression had been necessarily decentralized, in the hands of the 'representatives-on-mission'. But the CSP, and in particular Robespierre, had not trusted the 'representatives' and one by one they were recalled: Dubois-Crancé, Fouché, Barras, Fréron, Tallien, Ysabeau etc.

– a long list. These men were resentful and frightened. When Barras arrived back in Paris he went to see Robespierre in his lodgings: Maximilien was meticulously cleaning his teeth and carried on with his toilet as if no one was there.[10] Robespierre tried his own agents – young Jullien replacing Ysabeau at Bordeaux – but there were not enough to do this systematically. The sedentary national agents who replaced the 'representatives' often did not have the prestige to rule an area. And Robespierre distrusted many of these, as we know from the directives from his police bureau.

The result of this distrust was the concentration of all repression in Paris. The provincial revolutionary tribunals were abolished by the decrees of 27 germinal/16 April and of 19 floréal/ 8 May 1794: henceforth all detainees were brought to Paris for trial – a process which took up much of Robespierre's time at the police bureau. An exception, however, was made in the case of two proconsuls who met with Robespierre's approval, Lebon and Maignet, who were allowed to set up tribunals at Cambrai and Orange respectively. Maignet convinced Couthon and Robespierre that it would require an army to escort the 12,000–15,000 prisoners from his area. Some 30,000 witnesses would also have to be transported and the Payan brothers, who devised the streamlined procedures of the Orange Tribunal, observed that 'this would include the small number of public functionaries who have remained loyal and those who have been "regenerated" and would lead to political disorganization' (11, 374). So the centralization of repression may have destabilized the provinces.

It certainly destabilized Paris. The prison system could not cope with the influx of provincial 'conspirators'. By June there were 8,000 prisoners in Paris. This administrative problem is probably the main reason for the draconian law of 22 prairial/ 10 June, which created a new crime of 'enemy of the people' and abolished the need for defence counsel and witnesses. In a celebrated article Lefebvre argued that the prairial law resulted from governmental panic at the attempted assassination of Collot and Robespierre on 4 and 5 prairial/23 and 24 May.[11] There certainly was hysteria: the 'assassin' of Robespierre was a 16-year-old schoolgirl, armed with a silver-bladed fruit-knife, who had wandered into Duplay's timber-yard 'in order to see what a tyrant looked like'. And this hysteria certainly accounts for the infamous decree of 8 prairial/27 May that no British or Hanoverian prisoners would be taken (on the grounds that William Pitt, through his agent the Baron de Batz, was behind the assassination attempts). However, the Orange Commission, which was the prototype for the post-prairial Tribunal, pre-dated the assassination attempts.

The prairial law ushered in the Great Terror: from its inception in March 1793 to the prairial law the Revolutionary Tribunal had sent 1,251 people to the guillotine; from 10 June to 27 July 1,376 perished. There was another dimension to the prairial law: Robespierre intended to remove parliamentary immunity and send a number of deputies, and notably the recalled 'repesentatives', before the Revolutionary Tribunal. He failed in this and in the process quarrelled with CSG (which had not been consulted about the law) and naturally alienated the Convention. He also quarrelled with his colleagues in the CSP and from 23 prairial ceased attending cabinet but continued to work in his police bureau on the third floor of the building. On 13 messidor/1 July, after Carnot had called him a dictator to his face, Robespierre secretly seceded from the CSP altogether. The prairial law began the process of unravelling the Jacobin dictatorship.

However, in this and the next chapter we analyse the working of Robespierre's bureaucratic power unclouded by the political conflicts which lay just beneath the surface. In this chapter we look at the development of Robespierre's patronage and particularly at Payan and the 'Commune Robespierriste' and Payan's input into the Orange Commission. In Chapter 9 we look at Robespierre's own work at the police bureau and his close collaboration with Herman, the commissioner for police and tribunals.

We are interested in the spirit as well as the mechanism of the operation: why men were arrested as well as how? How did Robespierre reach out to the provinces and how did they reach back to him, how were men recruited and assessed? We note a new spirit affecting the way the Robespierrist bureaucrats went to work and the values they sought to impose on their employees and on the Republic, a conscious rejection of the manners and mannerisms of the *ancien régime*. Payan pre-eminently claimed the power to modify thought: what he called 'moral as well as physical and material centralization'.

*Section II: The extension of Robespierre's power base*

. . .

## THE TWELVE COMMISSIONS

On 12 germinal/1 April, two days after the arrest of Danton and eight days after the execution of Hébert, Carnot made a rare visit to the Convention to propose the replacement of the six ministries by 12 executive commissions. His main target was the war ministry, which had distributed Hébert's *Père Duchesne* to the troops and was riddled with men from the Cordelier group. The dismantling of the war ministry had been proceeding throughout the winter and, as we have seen, the threat this posed to their power base had played a part in the Hébertist insurrection. Concommitantly the CSP's war bureau under Carnot's general direction expanded from four employees on 14 frimaire to 63 by 9 thermidor. Though the Hébertist war ministry was Carnot's main concern, two Dantonistes were ministers of the interior and of foreign affairs. The new commissioners were bureaucrats responsible to the CSP: Lerebours, for example, the commissioner for public assistance, reported regularly to Robespierre tête-à-tête.

With two important exceptions, in filling the new commissions members of Robespierre's faction swept the board. The exceptions were the commissions carved out of the old war ministry and the finance commission. Carnot placed his man, General Louis-Antoine Pille, at the head of the ninth commission, for the organization and movement of armies. This commission was essential to Carnot's 'organization of victory'. But it also had political implications. Robespierre suspected that Carnot might direct an army to march on Paris. What Carnot did do, through Pille, was systematically to send Parisian artillery units loyal to Robespierre to the front. Artillery units were the key to control of Paris. Robespierre, however, managed to put his own men in as Pille's deputies (each of the 12 commissioners was assigned two such, one of whose counter-signature was required on executive orders). One of these deputies was Prosper Sijas, a prominent speaker in the Jacobins who perished with Robespierre on 10 thermidor. Sijas was another man tarred with Hébertisme (through his association with Vincent) whom Robespierre befriended. The other 'adjunct' was Boullay. A further 20 clerks were Robespierristes, or at least were purged after thermidor. As long as Robespierre lived, resistance by his adherents in Pille's commission prevented it from functioning properly.[12]

The functions of the former war ministry were scattered among seven of the new commissions, many headed by Robespierristes: Jean-Baptiste Charigny, for example, on Robespierre's 'list of patriots', became commissioner for military transport;[13] military construction came under the public works commission headed by the Robespierriste Fleuriot-Lescot; and military police under Herman's commission.

A second exception to Robespierre's control of the new executive commissions was finance where the influence of Cambon of the Convention's finance committee secured the appointment of Lhermina. Robespierre was to denounce Cambon and the 'hypocrite' Lhermina on 8 thermidor and Claude Payan gave a classic Robespierrean potted revolutionary biography of Lhermina in his notebook:

> Lherminas, appointed by Cambon. Lherminas the hypocrite placed by Danton, expelled from the Jacobins in the purge of 1792 for only giving patriotic contributions totalling 36 livres though he enjoyed 15,000 livres of *rentes* and a salary of 12,000. Got back into the Jacobins through the protection of Brichen, himself expelled by Robespierre, and of Leclerc, who was guillotined. His section of the war ministry signed the petitions of 20,000 and 8,000. (II, 390)

Of the other commissions, Herman headed the first commission, that of 'administrations civiles, police et tribunaux'; this was in effect the ministry of the interior and justice combined, and Herman was also to become Robespierre's right-hand man in implementing the measures taken by his police bureau. The elder of the Payan brothers, Joseph, headed the second commission, that of 'instruction publique' (in effect propaganda), to be joined later by young Jullien as his deputy. Police and propaganda were for Robespierre the key areas of government. In addition Gatteau, another war ministry radical,[14] became head of the third commission, that for 'agriculture and arts'. Fleuriot-Lescot (before the Revolution an architect's clerk) became commissioner for public works, before being elevated to the mayoralty of Paris. Lerrebours became commissioner for public assistance. Finally the twelfth commission, that of foreign affairs, went to Buchot.

Who were these men? They all figure on a series of lists which were found in Robespierre's papers and published by Courtois. G. Walter says that Robespierre drafted the first three of these lists (the fourth concerns the Revolutionary Tribunal) in 'the summer of 1793',[15] but they can be dated from internal evidence fairly precisely to the fortnight between the abolition of the ministries on 12 germinal year II and the filling of the new commissions on 29 germinal/18 April.

.   .   .

## THE LIST OF 'PATRIOTS WITH MORE OR LESS TALENT'

The first list headed by the words 'Patriotes ayant des talents plus ou moins' contains 116 names, headed by Herman, Buchot, Dumas, the two Payans, Jullien, Moenne, Jacquier, Lerrebours, Thullier and Gatteau (II, 7–10).

A second (slightly later) list is explicitly related to the new commissions (II, 10–11). This contains only 27 names as follows:

Commission des corps administratifs, Herman, Lanne.
Instruction publique, Payan, Jullien ou Lerrebours.
Transports et Messageries [military transports], Mathon, Mercier,
  Joannot.
Agriculture et arts, Gatteau, Thullier.
Approvisionnements, Piquet, Champion, Humbert.
Marine, d'Albarade.
Guerre, Pyles, Boulet.
Affaires étrangères, Buchot, Fourcade.
Maire, Fleuriot.
Agents nationaux [of the Commune], Payan, Moenne, Lubin
  fils.
Département [of Paris], Campion, Jacquier.

All but the last three obviously relate to the new executive commissions. Robespierre's use of an undifferentiated 'Guerre' suggests an undivided war commission, and this may be significant. Some mentioned in the first list are moved or dropped: Mercier is moved from 'administration' to 'transports'; Cambon's influence keeps Pochet and Verdier out of the finance commission. And the second list is itself provisional: for example Lerebours mentioned for public instruction or public assistance is appointed to the latter.

It is significant that Fleuriot-Lescot is pencilled in for mayor of Paris some six weeks before his actual appointment: Pache was finally arrested on 21 floréal/10 May and though Robespierre prevented his appearance before the Revolutionary Tribunal,[16] his fall was clearly long premeditated.

Robespierre's third list, headed by Herman, contains only eleven names and differs from the other two in that Robespierre ascribes moral and intellectual qualities (albeit of a stylized kind) to this inner band of apostles (II, 11). The full list is:

Herman: enlightened, honest, capable of the highest offices.
Dumas: energetic and honest, capable of the most important functions.
Payan, the elder, *idem.*
Payan, the younger, *idem*, national agent of the Commune of Paris.
Moenne, *idem*, deputy national agent.
Jullien, fils, *idem.*
Buchot, *idem.*
Campion, pure patriot, good for administration.
Gatteau, *idem.*
Thullier, *idem.*
Saint-Just's brother-in-law, energetic patriot, pure, enlightened.

We have seen that at the end of 1793 Robespierre was busy building up a nationwide network – the 'inventorying and classifying' of men – based on information from local 'patriots' as to their Revolutionary biography which doubtless furnished the elements for the lists under consideration. The 1794 lists nevertheless have an improvised quality and Robespierre often has to rely on the recommendations of his close followers. He had to move quickly to take advantage of the patronage opportunity presented so unexpectedly to staff a political bureaucracy.

There was some difficulty in doing this in any case. Robespierre's first list is famously headed 'patriots with more or less talent'. Patriotism is the most important quality and, as with the early apostles, there is the expectation that revolutionary spirit will supplement the other qualities. But a degree of literacy was necessary in a bureaucracy and one wonders how some of the cobblers, unemployed ormolu chasers, wig-makers and jewellers among the 116 names coped. By the summer of 1794 there was a distinct shortage of patriots with talent (the canons of patriotism had narrowed, the pool of talent remained static). We saw how established members of the Paris Jacobin Club could not be spared for the administration of Lyon; similarly the idea of stiffening the personnel of the Orange Tribunal with some Parisian Jacobins had to be abandoned because every last one of them was employed in the metropolitan bureaucracy and there were none to spare.

Some of the men on the lists, such as Payan and Herman, were personally known to Robespierre. Others were friends of friends and the recommendation is sometimes indicated on his first list. Gravier, from Lyon, and Payan, from Valence, were important providers of imports from the Rhône valley, who could be trusted not to lose their patriotic flavour with travel. On his appointment as national agent of the Commune in germinal, Payan asked Gravier for a list of Lyon patriots, and of these, Fernex ended up in the Orange Commission (see below) and Emery and Fillion as jurors in the Revolutionary Tribunal; Gravier also sent two sets of recommendations direct to Robespierre, which resulted in F.C. Place, Thonion and Ragot (who had been imprisoned by the Temporary Commission) being added to Robespierre's list of patriots.[17]

The case of Lerebours, who became commissioner for public assistance, is exemplary. Lerebours was president of the Jacobin Club at Pontarlier (Doubs) and deputy public prosecutor in the *département*. He was recommended to Robespierre by the 'representatives' in the Doubs. He was summoned to Paris by the CSP and interviewed by Robespierre who told him:

> You have ardour and energy, the qualities we need. We have been informed of your particulars. The CSP is appointing you commissioner of public assistance. Install yourself in the Rue de Varennes today. Come now, no hesitations, the Committee is counting on you. Duty comes first when it is a question of serving the Republic.[18]

One might wonder why Robespierre's colleagues allowed him to fill the executive commissions and, as we shall see, the Commune with his adherents. We have suggested that this was the price paid to secure his consent to the extermination of the factions. But equally the truth could have been much more prosaic: Robespierre was the only member of the CSP to bother with personnel; the only one to act like an eighteenth-century English political manager, bothering as he himself put it in his notebook to 'discover and . . . inventory the men worthiest to serve'. Billaud himself observed that he and his colleagues (in contrast to Robespierre) were not really interested in patronage, in

> seeking to create devoted followers for ourselves by appointing our acquaintances to the jobs at our disposal or by recommending them to others. None of us, perhaps, has appointed or caused to be appointed a single public functionary.[19]

This is borne out by another member of the CSP, Prieur (de la Côte d'Or):

> They [Collot and Billaud] did not possess any entourage which could have facilitated such a scheme. We saw them in their rare moments of leisure seeking out solitary places, walking alone with their wives, women of no standing.[20]

## *Section III: The Robespierrist Commune*

. . .

## PURGE OF THE COMMUNE AND DESTRUCTION OF DEMOCRATIC RIGHTS

The Commune was at the heart of Robespierre's power. Its Provisional Executive Committee ran the rising of 9/10 thermidor. Its personnel suffered the most from his fall. The Commune had also been the centre of Robespierre's power during the First Terror, August–September 1792; a brief exercise of a power which, arguably, was not equalled until the red summer of 1794. But in the interval the Hébertistes had captured the Commune. On 28 ventôse/18 March Chaumette, the national agent of the Commune, was arrested, following the execution of his deputy, Hébert, and ten sectional delegations sycophantically congratulated the Convention. Bourdon de l'Oise, one of the most outspoken Dantonistes, rubbed salt in the Commune's wounds by asking why the Commune had not itself sent a deputation. In the circumstances he thought it appropriate for the CSP and the CSG 'to proceed with the minimum delay to an examination of the conduct and a purging of the constituted authorities of Paris which, in these circumstances, have kept silent on recent events'. This proposal, which was decreed, may have saved Bourdon from the guillotine. Robespierre interpreted the Convention's decree, which provided for a once and for all purge, as a permanent right to remodel the municipal government and do away with the right of election.[21]

Robespierre had a nucleus of survivors from his time in the Commune still there, of which the following figured on his 'list of patriots': Robert Arthur and René Grenard, elected by Robespierre's *section*, Piques, manufacturers of coloured prints; J-B. Bergot, of the Mauconseil *section*, an employee in the Leathermarket, who had signed the famous petition of 31 July 1792 demanding the dethronement of Louis XVI; Claude-François Teurlot, a clockmaker from the Faubourg Saint-Antoine; Jacques-Claude Bernard, a former priest who had been deputed by the Commune to escort the king to the scaffold, elected by the Montreuil *section*; Antoine Simon, a cobbler, who represented the *section* de Marat; M-M-A. Mercier, a bookseller, Finistère; finally Lubin (Champs-Elysées) and Fleuriot-Lescot (Muséum). It was a base upon which to build.

The task fell to Claude Payan. On 10 germinal/30 March the CSP appointed Payan national agent of the Commune in succession to Chaumette. He quickly asserted himself over his nominal superior, the lame-duck mayor Pache and his successor Fleuriot-Lescot. The same day that it appointed Payan, the committee replaced seven members of the municipal police administration, three of the new appointments, Beaurieux, Bergot and Teurlot being on Robespierre's 'list of patriots'.

However, the major reorganization of the Commune's personnel was carried out, by a decree of the CSP dated 15 prairial/3 June, on information supplied by Payan, who by then had had time to familiarize himself with his Communal colleagues. Payan's notebook contains details of 19 names to fill the vacancies and of these 13 were finally chosen. Three were former colleagues of his on the Revolutionary Tribunal. Another appointment was of Tombe, who had been secretary to the Évêché committee which had organized the *journée* of 31 May. Payan's guiding principle for selection seems to have been 'patriotism' rather than 'talent': the tailor Joseph Soulié was appointed despite being illiterate – Payan overrode his doubts with the assurance that his patriotism would supplement his deficiencies (II, 385–6).

The law of 23 ventôse had given the CSP the right to dismiss members of the general council but the CSP further overrode the right of the *sections* to elect the replacements and made them itself on Payan's recommendation. Moreover it did not even bother to nominate the 'representative' of a particular *section* from the *section* in question. Thus we see on Payan's list, 'Aubert, member of the comité révolutionnaire of the Poissonière Section, for [i.e. to represent] Brutus [*section*]' (II, 386). Democratic control was further reduced by some procedural changes Payan introduced. On 23 floréal/12 May he cut the number of meetings of the general council of the Commune from eight to five per *décade* to allow council members to attend the Jacobins.[22] Indeed on 16 germinal/5 April, within days of his appointment, Payan told the general council that 'since there was no pressing business of general interest' he would regale them with some reflections on the crimes of the Dantonistes whom he confidently predicted would be found guilty by the Revolutionary Tribunal later that day.[23] Gone were the lively days when Lubin would lead the meeting in renditions of patriotic hymns with his fine operatic tenor voice. A. Soboul argued at some length that Payan alienated the *sans-culottes* by infringing their democratic rights and that this was reflected in the poor turnout for Robespierre in his hour of need on 9 thermidor.[24] Payan also hurt the *sans-culottes* in their pockets.

.   .   .

## PAYAN'S ECONOMIC POLICY

When the Commune had been run by Chaumette and Hébert, the prices side of the prices and incomes policy (maximum) introduced in 1793 had been strictly enforced but that on wages ignored. After their fall the *sans-culottes* were squeezed on both fronts. The CSP was trying to revive trade with neutral countries and that meant that the virtual proscription of merchants had to end and legislation introduced by Barère on 30 ventôse/ 20 February allowed them to make a decent if restricted profit. On 26 ventôse/16 March Robespierre denounced a petition demanding that all merchants should be excluded from public office whilst the war lasted.[25] Payan in turn fulminated against 'the destruction of commerce by the blanket condemnation of every citizen engaged in it'.[26]

Payan believed, as Robespierre had at the time of the sugar riots in February 1793, that money matters were beneath the dignity of the real *sans-culotte*. Like Hanriot, who included homilies in his orders for the day, he believed in 'poor *sans-culotte* democrats'.[27] Payan launched a campaign against the 40 sous given for attendance at sectional meetings; his diary notes:

> 1,200,000 livres: 40 sous a day for the poor of the *sections* who go to the assemblies adds up to 1,200,000 francs at least; immoral wage proposed by Danton. The *sections* of Droits de l'homme and Sans-Culottes have never wanted to receive a penny.

That gave him the idea of involving the two *sections* in a propaganda exercise – the renunciation of their 40 sous. But they were slow to take the hint (II, 379–81 and 384).

With 750,000 able-bodied men at the front, labour was scarce and there was pressure for a rise in wages. On 2 floréal/ 21 April 200 tobacco workers petitioned the Commune for an increase in their wages. Payan's deputy told them that that was between them and their employer but this was not enough for Payan. He dredged up the Loi Le Chapelier of 1791 against professional associations, arrested five men and sent a report to the CSP's police bureau, still in the hands of Saint-Just. Even Saint-Just was shocked by Payan's severity and ordered:

> Write to the [municipal] police to discover the authors of the gathering and the legitimacy of their demands, and tell them that it is the causes of the assembly that must be dissipated and justice must be done to them where it is due.[28]

Soon disgruntled workers passed from meetings to strikes and in his notebook Payan advanced an argument familiar today, 'To the workers: you say you do not earn enough and yet you are able to remain for several days in idleness' (II, 395). No wonder the previous autumn the print workers on his journal the *Antifédéraliste* had 'suddenly abandoned him'! When strikes occurred in concerns of national importance, such as *assignat*-printing and armaments, it was not just a question of the Loi Le Chapelier but the Revolutionary Tribunal and the guillotine. They were, as Barère reminded the Convention on 22 prairial/ 10 June, counter-revolutionaries. By 18 messidor/6 July the climate had so worsened that Saint-Just, back in charge of the police bureau, directed that even striking *faience* (pottery) makers were to be sent before the Revolutionary Tribunal.

.   .   .

## THE 'CENTRALIZATION OF MORAL GOVERNMENT'

The Payan brothers believed unashamedly in the merits of propaganda. Joseph Payan as commissioner for public instruction commissioned patriotic poems and one of his last public acts, on 7 thermidor, was to cancel some alterations made to Bernard's lyrics for the opera *Castor and Pollux* which had written out the Deity.[29] On 9 messidor/27 June Claude Payan urged Robespierre to

> Decree . . . that public functionaries, who are the ministers of morality, should be directed by you; so that they serve to centralize public opinion and make it uniform; that is to say centralize moral government whereas you have only centralized physical government, material government. (II, 365)

Robespierre had mentioned this objective in his report of 5 nivôse/25 December 1793: 'The function of the government is to direct the moral and physical forces of the nation towards the goal of its institution' (10, 274), but Payan felt that this objective had not been met.

Claude sought to impart his own distinctive moral tone to the Commune and indeed to the capital, through his homilies to the general council, dutifully reported in the *Moniteur*. Most aspects of life were covered from the place of women in a revolutionary society to a consideration of whether *male* domestic servants were compatible with a free society. His speech in the Temple of Reason on 30 germinal/19 April anticipated Robespierre's inauguration of a state religion with its distinctive festivals.[30] And on 9 messidor/27 June Payan urged Robespierre, instead of sulking at the sabotage of his state religion, 'to organize public festivals, and decree that the smallest details be determined with care and precision' (II, 363). Payan, as we shall see with the Barra and Viala festival, would practice what he preached.

.   .   .

## COMMUNITY DINNERS

So the summer passed in days of profitable labour wound up with visits to the patriotic theatre. Towards the end, in messidor, Payan was much exercised by a spate of community dining or *repas fraternels*. His allocution to the general council, on 27 messidor/15 July, concerned them. At various points throughout the Revolution citizens had come together to celebrate the various victories over internal and external enemies; in the summer these tended to be held outside, they were like English street parties. In his speech of 18 floréal/7 May Robespierre had likened one of the 40 festivals he planned, the one devoted 'to humanity', to a 'banquet fraternel et sacré'. In messidor there were two things to celebrate, the decisive victory of Fleurus on the 8th and the fifth anniversary of the storming of the Bastille on the 26th.

If there was anything sinister in this, several prominent Robespierristes were at first taken in. Garnier-Launay, a judge in the Revolutionary Tribunal and reputedly a member of his personal bodyguard, organized a dinner in his *section* for the 27th. He was a bit uneasy so he had a word with the president of the Tribunal, Dumas, who 'confirmed his fears about the way in which our enemies could exploit these perfidious dinners'. It was too late to call the dinner off, so he attended without sitting down or touching the food and drink. It was only when Robespierre denounced the dinners in the Jacobins on the 28th that Garnier realized just how far he had strayed from the line of orthodoxy – that he was not, in short, *au courant*. He didn't dare face Robespierre after the meeting, but when he got home, he sent him a grovelling letter of apology with the promise to recant in the general assembly of his *section* that evening (I, 231–4).

Hanriot also at first praised the banquets. One of his daily orders to the National Guard recommended that at the trestle tables there should be one candle for every six diners with one bottle of wine between two (half a bottle would not have been enough for Hanriot himself). Not before 1 thermidor/19 July did he express 'the hope that an end to these banquets has arrived'. Herman also fell for the trap. He organized a modest celebration: 'my brother, his wife, his cousin (there by chance) and two office-boys [from work] and their wives, were the only guests'. The food consisted of 'a bit of cold beef, a plate of *haricots verts* and a salad'.[31] Even Payan confessed in his address that he had attended a banquet and come away with a warm feeling inside at the display of fraternity. It was only when he got home that doubts entered in. What doubts?

Payan told the Commune that the banquets had often been laid on by the master of the house for his family and servants, who for the night were in fraternal spirit treated as equals. This, according to Payan, was just like donning the *bonnet rouge* or even giving to the poor, 'external acts in which patriotism and fraternity did not reside. It is so easy for these gentlemen to have nothing but their clothes or a few habits to change.' 'Does Fraternity consist in eating with your domestics, *since you still have them*?' (my italics). Moreover, 'Which of you, having drunk to the Republic with "moderates", will denounce them tomorrow with the same courage?'[32] Robespierre was to para-phrase this point in his speech to the Jacobins of the 28th: 'How indeed could one mistrust a man with whom one had drunk from the same cup, on the lips of whom one had found the language of patriotism?' (10, 534). Robespierre went fur-ther and saw each trestle table as a 'coterie' – a faction com-posed of '*intrigants*'. These separate tables, he said, should be contrasted with the Festival of the Supreme Being where everyone was under one blue sky and there were no '*intrigants*' present.

Payan, however, was not primarily interested in seating arrangements. The clue to his fundamental objection is given in a speech of 24 messidor/12 July where he complained that Parisians were becoming soft and lazy as a result of the milit-ary victories, and were beginning to look forward to peace. By rights peace would mean the end of *gouvernement révolutionnaire*, which one sectional activist openly proclaimed to be 'infinitely burdensome'. The *repas fraternels* were held in conjunction with petitions in favour of implementing the constitution: one opened by the Montagne *section* collected 10,000 signatures between 1 and 10 messidor/19–28 June when it was forcibly closed by the CSG. The implementation of the constitution would entail the replacement of the Convention which had drafted it and it is no accident that the commonest accusation Fouquier-Tinville devised in the summer of 1794 was that of seeking to dissolve the National Convention. The 'moderates' in the *sections* who detested the *gouvernement révolutionnaire* as an infringement of political and economic liberty and the *sans-culottes* who had lost all political initiative to the Jacobin dictatorship both had an interest in ending emergency government.[33] The community dinners were a recreation of the popular societies the government had forced to disband; an example of the ingenuity the *sans-culottes* displayed in the defence of their political rights.

Payan was determined to perpetuate the *gouvernement révolutionnaire* and he found an ingenious way of rationalizing his preference. Playing with words he introduced the notion of the Home Front and exhorted Parisians to 'win great internal victories' – 'peace will rise triumphant out of the depths of the tomb of *all* the internal enemies you have thrown into it'. The *repas fraternels* undermined this thesis: for if everyone was a friend there were no more enemies. So Payan urged:

> Let us shun all these reunions with the partisans of despotism. Let us shun this system whereby people want to persuade us that there are no more enemies in the Republic![34]

The Robespierrist historian Ording argued that Robespierre and Saint-Just did intend to implement the Constitution (and thereby end the Terror) once peace had been signed; but for that very reason the Terror was accelerated so that enough people would be guillotined to provide property for their social policies.[35] This ghoulish interpretation, which does Robespierre's reputation no favours, is wide of the mark. Robespierre's policy was the same as Payan's: war is against internal enemies as well as external. The former are defined as the immoral. On 18 floréal/7 May he said, 'the enemies of the Republic are all the corrupt men. . . . It is a small thing to crush the kings; . . . Let us distrust the very intoxication of our successes' (10, 462). This introduces a new concept, that of a war on immorality. Such a Manichaean struggle between good and evil was a permanent one which had nothing in common with the original aim of *gouvernement révolutionnaire*: temporarily disabling those who were a threat to the war effort and deporting them at the peace (as envisaged by Saint-Just in the ventôse laws).[36] For Robespierre and Payan, *gouvernement révolutionnaire* was no longer a provisional form of government. In token of this on 16 floréal/5 April Payan told the general assembly of the Faubourg Montmartre *section* that under the *gouvernement révolutionnaire* they were not allowed to use the expression 'primary assembly'.[37] When constituted as an electoral body, the general assemblies called themselves 'primary assemblies'. Now there would be no more elections, so why keep alive the embarrassing memory of a right?

There is an alternative interpretation of the community dinners. Barère saw them as part of the Robespierrist preparations for 'a new 31 May' directed against the Convention.[38] This would explain why such Robespierristes as Herman, Garnier-Launay, Hanriot and even Payan himself began by welcoming the banquets. Wasn't an alliance with the moderates merely a replication at local level of Robespierre's new tactics in the Convention of appealing to the Right? Could it be that Payan judged that the dinners were getting out of hand, accelerating the preparations for insurrection too far? Did Robespierre (who started condemning the banquets on 27 messidor) want the brake applied, as before the risings of 31 May and 10 August? Had he done a deal with Barère who to placate him had Dubois-Crancé recalled from his mission in Brittany on 26 messidor?

## Section IV: Payan, Robespierre and revolutionary justice: the Orange Commission and the law of 22 prairial

On 20 germinal/9 April Maignet, Robespierrist 'representative' in the Vaucluse and Bouches-du-Rhône, in a letter to Joseph Payan first mentioned his ideas for a revolutionary tribunal in the territory of his proconsulate. The result was to be the Orange Commission established by a decree of the CSP dated 21 floréal/10 May which became the prototype for the reorganization of the Revolutionary Tribunal under the law of 22 prairial. Lacking local knowledge, Maignet asked Joseph Payan to supply him with the names of 'twelve frank republicans' to staff this body and/or become local national agents. Payan scribbled a hasty reply, telling Maignet that he had just been summoned to Paris by the CSP (in fact to be made commissioner for public instruction), giving a quick list and saying that he would consult his brother Claude on his arrival. In the meantime he recommended him to study the minutes of the two Congresses of popular societies held in Valence in 1793, which should provide him with 'some names and information'. In the words of Maignet's secretary Lavigne, writing to Couthon, the two brothers 'furnished him [Maignet] with a little council of energetic patriots' (II, 414).

A new provincial tribunal went counter to the CSP's policy of concentrating political justice in Paris but Maignet had the backing of Couthon, with whom he had worked in the suppression of Lyon. Maignet convinced him that it was best to create an example of terror in the locality. Maignet's letter also informs Couthon that his personal supplies of 'sugar, coffee, and olive oil are en route' (11, 374). Before deciding, however, the CSP expressed a desire to consult the Payan brothers, with their local knowledge, and now reunited in Paris. At this stage Robespierre was not very enthusiastic about the Orange Tribunal – Payan had to ask him to attend the CSP's sessions concerning it (II, 411) – which is surprising given that it was to be the prototype for the prairial law. The Payans recommended that the tribunal should meet at Orange rather than Avignon (as Maignet had tentatively suggested) because the patriotic level of the latter had declined. Another reason, which they gave to Maignet but not the CSP, was that the personnel they were going to recommend, mostly from their acquaintances in the Drôme, though excellent patriots were not prepared to displace themselves as far as Avignon (II, 373–4, 411–14).

The Payans' other suggestions concerned organization and personnel. The essence was that 'The tribunal must judge *révolutionnairement*, without a written preliminary examination and without the presence of jurors', which the CSP accepted. In a letter to one of the new judges, Payan gives his own contextual definition of the technical term '*révolutionnaire*': a 'revolutionary' tribunal is one 'which should go straight to the facts and strike conspirators without mercy' (II, 370–1). Most of the Payans' recommendations as regards personnel also were accepted. Viot, a member of the departmental directory of the Drôme and recommended by Joseph Payan as a 'pure and firm patriot', became public prosecutor (II, 358); Fauvety became president of the tribunal, and Meilleret, a doctor, a judge. Another judge was Roman-Fonrosa, a 60-year-old district judge, a graduate of the university at Orange, who had been mayor of the town in 1790. The influence of Robespierre is also present – of the six senior appointments, four, Viot, Roman, Fernex and Ragot, feature on his list of patriots. Joseph Fernex, a former silkworker from Lyon and correspondent of Robespierre, 'savage, living on his own, with no contact even with the other four judges', was the most implacable of them all. Joseph Ragot was a carpenter, also from Lyon, allegedly drunk during most of the hearings: when Meilleret woke him up to ask his opinion, he would draw his hand across his throat with the words, 'la mort'. Fauvety, the president, had previously been appointed as a juror in the Paris Revolutionary Tribunal on Robespierre's recommendation.[39]

Despite Robespierre's initial lack of enthusiasm about the Orange Tribunal, he soon realized its possibilities and made the project his own. The CSP's instructions to Maignet on the organizing principles behind the Orange Commission, though derived from Payan, are written by Robespierre, couched in his catechistic style. The task of the members of the new tribunal was to 'judge the enemies of the Revolution'. These are defined as, 'all those who, in any manner and no matter with what mask they have concealed themselves, have sought to thwart the progress of the Revolution and prevent the strengthening of the Republic'. The proof required for conviction of this crime, Robespierre continued, 'is such information of any kind as is capable of convincing a reasonable man and a friend of liberty' and 'The penalty for this crime is death'. The idea of a tribunal judging only one crime and applying only one sentence is not fully present in Payan but by presenting this new principle in a throwaway line, Robespierre did not make himself sufficiently clear: the Orange Tribunal passed a range of sentences and two of the five judges were to reject the notion that there were not degrees of guilt.

The judges who partially thwarted Robespierre's intentions were two of the Payans' recommendations, Meilleret and Roman-Formosa, and Claude's advice to the latter provides insights into Payan's character and his conception of the principles on which the tribunal should have proceeded. The president of the Orange Tribunal had told Payan that though Roman was 'an excellent judge' he was 'a desperate formalist and slightly beneath the required revolutionary level' (I, 188–90). This prompted Payan to send Roman a gentle reprimand, in which he turns on its head the old adage that it is better that a hundred guilty men should go free than that one innocent man should perish: 'People are ceaselessly telling the judges: take care to protect the innocent; and I say to them, in the name of the *patrie*: tremble to save the guilty'. Payan begins by reminding his 'dear friend' that commissions charged with punishing conspirators bear absolutely no comparison with the tribunals of the *ancien régime* or even with those of the new. There must not be any forms; the judge's conscience is there to replace them. It does not matter whether an accused has been interrogated in such or such a manner. . . . In a word these commissions are *revolutionary* commissions, that is to say tribunals which should go straight to the facts and strike conspirators without mercy: they should also be *political* tribunals; they should remember that everyone who has not been for the Revolution has been by that very fact against it because he has not done anything for the *patrie*. (II, 370–2)

Payan's last reflection has much in common with the ideas of Robespierre and particularly Saint-Just but takes them further, for neither as yet had advocated *death* for being 'lukewarm' towards the Revolution.

The stress on the conscience of the judge rather than legal proof is quintessenially Robespierrist and indeed Robespierre made his own political judgements in this fashion; in December 1793 he had said 'that he was so wearied by the succession of intrigues that he had seen, that now he just relied on his heart and his conscience' (10, 246). Couthon also talked about 'the instinct of patriotism'.[40] It appears as a gut reaction but is in fact arrived at by the subconscious processing of thousands of cases over the five-year period. We may doubt whether any of Robespierre's guilty men were guilty of any crime but we must agree that they all fell into the same category.

Payan also has a peculiar definition of '*révolutionnaire*' and a keen sense that the tribunal should be political not judicial. He ends his letter by urging Roman to 'read these words constantly and above all before passing judgement on the scoundrels you have to strike down', but then, perhaps thinking that this is a bit pretentious, crosses it out – Payan never had the time to revise his letters. His letter contained a hint of menace – 'all those who claim to be wiser or more just than their colleagues are adroit conspirators' – so Roman sent a lengthy reply.

Dated 30 messidor/18 July, it must have been one of the last things Payan read (II, 405–10). It is a careful but brave letter. Roman distinguishes between the literate and the illiterate and stresses that in the latter case, forms are necessary to protect innocence. In such cases he thinks it necessary to have at least a brief preliminary enquiry to sift the evidence and above all weed out denunciations arising from local or professional animosities. This was a real problem and the public prosecutor, Viot, sent Payan a letter saying that there were 30 '*monnediers*' before him who had committed 'only crimes not political errors' and were the victims of factional fighting between themselves and the rag-and-bone men. If the accusations of either side were to be believed they should all be guillotined but if one went on like that there would soon not be any patriots left. Viot's letter was dated 9 thermidor (II, 425–7).

Roman also wanted to distinguish between ringleaders and those who had merely been led astray and, he told Payan, 'I dare to say that when in my heart I have had this conviction, I have voted for lesser penalties or acquittal'; this also when his local knowledge (which after all Robespierre was always urging people to apply) led him to suspect malicious testimony. And Roman was as good as his word: between 1 messidor/19 June and 17 thermidor/4 August the tribunal found 432 people guilty, but of these a hundred suffered imprisonment or fines rather than the guillotine.[41] Roman also saved the lives of people in prison in Valence by preventing their transfer to the Orange Tribunal on the grounds that the prisons in Orange were full. Someone seated under the Roman arch at Orange later testified to having heard Roman, on a solitary evening stroll, exclaim: 'My God! Still more executions! Hasn't there been enough blood spilled yet?'[42]

Roman's bravery saved his life in the thermidorian reaction when most of his colleagues lost theirs. Local historians in the nineteenth century loved to dwell on the Christian resignation to their fate displayed by these ex-terrorists on the scaffold; Ragot, for example, 'weeping for his transgressions and bathing the crucifix with his tears'.[43]

·  ·  ·

## THE LAW OF 22 PRAIRIAL

The Orange Commission inspired the changes made to the Revolutionary Tribunal by the law of 22 prairial/10 May. The essence of both tribunals was to replace, as protection of innocence, the legal forms of the *ancien régime* with the ability of the judges and 'patriotic' juries to 'sniff out patriotism' and distinguish it from the counter-revolutionary mentality. In the ordinary law courts, Couthon, who presented the law to the

Convention, conceded that 'a certain luxuriance of forms' could be tolerated, even 'the obstacles of chicane and of the former jurisprudence'. But when dealing with 'enemies of the people' all this time-wasting had to go: 'The delay in punishing the enemies of the fatherland must be no longer than it takes to recognize them: it is less a question of punishing them than of annihilating them' (10, 484).

The procedures of the Orange and prairial courts were similar, except that whereas the Orange Commission had witnesses but no juries, the prairial law provided for juries but no witnesses (unless the prosecution thought that these would reveal 'accomplices'). As with the Orange court there was only one penalty, death, and no preliminary investigation, but unlike the Orange court there were no Roman-Fonrosas to bend the rules in a humanitarian direction.

Article I of the law of 22 prairial reduced the personnel of the Revolutionary Tribunal from 83 to 71, the judges being reduced from 16 to 12 and the jurors from 60 to 50.[44] Partly it was a question of dismissing moderate judges.[45] But more one suspects that the expansion of Robespierre's power base left gaps as the 'patriots' were appointed to higher posts, the juror Lanne, for example, having been promoted as Herman's deputy and Fauvety as president of the Orange Commission. For as one of Robespierre's opponents said: 'count the Robespierristes; this party will end for want of numbers'.[46] Even with the reductions, Robespierre had to find 21 new jurors, which was not easy. Yet he was choosy: Amar and Moyse Bayle of the CSG claimed that 'they had put forward 21 names ... but that Robespierre had rejected them all and only allowed his creatures'.[47] Subleyras was appointed from the list of patriots, and Garnier-Launay promoted judge, but for the rest Robespierre had to rely for the most part on provincials recommended by the Robespierrist network, like a country cousin of Duplay's, L'Aveyron, described as a farmer from Creteil.

The main contingent came from the Rhône mafia: seven men, including recommendations of the Payans, Debeaux and Gouillard, from Valence, and the three extra 'friends of Chalier', from Lyon, we have noted. The appointment of so many Lyonnais also meant that the 'friends of Chalier' would be pronouncing on their personal enemies, for Achard was busy gathering materials together for an indictment, so that 'it won't be my fault if you don't have the sweet satisfaction of pronouncing on individuals whose patriotism is no deeper than their mask' (II, 222). The most prominent of these 'individuals' was Fouché.

. . .

## NOTES

1. A.C. Thibaudeau, *Mémoires sur la Convention et le Directoire*, ed. Berville and Barrière, 3 vols (1824), I, p. 49.
2. Saint-Just, *Oeuvres complètes*, ed. Ch. Vellay, 2 vols (1908), II, pp. 508, 478.
3. J. Vilate, *Les mystères de la Mère de Dieu dévoilés* (year III), p. 63.
4. Prince de Hardenberg, *Mémoires*, published by P.J.B. Buchez and P.C. Roux, *Histoire parlementaire de la Révolution française*, 40 vols, (1834–38), XXXII, pp. 389–90.
5. J.M. Thompson, *Robespierre* (1988), p. 504.
6. Vilate, *Mystères*, p. 63.
7. J.W. Croker, *Essays on the Early Period of the French Revolution* (1856), pp. 390–2.
8. M. Lyons, 'The 9 Thermidor: motives and effects', *European Studies Review* (1975), pp. 123–46.
9. Saint-Just, *Oeuvres complètes*, II, pp. 477–91.
10. Barras, *Memoirs*, trans. C. Roche, 4 vols (1895), I, pp. 183–6.
11. G. Lefebvre, 'Sur la loi du 22 prairial an II', *Annales historiques de la Révolution française* 23 (1951), pp. 225–56.
12. H. Brown, *War, Revolution and the Bureaucratic State: Politics and Army Administration in France, 1791–1799* (1995), p. 136.
13. M. Eude, 'La Commune Robespierriste', *Annales historiques de la Révolution française* XI (1935), pp. 529–56, at p. 548.
14. Brown, *War*, p. 93, where he is spelled Gateau, as in cake.
15. G. Walter, *Robespierre* (1946), p. 546.
16. On Pache see M. Eude, 'La Commune Robespierriste', *Annales historiques de la Révolution française*, XII (1936), pp. 132–46.
17. E. Herriot, *Lyon n'est plus*, 4 vols (1939), IV, pp. 27–8.
18. E. Hamel, *Histoire de Robespierre*, 3 vols (1867), III, pp. 494–5.
19. J-N. Billaud-Varenne, *Mémoire inédit*, ed. Ch. Vellay. *Revue historique de la Révolution française* (1910), pp. 7–44, 161–75 and 321–36.
20. G. Bouchard, *Un organisateur de la victoire: Prieur de la Côte-d'Or* (1946), p. 447.
21. P. Sainte-Claire Deville, *La Commune de l'an II* (1946), pp. 146–8.
22. *Moniteur*, XIX, p. 49; Deville, *Commune*, p. 171.
23. *Moniteur*, session of 16 germinal.
24. A. Soboul, *Les Sans-culottes Parisiens en l'an II* (1958), *passim*.
25. *Moniteur*, XIX, p. 734.

26. Soboul, *Sans-culottes*, p. 941.
27. Soboul, *Sans-culottes*, p. 947.
28. Archives Nationales F7 4437, entry for 5 floréal.
29. *Moniteur*, XXI, for 8 thermidor.
30. Eude, *Commune* (1936), p. 156.
31. Soboul, *Sans-culottes*, p. 985; H. Campardon, *Histoire du tribunal révolutionnaire de Paris*, 2 vols (1975), II, pp. 334–5.
32. Eude, *Commune* (1936), p. 305.
33. Soboul, *Sans-culottes*, pp. 980–5.
34. *Moniteur*, XXI, p. 238.
35. A. Ording, *Le bureau de police du Comité de Salut Public* (1930), p. 174.
36. F. Ferer, *The Frozen Revolution: An Essay on Jacobinism* (1987), pp. 110–111; (10, 462).
37. Soboul, *Sans-culottes*, pp. 954–5.
38. Barère, *Memoirs of Bertrand Barère*, 4 vols (1896), II, p. 170.
39. S. Bonnel, *Les 332 victimes de la Commission populaire d'Orange en 1794* (1888), p. 27.
40. *Moniteur*, XXI, p. 66.
41. F. Brunel, *Thermidor: La Chute de Robespierre* (1989), p. 66.
42. Bonnel, *Victimes*, p. 24.
43. Bonnel, *Victimes*, p. 27.
44. H. Calvet, 'Une interprétation nouvelle de la loi de Prairial', *Annales historiques de la Révolution française*, 22 (1950), pp. 306–19, at p. 312.
45. Campardon, *Tribunal*, II, p. 341.
46. J. Michelet, *Histoire de la Révolution française*, ed. G. Walter, 2 vols (1952), II, p. 951.
47. L. Lecointre, *Les Crimes des sept membres, des anciens comités de salut public et de sécurité générale* (1795), p. 72.

*Chapter 9*

# THE DAILY EXERCISE OF POWER II: ROBESPIERRE, HERMAN AND THE POLICE BUREAU

Robespierre's involvement with the Bureau de surveillance administrative et police générale was, in common with many of his accretions of power in the spring of 1794, largely accidental. He told the Convention on 8 thermidor/16 July,

> I was charged momentarily, in the absence of one of my colleagues, with supervising a bureau of general police, recently and feebly organized by the CSP. My short tenancy resulted in just thirty decrees, either freeing persecuted patriots or securing the arrest of a few enemies of the Revolution. (10, 565)

Though this statement contains spectacular lies, it does also contain a germ of truth. For the police bureau was the brain-child not of Robespierre but of Saint-Just and he did only look after it during the 'absence of his colleague' on mission with the Army of the North – but the absence lasted two months.

Saint-Just ran the bureau on his own from 4 to 9 floréal/23–28 April; from 9 to 13 floréal he shared the work with Robespierre but this can best be regarded as briefing him prior to his departure for the front. Robespierre ran the bureau alone from 14 floréal/3 May to 11 messidor/29 June, a period of seven weeks, except that the entries for 16 prairial/28 June are all in Saint-Just's hand, a fact overlooked by A. Ording.[1] On 12 messidor, after his final return from the front, Saint-Just and Robespierre shared the work. Since, however, Robespierre seceded from the CSP on the 13th, this day can be regarded as Robespierre in turn briefing Saint-Just after a long absence. Thereafter Robespierre took no further part in the running of the bureau.[2] Nevertheless it remains the fact that Robespierre ran the bureau for seven weeks, most of its existence, and he certainly stamped his imprint on it.

Saint-Just's conception of the role of the police bureau differed markedly from Robespierre's. For Saint-Just the main threat to the Revolution in 1794 came from delinquent and corrupt officials, so the role of the bureau was to purge the civil service. Robespierre cast his net wider; he was particularly keen to use the bureau to repress the nobility and further his religious policy. By the same token, Robespierre's conception of the role of the bureau challenged the jurisdiction of the CSG, Saint-Just's didn't. Whereas Saint-Just referred eight cases to the CSG during his five-day spell in charge of the bureau in floréal, Robespierre only sent four their way during the whole time he was in charge. His last reference to the CSG was on 24 floréal; thereafter he relied exclusively on Herman's services, above all to bring suspects before the Revolutionary Tribunal which came under his jurisdiction as commissioner for police, administration and tribunals.[3]

Robespierre had to use the bureaucracy of either the CSG or Herman's commission because the police bureau had only a skeleton staff whether in Paris or in the provinces. A decree of the CSP dated 2 messidor expanded this with the bureau headed by Lejeune with two assistants, one of whom was Duplay's nephew. They presided over four divisions which divided up the country according to *département*. They were to work from 8.30 a.m. to 3.30 p.m. and one-fifth to take it in turn to do an evening shift. When this decree was implemented we do not know, but on 5 messidor/23 June Robespierre complained:

> The lack of dossiers which are mentioned but are often found to have gone astray perhaps stems from the poor organization of the bureaux which means that the dossiers are not put back where they should have been left.[4]

By 5 messidor Robespierre was getting to the end of his tether. The bureau had eight agents in the country, charged with surveillance but with no executive powers. After sending in their reports they were sometimes empowered by the CSP to take action in a particular case – the CSP was moving away from giving delegated authority. The original appointments were made by Saint-Just and included Eve Demaillot, Saint-Just's schoolmaster, Garnerin, his childhood friend (whom

Robespierre put on his list of patriots), Vielle, the mayor of Soissons, and Lambert, a plain shepherd Saint-Just had met at a relay-post in his native Étoges. Saint-Just had been impressed by Lambert's republican spirit and recommended him to Robespierre, who not only put him on the list of patriots but invited him to be a juror on the Revolutionary Tribunal. Considering that as a semi-literate shepherd he had 'less rather than more talent' Lambert declined and was instead made the the bureau's agent in the *départements* of Marne and Ardennes. He defined his task to the Jacobin Club of Rheims as follows: 'I was also charged to give the CSP all the information I could about brave *sans-culottes* in a position to fill the jobs from which the government wanted finally to expel the *muscadins* [fops]'.[5]

By the summer of 1794 the Jacobin dictatorship relied on an increasingly narrow base, not just of supporters but of those to staff the bureaucracy – indeed the two categories became almost interchangeable. Those who had the necessary education and therefore some wealth suffered increasingly from what Robespierre called 'aliénation d'esprit' or were presumed to suffer from it. So the government had increasingly to rely on shepherds and their recommendations. This acute shortage of patriots with talent accounts (since the Robespierristes were not interested in money) for the widespread occurrence of pluralism. Lambert was mayor of Étoges as well as the agent of the police bureau; and young Jullien in addition to being Joseph Payan's deputy at the commission of public instruction was on 29 floréal/18 April given a roving commission by the CSP and brought about the recall of the representative Ysabeau from Bordeaux who, he claimed, was living in the lap of 'asiatic luxury'. Worn out with overwork, Jullien applied for a few days holiday in the Pyrenees (III, 8 and 35–40).

· · ·

## ROBESPIERRE AT HIS DESK

The two months Robespierre spent at the police bureau was the only time he had had a regular administrative job. Since 1789 he had been a professional politician. His entry into the CSP in July 1793 had not really changed his lifestyle: he continued to concentrate on ideology, on making speeches at key turning-points in the Revolution, but now from a governmental rather than an oppositional standpoint. He had also been increasingly regarded as an expert in personnel, and his work at the police bureau was in some ways an extension of this.

At work at his desk we see him in almost intimate or at least unguarded conditions. Robespierre's speeches, necessarily designed to create a certain impression, tell us little about the man. That is why Croker could say, 'Of no one of whom so much has been said is so little known'.[6] But Robespierre's directives from the police bureau were not designed to impress and, though laconic, they are long enough to reveal his personality, principles and prejudices. We learn, for example, that he has a filthy temper and that no detail was too small to occupy the man known for the enunciation of lofty general principles. Also Robespierre's impact and lack of it through the police bureau is demonstrable in a way that the effect of his set-piece speeches is not. Robespierre makes a speech about virtue and a hundred heads fall. No. But Robespierre directs Herman to have a man sent before the Tribunal for cutting down a tree of liberty and it happens – unless, as occurs towards the end, his governmental colleagues block his directive.

Robespierre's business activity at the police bureau was generated entirely by informers. A minority regime such as the Jacobin one with so few agents could only sustain itself because large sections of society were prepared to denounce their neighbours. In this sense Robespierre's work at the police bureau was not trivial – it touched the heart of power. Every morning when he arrived at his desk the chef de bureau, Lejeune, placed before him a digest of the denunciations which had been sent in from every corner of France. Lejeune later claimed that there was a total of 20,000 of these,[7] but this is impossible to verify: the digests have survived but not the raw material. The reports were written on the right-hand of the page leaving a margin for Robespierre's decision as to what if any action should be taken. In some cases Robespierre asked for more information about the 'patriotism' of the denouncer or the denounced or brought one or both parties to Paris. In others he empowered the relevant official (in the vast majority of cases Herman) to make an arrest. Robespierre's directives did not technically have executive force until they had been counter-signed by (in theory) a minimum of two colleagues in the CSP, which converted them into decrees of the CSP. We have concluded that whilst Robespierre remained in charge of the police bureau, the counter-signatures were given 'on the nod'.

The denunciations fell into two categories, those from officials, including the bureau's eight agents in the provinces, and
those from private persons (and the latter can be further sub-
divided into the signed and the anonymous). Most came from
officials across a wide spectrum: there were denunciations from
the few representatives still left on mission; from Robespierristes
such as Herman, Payan and Garnerin, the latter sent to Alsace
with funds of 50,000 livres signed for by Robespierre;[8] from the
CSP's ten Parisian police spies under Guérin. Large numbers
of denunciations came from national agents and surveillance
committees up and down the country, most of whom were not
personally known to Robespierre.

As early as 1789, Mirabeau had said, 'delation, a horrifying
act under despotic rule, must be seen as the most important
of the new virtues and the palladium of our nascent liberty
given the perils that surround us'.[9] Robespierre also, following Mirabeau and especially Marat, regarded informing as a
patriotic duty; it followed naturally from his belief in endless conspiracy; no odium attached to the trade. The parallel
Desmoulins drew between the French informer and the *delator*
of imperial Rome must have infuriated Robespierre. However, though Robespierre regarded delation as a duty, it had
to be performed in the right spirit. A note in his papers on
the qualities of the ideal police force observes, 'Every informer,
in short, who acts only out of self-interest, in the hope of a
reward, is a false republican'.[10] Though Robespierre did not
write this, those were his sentiments. This view contrasts with
the traditional police mentality, shared by the CSG, of 'set a
thief to catch a thief', the employment of royalists to catch
royalists and the use of *agents provocateurs*. This different mentality, in addition to jurisdictional jealousy, was a source of
friction between Robespierre's police bureau and the CSG.[11] It
is another example of Robespierre's stress on patriotism rather
than professionalism.

However much Robespierre may have been interested in the
philosophical question of whether a man who denounced for
money could be a pure republican, his major worry was denunciations from those whose revolutionary profile was suspect.
The most suspect kind of denunciation came from Robespierre's
*bête noire* in his last months, people whom he termed 'contre-
révolutionnaire – tendance Hébertiste', often 'étalant un grand
luxe', and even 'un luxe asiatique' like Ysabeau. By the summer

of 1794 there was no open opposition to the Jacobin dictatorship. Any opposition therefore had necessarily to take the form of conspiracy or hypocrisy. (If an opponent dared not take any action, overt or covert, his opposition might manifest itself in 'aliénation d'esprit' or 'looking at a tree of liberty with indifference'.)

Hypocrisy resulted not only from dictatorship but from the fact that Robespierre increasingly regarded himself as having enemies only to his Left. The only way in which Robespierre could logically denounce someone to the Left of him was by saying that his radicalism was a hypocritical cover or 'mask' for counter-revolutionary activity – hence the term 'contre-révolutionnaire, tendance Hébertiste', much as that seems like a contradiction in terms. The concept of hypocrisy was also a useful device for Robespierre in explaining how he had been taken in by people whose counter-revolutionary qualities had only emerged later, men such as Brissot and Danton, and for invalidating their earlier achievement, de-pantheonizing them. Hypocrisy (and conspiracy) were by their nature more difficult to detect than straight opposition and Robespierre had to apply certain procedures to elucidate the truth. There was only one truth that mattered to Robespierre: is a man a patriot without guile?

The rest Robespierre considered to be counter-revolutionaries or 'modérés', often with a 'moderate' past. Recently, however, these 'patriotes d'un jour' had tried to be *plus Robespierriste que Robespierre,* and by an exaggerated patriotism sought to alienate the people from the Revolution and thus effect the counter-Revolution, their ultimate goal. Saint-Just described the phenomenon graphically in his fragmentary 'Republican Institutions' as 'red caps worn by intriguers' and it is significantly these words that immediately follow his famous lament, 'The Revolution is frozen'.[12]

.  .  .

## SOME CASES

On 8 prairial/27 May Robespierre received a denunciation of two ex-noblemen accused of 'dangerous excesses and putting terror on the agenda'; without hesitation he ordered the local national agent to arrest them. On 15 prairial/3 June Robespierre was confronted by a petition from the Jacobin

Club of Vienne le patriote inviting the Convention to pass a decree including priests within the provisions of the law of 27 germinal, that is obliging them to vacate Paris and military towns and report to the authorities daily, as nobles were compelled to do. Robespierre immediately smelt a rat (what were they doing in any case calling Vienne 'le patriote'?). His directive went: 'This initiative proves that this society is led by *intrigants*'. Robespierre had been using the word '*intrigant*' for years but after the fall of the factions he uses it interchangeably with 'Hébertiste' to mean someone who was pursuing his devious ends under the cover of a patriotic mask. But there was an easy way for Robespierre to confirm his suspicions about the Vienne Jacobins: 'This address', he ordered, 'must be sent to Payan for him to give information on this point'. He came from those parts and would be able to ascertain the 'esprit' of the Vienne Jacobins; if it was bad, so would their petition be.

Similarly, when the popular society of Valence denounced the quartermaster of the Armée des Alpes as 'immoral' and the adjutant-general as 'inept', Robespierre directs: 'ask Payan what is the *esprit* of the Valence society?'. Payan had presided over a congress of popular societies at Valence in 1793 and his brother kept a file on the participants. There is a certain unreality about these two cases which symbolizes much of Robespierre's activity. He considered that he had a duty to discover whether the popular society was acting in the right frame of mind before taking action which would cost the man denounced his job or even his life, but he never questioned that provided the Valence society had the right 'esprit', a moral quality, it would be able to ascertain the technical competence of a staff officer. He was not primarily interested in technical competence.

When local knowledge was not to hand, the resources of Herman's bureaucracy were enlisted. The popular society of Rebais, congratulating the Convention on its decree enjoining members to give an account of their political conduct and fortune before and after 1789, asked that it be extended to all public functionaries. Robespierre smelt an 'Hébertiste' rat in such exaggerated patriotism and on 25 prairial he directed that, 'Herman enquire as to the *esprit* of this popular society of Rebais and those who direct it'.

The Hébertistes/*intrigants* were the worst offenders precisely because he saw them as a threat to his religious policy – arguably the only policy he had in the summer of 1794. Robespierre was touchy on anything connected with religion. The surveillance committee of the Muscius Scaevola *section* found a hymn to the Supreme Being in someone's pocket – Herman had to enquire about the man concerned. On 11 prairial/30 May Robespierre was informed that a national agent had sent a circular to all the national agents in his *arrondissement* asking for their views on freedom of worship – Robespierre insisted on having the circular tracked down and brought to him. The mayor of Mont-Rouge was accused of 'incivisme' during the local Festival of the Supreme Being; more specifically he was accused of saying 'as he watched the citizens dancing, "this rabble don't wear underwear, see how they dance"'. Unfortunately, no one would testify against him. On 28 prairial/16 June Robespierre directed: 'Arrest the mayor of Mont-Rouge and have Herman interrogate him'.

Robespierre had to deal with a more serious denunciation on 30 prairial/18 June. Several citizens of 'certified civism' in the Bouches-du-Rhône *département* denounced three reactionaries-turned-ultra, including two ex-priests. One of them, called Bourges, 'at the end of an orgy' got everyone present to swear not to recognize the divinity and proposed the massacre of all detainees. He had said at a meeting of the club that probity had been made the order of the day in order to operate the counter-Revolution. This was serious: an Hébertiste attack on Robespierre's state religion and on his reign of virtue. However, the remedy was to hand in the shape of 'representative' Maignet. Robespierre directs: 'Send [the file] to . . . Maignet, with the invitation to report on the measures taken'. No doubt these measures would culminate in the appearance of Bourges and his colleagues before Maignet's Orange Tribunal.

Again on 13 prairial/1 June when the national agent of Senlis reported officiously on the success of his campaign to stop peasants going to church on ci-devant Sunday, he got a dusty response from both Saint-Just and Robespierre (manning the bureau together that day). Saint-Just directed: 'write to the national agent that he should confine himself to his functions as prescribed by the law, respect freedom of worship and do good without false zeal'. Robespierre, however, went further: 'get information on the principles of the national agent'. For Saint-Just the hapless man was merely officious, for Robespierre most likely a counter-revolutionary.

. . .

## RESISTANCE TO ROBESPIERRE'S DIRECTIVES

All these cases were of minor importance (except to the individual concerned and for the ripples of terror emanating from each) but the case of Robert had a more general political bearing. Jean Robert, a Paris wine merchant from the Unité *section*, was incarcerated in Les Carmes. Hoping to obtain his release he sent a petition to the CSP accusing the members of the surveillance committee of his *section* of 'Hébertisme'. Some of the people associated with the committee had indeed been involved in the germinal trials, Lacroix had been executed, Berryeter acquitted. Berryeter was for Robespierre the archetypal Hébertiste/*intrigant*: a déclassé noble exhibiting signs of exaggerated patriotism. Though Robert's accusations were stale, Robespierre was keen to revive an affair which the CSP and CSG had dropped in April. On 3 messidor/21 June he directed: 'send to [Herman] to interrogate Robert and seek further information on the facts some of which are notorious and on the persons denounced'.

However, the directive was not sent to Herman until 21 messidor/9 July and it is unlikely that he took any further action. There are two possible explanations for this delay. One is that a three-week time-lag was typical by the beginning of messidor, given the increasing volume of business put before Robespierre at the bureau. The other is that we are entering on the period when Robespierre's colleagues were blocking the implementation of his directives. The second interpretation is lent weight by the fact that one of the members of the surveillance committee in question, Albert, was an agent of the CSG.[13]

A case of even greater political importance was that of the surveillance committee of the Indivisibilité *section*, because it was through such committees that Paris was controlled and its armed force mustered. In this case also Robespierre encountered opposition both from his colleagues in the CSP and the CSG, which had employed several members of the surveillance committee on missions in the provinces. When Robespierre sat down at his desk in the bureau on 1 messidor/19 June he read a denunciation of the said surveillance committee sent in by Perrier, the president of the *section*'s general assembly. Perrier was a Robespierriste who worked in the commission of public information under Joseph Payan. He had the classic Robespierrist mind-set, as is evident from the nature of his denunciations. One of the men was denounced for saying 'that Robespierre despite his f . . . . ing decree on the Supreme Being would be guillotined'. The committee as a whole had declined to congratulate the Convention on the decree recognizing the Supreme Being. They also 'gave each other splendid dinners' – always a suspicious act for the Robespierristes. They were also accused of 'Hébertist' tendencies, not just atheism but taxing the rich and saying that the 'popular societies' would soon be restored. On the 6 messidor/24 June Robespierre directed: 'arrest all the individuals mentioned in this article'. And arrested they were, on the 9th, by Herman's 'civil commission'. However, the minute of the arrest warrant is signed by Robespierre alone, since his colleagues refused to counter-sign it. On 12 messidor/30 June the detainees appealed to the CSG for their release, recalling their past services as under-cover agents for the police committee. Robespierre's secession from the CSP on the 13th left the way clear for his enemies. On 21 messidor/9 July a joint session of the CSP and CSG issued two decrees, one liberating the members of the surveillance committee, the other arresting Perrier himself. Saint-Just, who maintained good relations with his colleagues, signed both these decrees. The other signatories were, for the CSP, Billaud, Collot, Carnot and Barère and, for the CSG, Vadier, Dubarran, Lavicomterie, Amar, Voulland, Louis, Jagot and Moise Bayle.[14] This is one of several cases of rival power centres arresting each other's agents, which often happened because of patriotic pluralism: the men from the Indivisibilité *section* were both sectional politicians and agents of the CSG. Such anarchy was symptomatic of the decline of the Jacobin regime. The law of 14 frimaire had not catered for conflict between the central institutions of government.

The Indivisibilité case has a bearing on the question of whether Robespierre's governmental colleagues shared with him responsibility for the work of the police bureau and thus for the terror in general. Robespierrist historians such as Mathiez and Ording and those who impeached Collot, Billaud and Barère in 1795 as accessories to Robespierre's crimes, argued that if they could stop Robespierre over the Indivisibilité case, they could have thwarted him in other cases had they wanted to. Skipping over that particular case, the accused argued that they bore only a technical collective responsibility for the work of the bureau. This case was put most forcefully by Carnot, who was not himself accused. He argued that each member of the CSP had his department, Carnot the army, Lindet 'subsistances', Collot compliance with 'revolutionary' laws, Robespierre police etc., and the counter-signatures were a pure formality:

> The signatures of the members of the former CSP (I am speaking of those who signed second) were a formality prescribed by the law . . . a purely mechanical operation. . . . The number of matters expedited each day generally came to 400 or 500. Each member dealt with . . . those attributed to his competence and they were taken for signatures generally towards two or three o'clock A.M.[15]

Carnot gave the example of his signing an order of Robespierre's for the arrest of one of his own officials because he did not have the time to read it. Robespierrist historians counter by saying counter-signatures meant what they said: a collective decision.

The common-sense conclusion – and the one borne out by the archives of the police bureau – is that as long as Robespierre enjoyed the confidence of his colleagues, they allowed him *carte blanche* in his fief, appending their signatures to convert his directives into executive decrees on the nod, as Carnot suggests. But that as he lost that confidence (and here a date of 22 prairial for the beginning of that process is indicated) they progressively blocked his measures. The most light is shed on the matter by the history of the last weeks of the police bureau. On 6 messidor/24 June Robespierre annotated several abstracts; the period 7–11 messidor is totally blank, no annotations no abstracts; on the 12th, the day before his secession, Robespierre worked off an enormous backlog, 67 items neatly laid out and numbered (Saint-Just dealt with 11). This suggests that Robespierre was planning his retreat and had arranged it with his staff.

A bureaucrat has written significantly at the beginning of the first sheet for the 12th: 'The measures in this report were not implemented' and later, 'delivered to the chef [de bureau, Lejeune] on 2 thermidor'. After Robespierre's secession, Saint-Just resumed control over the bureau assisted by Couthon but their marginal comments taper into silence after 24 messidor/ 12 July. The reports, however, (which Lejeune continues to lay out until 18 thermidor) go on and indeed increase. Partly as a result of bureaucratic momentum, partly as a result of the re-organization decreed by the CSP on 2 messidor, the volume of reports increases from 419 in floréal, to 807 in prairial, 1,851 in messidor and 700 for the first ten days of thermidor.[16]

The explanation is provided by a passage in one of Billaud-Varenne's defence memoranda:

> In the last period of the reign of the triumvirate Saint-Just proposed most urgently that we take over the running of the police bureau. This proposition was forcefully rejected *as was the decree which he simultaneously asked for to ratify the operations of this bureau.*[17]

Barère puts it rather differently:

> At the end of messidor the CSP as a result of the complaints of the CSG decided to hand over the bureau de police together with its papers and clerks to the CSG. This was carried out.[18]

According to Courtois what actually happened was that on 10 thermidor, the day of Robespierre's execution, Collot d'Herbois,

> In order to pretend he was not in collusion with Robespierre, went to the police bureau and angrily told the officials to bring all the boxes to the CSP: 'There we have the Bastille of Robespierre and his agents'.[19]

After three or four days, however, Collot sent the boxes back to the bureau unread. This squares with the archival evidence that the files of the bureau were never handed over to the CSG (there are 700 reports covering the first ten days of thermidor) but that its activities ended on 10 thermidor/28 July (when Collot seized the boxes). Collot sent them back a few days later and one last marginal comment (from a bureaucrat?) was added – 'this man was executed on 12 thermidor'. The rest is silence.

This conclusion is not entirely to the vindication of Barère, Collot and Billaud, for if, as I suggest, they were able to restrain Robespierre's activities from, say, 22 prairial on, and block Saint-Just's from 13 messidor, why did they not act sooner? They would presumably reply that as long as Robespierre was engaged on trivial cases such as selling trees of liberty for timber they could afford to leave him alone but that with the advent of the Grand Terror, inaugurated by the law of 22 prairial, they moved to thwart him. In that case, counter their accusers, how came it that the acceleration of the Terror occurred precisely after Robespierre had seceded from the CSP? And if the members of the CSP were able to block the trivial directives coming from the police bureau, why did they not stop the show trials? The answer lies in the person of Herman, the commissioner for administration, police and tribunals, who developed an autonomy both from the CSP and its police bureau. Herman is the subject of the next section.

. . .

## HERMAN'S CHARACTER

The two key men in the operations of the police bureau were Robespierre and Herman, to whom the vast number of Robespierre's references at the bureau are made – 201 of them, including 40 on 19 prairial/7 June alone. (Herman is followed at a great distance by Lindet in charge of the CSP's bureau de subsistances, who is favoured with 33.) Herman did not belong to the bureau but headed the commission des administrations civiles, police et tribunaux which had replaced the ministry of the interior on 1 floréal/20 April. Herman had himself been the last minister of the interior, from 15 to 30 germinal/4–19 April, and conjointly the last foreign minister. He was a key official: it was he who formally presented Fleuriot-Lescot as mayor to the Commune. Before that, as we have seen, from 28 August 1793 he had been president of the Revolutionary Tribunal. All Herman's appointments were due to Robespierre, though he subsequently claimed that he was 'no wiser' about why he was promoted to head the commission civil than about the reasons for his original appointment to the Tribunal; but, he added, 'I was vain enough to think that I owed this mark of confidence to the CSP with whom I had dealings whilst at the Revolutionary Tribunal'.[20]

In fact the contemporary view was that his promotion was due to the letter he wrote to the CSP which resulted in the decree curtailing Danton's defence.[21] He was made minister of the interior the day after Danton's conviction. Herman himself argued that the CSP shifted him from the Revolutionary Tribunal because it knew that he would resist the planned intensification of the Terror![22] In fact Herman merely moved to an earlier stage in the production process.

Robespierre and Herman were soul-mates. To appreciate this compare the following observations on Herman's mind-set with this extract from Robespierre's speech of 17 pluviôse/ 5 February:

> In our country we want to replace egoism with morality, honour with honesty, the tyranny of fashion with the rule of reason, contempt for misfortune with contempt for vice, insolence with self-respect, vanity with greatness of soul, love of money with love of *gloire*, good company with good people, intrigue with merit, wit with genius, show with truth, the tediousness of dissipation with uncloyed happiness, the pettiness of *les grands* with the greatness of man, an aimiable, frivolous and wretched people with one that is magnanimous, strong and happy – that is to say all the vices and stupidities of the monarchy with all the virtues and miracles of the Republic. (10, 352)

Every Robespierrist virtue is found in Herman, even in exaggerated form. He was deeply puritanical. At his trial in 1795 he said,

> I admit that I gave orders that only people dressed as sans-culottes and especially only women of the people should be admitted to the precincts of the Administrations civiles. I wanted to avoid seduction. I had to give preference to petitioners who could not read or write; the others could send me their petitions.[23]

He submitted a report to the police bureau on an employee in the war office who had written a letter to a friend in 1792 saying that 15 minutes spent with a charming lady at his public audiences meant more to him than 'the ten thousand men I hear every week'. 'These two phrases', Herman reported, 'seem to me to characterize the whole man. . . . It is impossible to be so frivolous and at the same time a patriot.'[24]

The solid female virtues were the ones for him. When already president of the administration of the Pas-de-Calais *département*, Herman married a humble dependant 'as much out of duty as attachment' from a family 'without an inch of land'. His ménage consisted of this woman, their 14-month-old son and his wife's sister 'whose manners were still so coarse that they would heretofore have shocked and even dishonoured the pettiest bourgeois'. The Hermans never ate out and entertained employees at home in frugal style. The number invited was restricted because Herman 'only possessed three dozen plates, five pairs of silver spoons and forks and three in pewter'.[25] Whereas Robespierre enjoyed modest comfort at his table, Herman favoured frugality. Indeed he arrested workers at the Imprimerie Nationale for striking over the length of their lunch-break and being 'slaves to gourmandizing'.[26]

Herman wrote to the CSP asking for pay differentials within the whole administration to be lessened:

> Under the reign of equality, can one allow there to exist an enormous disproportion between two men who, living the same life-style under the republican regime, are presumed to have virtually the same needs?
> What about talents, people will say? . . .
> One owes oneself to the Republic just as one is, with one's faculties more or less developed.[27]

In a memorandum sent to his employees on 1 prairial/20 May Herman proclaims that 'The Revolution gives happiness to whomsoever would set it within himself'.[28] A man who 'comes like an automaton to work every morning because the hour has struck so that people can see that he's there' is 'no friend of liberty'. Both the style and the substance of work must be right. As regards style,

> Above all we must throw out the old clothes, leave behind that mannered politesse which contrasts so strongly with the bearing of a free man and which still recalls the time when there were masters and slaves.

Herman then addressed 'the substance of one's work':

> Here, too, there are many things to forget. If there are any former legists among you, they must break with all those who still talk the old formalist nonsense. They must leave behind all the legal quibbles [arguties de palais], all the adages of the Bar and above all not forget that they are not paid to be defence counsel but impartial reporters. You must, like the present government, clear a path through the ruins so as always to reach the goal swiftly and surely.

Here we meet again the Robespierrist denunciation of 'formalism', such as Payan employed when chastising Roman-Fonrosa for affording legal guarantees to the defendants before the Orange Tribunal. Herman employs Robespierre's favourite expression, 'arguties de palais', doubtless thinking back to those same procedures they had confronted together in the Council of Artois, as young men 'clearing a path' through the thickets of the *ancien régime.*

.   .   .

## THE CIVIL COMMISSION

The scope of Herman's civil commission was vast and though he was downgraded from minister to commissioner, Herman's association with Robespierre meant that his activity increased. His complicated new title – commissaire des administrations civiles, police générale et tribunaux – was actually descriptive of what he did. Police – and Robespierre often refers to Herman as the 'commissaire de police' for short – meant what it said: Herman headed the 'commission de police' just as Robespierre headed the 'bureau de police'. But it must be borne in mind that there were two other important police authorities: the hostile CSG and the Commune's 'administration de police', which worked under Payan's eagle eye. The latter of course was a strictly Parisian organization whereas the CSG, the bureau de police and the commission de police were national. The reason for such a proliferation of police activity is not hard to find: it was now the main activity of government.

The first handle to Herman's title, commissioner for 'civil administrations', corresponded to Saint-Just's original conception of the work of the bureau de police: curbing delinquent officials. The most common task Robespierre assigns Herman in respect of administrative bodies is to enquire as to the 'esprit' of their members and if it is defective to replace them.

How did he set about placing and replacing? It is unlikely that he had for the whole of France a register of safe candidates such as Payan had at his disposal for Paris. The procedure is likely to have been that described by J-N. Thierret-Grandpré, one of Herman's divisional chiefs, in testimony during Herman's trial. Grandpré gives the example of the replacement of the president of the tribunal and the national agent of Saint-Briez (Moselle):

> Herman, who knew that the majority of the popular societies were composed of Robespierre's creatures, made use of these societies to place or displace, in the administrative bodies, all those who

could further or thwart his aims. He wrote to the [popular] society of Briez which, at his request, proceeded to the election of two citizens.

Unfortunately they broke the law by electing two men who had held office during the Prussian occupation in 1792. They were denounced but Herman minuted the denunciation 'no action to be taken'. When Grandpré took up the matter with Herman,

> He replied coldly that this warning carried no weight and that the details given by an individual could not be compared to the motives which had determined the choice of a popular society composed of a great number of individuals and that the matter must be allowed to rest.[29]

. . .

## PERSECUTION OF THE NOBILITY

Herman became the Chérin of the Terror. Just as, under the *ancien régime*, that court genealogist had exercised the power to block or open avenues to promotion through his investigations, so Robespierre deferred to Herman the even more critical question of whether someone qualified as a *non*-noble and so escaped the dread provisions of the law of 27 germinal. Some of the cases were as tricky as those Chérin had had to grapple with. The most vexed question was that of mixed marriages, between nobles and commoners, and the same forensic skills were lavished on these hard cases as on those of marriages between Aryans and Jews in Nazi Germany. Thus on 6 messidor/24 June Robespierre sent Herman the petition, on behalf of her daughter, of a non-noble woman who had married a nobleman. The said daughter had in turn married a commoner and considered that the law of 27 germinal obliging nobles to leave Paris did not apply to her. Accordingly she had stayed put but had nevertheless been arrested.

Robespierre had views on this knotty problem because he had lent decisive support to an amendment to the law of police générale, that a noble woman who married a *roturier* (commoner) had performed an 'estimable' act and should be exempt from the provisions of the law. But in the contrary case, where a *roturière* woman married a noble, the woman should be punished for her 'criminal pride' by being subject to the law. In fact this second category was not legislated for and Robespierre took the view that such mixed marriages should not be penalized or there would be a spate of divorces (10, 438).

The case in question (a noble woman marrying a *roturier*) clearly came under the amendment; nevertheless, Robespierre referred it to Herman for a decision. Another person simply wrote in claiming that they were not noble; Robespierre directs: 'refer to [Herman] for the reply'. Often, though, Robespierre had no doubts in his mind and didn't need to apply to Herman. And generally his verdicts were harsh, going further even than the law of 27 germinal. Thus he orders the arrest of a 70-year-old Westphalian count who had lived in France for 49 years: his age and residence should have exempted him from the provisions of the law. On another occasion the commune of Faucon said they only had one nobleman who fell within the provisions of the law of 27 germinal. Did this chevalier have to bother reporting to the authorities? He did indeed, and for his pains Robespierre directed that 'this ex-noble must be transferred [to prison] in Paris'. But the chevalier was lucky – the official at the bureau notes: 'it has not been possible to locate the *département* in which Faucon is situated'.

. . .

## THE PRISON 'CONSPIRACIES'

Herman was also commissioner for 'tribunals' and this meant pre-eminently the Revolutionary Tribunal. In this capacity he took the initiative in the 'prison conspiracy' trials of prairial and messidor. These so-called 'conspiracies' are also exemplary of how the police bureau worked. The first batch of cases was initiated by a denunciation from an inmate of the Bicêtre prison who informed the CSP of a conspiracy to break out of prison. The denunciation was passed on to Lejeune of the police bureau and when Robespierre arrived at his desk on 14 prairial/2 June Lejeune's abstract of the denunciation was waiting for him. On the 19th Robespierre turned the matter over to Herman, in a letter counter-signed by Barère for the CSP as a whole. Robespierre asked Herman to investigate only whether there were plans for a prison break-out. As Thierret-Grandpré put it, '[Herman] should have confined himself to these measures'.[30]

However, not content with this, Herman proceeded to transform the 'conspiracy' to break out into one to massacre the entire Republican establishment with cannibal intentions. On receiving Herman's report on 25 prairial/13 June the CSP ordered the transfer of the accused to the Revolutionary Tribunal and added significantly that should Herman's researches yield any further accomplices, he could deliver them to the Revolutionary Tribunal without referring back to the CSP. This yielded a further 36 cases to add to the 37 condemned to death on 28 prairial/16 June. The fairly slow initial procedure meant that these cases were heard in accordance with the law of 22 prairial. They were convicted

> of being declared enemies of the people in forming, proposing or joining a plot, of which the object was . . . to force the gates of the said prison, and then to stab with poignards the representatives of the people, members of the CSP and CSG, to tear out their hearts, to broil and eat them, and to put the most patriotic representatives to death in a barrel lined with nails.

Croker asks, 'in what other court . . . would such charges even have to be defended?'.[31]

Building on the latitude the CSP had granted him, Herman suggested that the same procedure could be applied to all the prisons, starting with the largest of the political prisons, the Luxembourg. In a report to the police bureau of 3 messidor/21 June, he suggested the possibility

> of purging the prisons in an instant and clearing the soil of liberty of this garbage, of these dregs of humanity. Justice would be done and it would be easier to restore order to the prisons.

And he sent Robespierre a draft decree empowering him to carry out investigations and to restore order in the prisons, the latter in conjunction with the Commune's police department, a joint operation involving several levers of Robespierre's political machine: Herman's bureau, the Commune, the police bureau and finally the Revolutionary Tribunal. Robespierre sent the decree back with his 'approuvé', signed it and got Billaud and Barère to counter-sign it.

On receipt of the CSP's decree, Herman's deputy, Lanne, proceeded to the Luxembourg and drew up a list of 159 names. The commission's report to the police bureau characterizes the 159 as agents of the guillotined General Dillon, who regretted that they could not assassinate patriots and lamented republican victories. Two copies of this list are extant, one signed by Lanne, the other by Saint-Just. On the former, a bureaucrat has written, 'It is to be noted that this decree is unsigned [i.e. by a member of the CSP] and the list of these prisoners was simply given to Fouquier-Tinville'. This irregularity (if it was one) was smoothed for the future by the CSP's decree of 17 messidor/5 June instructing Herman's commission to send future lists straight to the Revolutionary Tribunal, which was ordered to try these cases within 24 hours. This decree is in Saint-Just's hand, with his signature and the counter-signatures of Billaud and Collot.[32] Shortly before (on the 13th) Robespierre had seceded from the CSP but there was no change in policies when Saint-Just resumed control of the police bureau. And Saint-Just had taken the lead in extending Herman's autonomous powers. Herman later attempted to justify his increase of the Terror with the same argument Payan used, that French victories had made the 'enemies of the people' more desperate and therefore more dangerous.[33]

.   .   .

## NOTES

Unless otherwise stated all Robespierre's directives from the police bureau are taken from the Archives Nationales F7 4437.

1.  See A. Ording, *Le bureau de police du Comité de Salut Public* (1930), p. 42.
2.  Ording, *Bureau*, pp. 42–3.
3.  Ording, *Bureau*, p. 85.
4.  Ording, *Bureau*, pp. 37–8.
5.  Ording, *Bureau*, pp. 140–1.
6.  J.W. Croker, *Essays on the Early Period of the French Revolution* (1857), p. 299.
7.  G. Walter, *Robespierre* (1946), p. 540.
8.  Walter, *Robespierre*, p. 537.
9.  Quoted by J. Guilhaumou, 'A discourse on denunciation' in K. Baker, ed., *The French Revolution and the Creation of Modern Political Culture*, vol. IV, *The Terror* (1994), pp. 139–55, at p. 140.
10. Cited in M. Lyons, 'The 9 Thermidor: motives and effects', *European Studies Review* (1975), pp. 123–46, at p. 136.
11. Lyons, '9 Thermidor', pp. 135–6.
12. Saint-Just, *Oeuvres complètes*, ed. Ch. Vellay, 2 vols (1908), II, p. 508.

13. For two widely differing interpretations, see A. Soboul, *Les Sans-culottes Parisiens en l'an II* (1958), pp. 831–2 and 971–2 and Ording, *Bureau*, pp. 116–19.

14. Soboul, *Sans-culottes*, pp. 973–4; Ording, *Bureau*, pp. 112–16.

15. Ording, *Bureau*, p. 30.

16. Ording, *Bureau*, p. 47.

17. J-N. Billaud-Varenne, *Mémoire inédit*, ed. Ch. Vellay, *Revue historique de la Révolution française*, 1910, pp. 7–44, 161–75 and 321–36, 16 (my italics).

18. *Réponse des membres des deux anciens Comités de salut public et de sécurité général . . .*, reprinted in *La Révolution française* (1898), p. 258.

19. Courtois, *Notes relatives au 9 thermidor*, in *La Révolution française*, 1887, 922, 988.

20. H. Campardon, *Histoire du tribunal révolutionnaire de Paris*, 2 vols (1975), II, p. 332.

21. Acte d'accusation notifié le 24 germinal, P.J.B. Buchez and P.C. Roux, *Histoire parlementaire de la Révolution française*, 40 vols (1834–38), XXXV, p. 31.

22. Campardon, *Tribunal*, II, p. 336.

23. Buchez and Roux, *Histoire parlementaire*, XXXV, pp. 50–1.

24. F7 3822, report of 5 thermidor, cited in Ording, *Bureau*, pp. 50–1.

25. Campardon, *Tribunal*, II, pp. 334–5.

26. Letter of 21 messidor, cited in Campardon, *Tribunal*, II, p. 349.

27. Campardon, *Tribunal*, II, p. 347.

28. Campardon, *Tribunal*, II, pp. 345–6.

29. Buchez and Roux, *Histoire parlementaire*, XXXV, pp. 50–1.

30. Buchez and Roux, *Histoire parlementaire*, XXXIV, pp. 429–30.

31. *Moniteur*, XXI, 4 messidor/22 June 1794, cited in J.W. Croker, *Essays on the Early Period of the French Revolution* (1857), p. 490, Croker's translation.

32. J. Saladin, *Rapport au nom de la commission des 21*, year III (1795), p. 164; Archives Nationales F7 4436A; Ording, *Bureau*, pp. 161–3.

33. Campardon, *Tribunal*, II, p. 335.

*Chapter 10*

# RESISTANCE, 22 PRAIRIAL/
# 10 JUNE–7 THERMIDOR/25 JULY

. . .

## THE LAW OF 22 PRAIRIAL:
## THE PARLIAMENTARY DIMENSION

All roads lead back to the law of 22 prairial. We have already examined its provisions and seen how it led to an escalation of the Terror. This in due course caused even the Parisians to tire of blood: the guillotine was moved from the present Place de la Concorde to the working-class district of the Faubourg Saint-Antoine and, when the accumulation of blood became a health hazard, to the Barrière de la trône on the outskirts of the city. We noted that the CSP as a whole was involved in this aspect of the prairial measures but that Herman developed a degree of autonomy which he used to intensify the Terror.

However, at the last minute Robespierre grafted another clause on to the prairial law, without consulting his governmental colleagues. This led to a rift between Robespierre and Couthon and the rest. (Saint-Just returned to the army on the very day the law was presented.) The seemingly innocuous clause 20 ran: 'The Convention repeals all previous legislation which conflicts with the present decree . . .'. Despite Robespierre's sleight of hand deputies realized that it was an implicit repeal of the provision in the constitution of 1791, repeated in that of 1793, that no deputy could be put on trial without a specific decree by parliament. The other clauses of the prairial law would also have ensured that once deputies were put before the Revolutionary Tribunal they would not have enjoyed the relative procedural advantages which but for Herman's skulduggery might have enabled Danton to 'get off'.

Robespierre was driven to insert clause 20 by two recent events. On 18 prairial/6 June his deadly enemy Fouché had been elected president of the Jacobin Club. An increasingly reclusive Robespierre had neglected the Jacobin Club, taking his mastery over the original basis of his power for granted. Fouché was the incarnate type of the recalled proconsuls whose heads Robespierre now sought. If he had any doubts they were dispelled two days later, on 20 prairial/8 June, when the atheist wing of the Mountain and some friends of Danton's taunted him during the inaugural festival of his state religion.[1]

Those deputies who felt they were threatened by clause 20 attacked the prairial law on the floor of the house, a rebellion unprecedented since the fall of the Girondins. Immediately after Couthon, the law's sponsor, had sat down, the 'Dantonist' deputy Ruamps sprang to his feet with the words: 'This is an important decree; I demand that it be printed and that there be an adjournment. If it were to be adopted without an adjourn-ment, I would blow my brains out'. His motion was seconded by Lecointre de Versailles (who later claimed that he was planning to assassinate Robespierre at the rostrum). Barère, who had just arrived from the CSP, proposed an adjournment of three days and Lecointre magnanimously said he would be content with two.[2]

This amicable solution was wrecked by an intervention by Robespierre, who left the speaker's chair to browbeat the deputies. He resisted Bourdon's compromise that the purging of the Revolutionary Tribunal should go through and the rest of the measure be subject to an adjournment. An adjournment would have defeated his purpose of smuggling clause 20 through. So he told the deputies:

> I demand that the draft-law be discussed clause by clause in this sitting. . . . I observe furthermore that for a long time the National Convention has been accustomed to discuss and decree on the spot, because for a long time it has been free from servitude to factions. . . . I demand that, without stopping to consider the pro-posed adjournment, the Convention discuss the projected law sub-mitted to it, if need be until nine o'clock tonight. (10, 486)

Here, far more than at the recent festival, Robespierre appeared to his colleagues as a dictator being dictatorial; keeping them in detention like naughty schoolboys until they had done his bidding and dangerously discarding the fiction of freedom of

debate by saying that it hadn't existed for months, which everyone took to mean since the purge of the Dantonist deputies
in April. At the end of the momentous parliamentary session
of the 22nd, Couthon asked the Convention for the monthly
renewal of the powers it had delegated to the CSP. The Convention complied.

On the 23rd, however, in the absence of any members of the
CSP, there was open rebellion. Bourdon de l'Oise observed
that he was sure that in passing clause 20 'the Convention did
not intend that the power of the Committees should extend
to the members of the Convention without a previous decree'.
He proposed that clause 20 be amended accordingly. Merlin
(de Douai), however, a right-centre deputy and a distinguished
jurisprude, proposed that Bourdon's amendment be rejected
as superfluous on the 'consideration' that parliamentary inviolability was already an 'inalienable right'. This motion was passed.[3]

On the 24th Robespierre was back in the speaker's chair in
the Convention and for a while he had to watch the tide reced-
ing further, sorely tempted to ring his bell. Two members questioned not just the content of the law but its very style and for
the first time a politician implied that the republican jargon
was becoming meaningless. Charles Delacroix wanted to know
the meaning of 'depraving morals' in the clause 'seeking to . . .
deprave morals and corrupt the public conscience and undermine the energy and purity of revolutionary principles' (reason-
ably since it carried the death penalty). And 'I'd like to know',
asked Mallarmé, 'just what is meant by the words: "the law
supplies defence counsel to calumniated patriots in the shape
of patriotic jurors"?'. Two Robespierrist deputies attempted to
give some definitions: 'We all know what a patriotic juror is: he
is a man on the side of the Revolution'. Another added: 'the
article is as clear as day. The law is designed to suppress the
chatter of lawyers whilst giving calumniated patriots, for their
defence, the conscience of a patriotic juror.' He concluded,
'I demand that there be no further explanations'. Nothing
deterred, an anonymous deputy with a genuine love of words
pointed out that the phrase 'patriotic juror' was tautologous
since jurors in the Revolutionary Tribunal were by definition
patriotic. Consequently he 'demanded that the word "patriot"
following that of "juror" be deleted'.

Couthon could contain himself no longer. The linguistic
foundations of the Terror were being undermined. If people

started using words with 'precision and clarity' as Mallarmé had asked, where would it end? He demanded an end not only to this nonsense but the repeal of Merlin's 'consideration'. He got his way but only by affirming that parliamentary immunity was 'a constitutional and fundamental law of liberty'. Robespierre agreed. It was a sort of infinite regression: Merlin had said that there was no need for the Convention to assert that it retained its immunities since these were inalienable. Couthon said it was a slur on the CSP to suggest that it had wanted to remove the Convention's inalienable rights by a sleight of hand. They had already said as much to the Convention's envoy, Audoin. And though such alienation had indeed been their intention, the result of their action was that parliamentary immunity had now *become* inalienable. Robespierre would have to go to the Convention directly for any future heads.[4]

Virtually no one defended the prairial law in the Convention; nor did sycophantic petitions flood in from the country praising the measure; members of the CSG were eloquently silent; Barère, out of government solidarity, proposed a compromise which was not acceptable to Robespierre. As Levasseur, a deputy favourable to Robespierre, later observed, the CSP (even though the splits within it were concealed) no longer had a 'base' in the Convention, there was no governmental faction.[5] Robespierre got his way by employing a 'sinister eloquence' as when he said that 'Tallien is one of those who speaks constantly and fearfully and publicly of the guillotine, as something which concerns him' (10, 496). The prairial law ruined Robespierre's credit in parliament. The rest of his fortnight as speaker must have been embarrassing, but at least he was relieved of the necessity of speaking. When it ended on 30 prairial/18 June he ceased attending, only returning to the Convention on 8 thermidor.

. . .

## CONSPIRACIES AGAINST ROBESPIERRE

The prairial law also led to a series of conspiracies by various deputies against Robespierre. All his political life he had railed against imaginary conspiracies, now there were several real ones. Their main organizer, if his later claims are to be believed, was

Lecointre, who planned to assassinate him on the floor of the House but was dissuaded by his co-conspirators. Lecointre's allies included Fréron, Barras, Tallien, Thirion, Courtois, Garnier de l'Aube, Guffroy and Rovère. The first three were recalled proconsuls but they were all Dantonistes. Another Dantoniste, Bourdon de l'Oise, who was the parliamentary leader of the group, for some time pursued a one-man conspiracy, making his will on 22 prairial and vowing to assassinate Robespierre with a blood-stained sword which had seen action during the storming of the Bastille![6] As Dantonistes they sought not only to avenge their leader's death but to implement his policy of ending the mechanism of the *gouvernement révolutionnaire* and its spirit, the Terror. Robespierre, as the figurehead of the system, was merely the first in the line of fire. They were at first unaware of the conflict within government which made their opposition less effective.

Fouché, however, whom Robespierre christened 'the conspirator-in-chief', made the lethal play of making overtures to Carnot, Robespierre's most serious opponent in the CSP. Fouché later claimed that he had first suggested to Carnot sending artillery units attached to the Paris *sections* to the front to weaken Robespierre's military power base.[7] Between the end of prairial and the beginning of thermidor Pille, commissioner for the movement of armies, acting under Carnot's orders, sent 12 artillery companies to the front, leaving some 30 behind. On 6 thermidor an angry Sijas told the Jacobins that another 4,000 of these gunners would be leaving for the front. The last such order was signed on 4 thermidor but others would undoubtedly have followed.[8] Pille rushed out a pamphlet defending his conduct on 5 thermidor.[9]

On 28 messidor/16 July Robespierre himself attacked Pille. In order to avoid the scrutiny of his two Robespierrist deputies Sijas and Boullay, Pille had had his orders counter-signed by another official but Robespierre had successfully raised the matter in the CSP (10, 532). He argued that Pille (and by implication Carnot) had become unaccountable. Robespierre warned the Jacobins against a military dictatorship and specifically that Pille's commission for troop movement would direct an army towards Paris. On 19 messidor/7 July Carnot had launched a paper for the troops, the *Soirée du camp*, designed to prepare opinion for an impending government crisis and to inculcate a spirit of professionalism rather than a volunteer mentality. Robespierre had always believed that a professional army would lead to a military *coup d'état*. He told the Jacobin Club that the victory of Fleurus had been won by the French people and not by 'a commissioner [Pille] or any other man whatsoever [Carnot]'.

At about this time Robespierre drew up a proscription list of six deputies. Carnot does not figure in it but three of those who do, Dubois-Crancé, Delmas and Bourdon de l'Oise, are criticized for their relationship with Carnot. Dubois-Crancé and Delmas both belonged to the Convention's military commit- tee, which worked closely with Carnot. Robespierre concludes his indictment of Delmas by saying, 'As a member of the mil- itary committee, he is in frequent contact with Carnot'. This is one of the most precise pieces of information we have about Robespierre's intentions. Coming at the end of what has the appearance of a formal act of accusation, it reads as if Carnot had already been sent to the scaffold as a counter-revolutionary! The impression that Robespierre regarded Carnot as his prin- cipal opponent seems to be confirmed by another accusation against Bourdon de l'Oise: 'He presented [the CSP] with a clerk whom Carnot placed in his secretariat, a man who was only dismissed after Robespierre's repeated protests' (II, 16–21).

Carnot also quarrelled with Robespierre over his running of the police bureau. On 23 prairial/11 June, after a violent quarrel with his colleagues over the prairial law, Robespierre ordered the arrest of two officials protected by Carnot.[10] Either because of inefficiency at the bureau or resistance from his colleagues the arrest was not effected until 7 messidor/25 June. On 12 messidor/30 June Carnot called Robespierre a dictator over the arrests; and, as we have seen, finding his directives in the police bureau increasingly blocked Robespierre secretly seceded from the CSP.

Apart from Carnot, Robespierre's main opponents from within the CSP at this time were Billaud-Varenne and Collot d'Herbois. Their opposition is harder to explain. Between Robespierre and Carnot there was a rooted antagonism and personal antipathy going back from beyond the time of Robes- pierre's joining the CSP and based on differences of style and substance (military strategy, professional military ethos, dislike, on Carnot's part, of the ethos of the Jacobin Club). But Billaud and Robespierre had many characteristics in common. Both were solitary men, Billaud having only five or six close friends with his only entertainment the occasional visit to his beloved theatre. Both were austere men, Billaud's lodgings in the Rue Saint-André des Arts being only slightly more commodious than Robespierre's in the Rue Saint-Honoré. Both saw themselves as theoreticians of the Revolution and both were of a sombre cast of mind. Collot d'Herbois too had been an early protégé of Robespierre's and corresponded with him in affectionate terms up to the beginning of 1794 and perhaps beyond.

However, Collot felt threatened by the attack on Fouché, with whom he had been on mission to Lyon. And Billaud developed a theory of 'dangerous popularity' in relation to Robespierre similar to the one advanced in the Jacobin Club by the Girondin Guadet in April 1792.[11] Both sought precedents in classical history and thought that Robespierre should be ostracized or exiled for the good of the Republic to which such popularity as his posed a threat. Billaud's opposition was dangerous because he was well aware of the practical bases of Robespierre's power – his 'levers' as he put it – and sought to undermine them. Billaud located Robespierre's power bases in the Commune, the National Guard, the Jacobins, and the Revolutionary Tribunal. He was also aware of Robespierre's use of patronage, for which, he claims with much justification, neither he nor his colleagues possessed either the aptitude or the taste. Billaud sought, at first unsuccessfully, to have Fleuriot-Lescot and Payan, Hanriot and his general staff dismissed and even arrested, and the National Guard restored to its 1792 organization without a permanent commander-in-chief. In addition Billaud and Collot boycotted the Jacobin Club.

Billaud also claimed 'to have sought the slightest pretexts . . . to reform or abolish the Revolutionary Tribunal'.[12] Robespierre referred to this manoeuvre in a speech to the Jacobins on 13 messidor/1 July, the day he had secretly seceded from the CSP (10, 512–16). Robespierre's governmental enemies had demanded the repeal of the prairial law, in whole or in part, thereby seeking, as Robespierre put it, 'to shield the aristocracy from the justice of the nation'. They sought to 'slander the Revolutionary Tribunal and the Convention's decree [of 22 prairial] concerning its organization'. The prairial law having empowered a further Robespierrist purge of the Tribunal, he now hints at a counter-purge: his enemies had sought to 'Destroy the Revolutionary Tribunal *or compose it of members agreeable to the men of faction*' (my italics). Saint-Just also claimed that, but for his efforts 'the Revolutionary Tribunal [would have] been suppressed or filled with the nominees of two or three members [of the Committee] ruling absolutely'. He implied that these included Billaud and Collot.[13]

.  .  .

## OPPOSITION FROM THE CSG

A key move on Billaud's part was to make contact on 22 prairial itself with the CSG, which Robespierre and Couthon had not consulted on the measure. The latter had intended by sleight of hand to exclude the CSG from cognizance of some of the cases covered by the law. In the draft law presented by Couthon on the 22nd, as it appears in the proofs of the *Bulletin de la Convention*, the CSG had no involvement in cases covered by articles 11, 15 and 18. However, without there having been any parliamentary discussion of this omission, in later versions the CSG was given joint supervision with the CSP over cases covered by articles 11 and 15. (On the 26th Vadier, in the Convention, had the CSG's role extended to article 18.)[14] It is highly likely that the role of the CSG was restored as a result of pressure from the CSP during the stormy meeting on the morning of the 23rd. So noisy was it that a large crowd gathered in the Tuileries gardens and the french windows had to be closed.

Four days later on 27 prairial/15 June the atheist Vadier, of the CSG, took a spectacular revenge on Robespierre for the slights his committee had sustained at his hands in recent months, by turning his report to the Convention on the Catherine Théot affair into a thinly veiled attack on Robespierre's state religion. Théot, an elderly prophetess, had predicted a divine manifestation for Pentecost, which happened to fall on 20 prairial, the day of the Festival of the Supreme Being. She had been arrested on 23 floréal/12 May and there is little doubt that Vadier now dragged up the case to embarrass Robespierre. And, with Robespierre sitting in the President's chair, he induced the Convention to send Théot before the Revolutionary Tribunal.

Robespierre was determined to stop proceedings which would have prolonged the ridicule and also have revealed that Catherine's disciples included the father of Fleuriot-Lescot, the Robespierrist mayor of Paris, and connections of his hosts the Duplays. Accordingly that evening he summoned Dumas, the Robespierrist president of the Revolutionary Tribunal, and Fouquier-Tinville, its more independent-minded attorney-general, to the CSP. Fouquier relates how all the members of the CSP filed out and left him alone with Robespierre who ordered him to hand over the file. He obeyed, though resentful at this attack on the independence of the judiciary and flouting of a decree of the National Convention.[15]

Furious at Fouquier's show of independence, Robespierre turned to Herman to supply him with a replacement. That high functionary in turn took soundings from a district judge:

> I believe you to be a good and enlightened patriot and am applying to you to ask, in the light of your republican conscience, to suggest to me a citizen fit to perform the functions of public prosecutor, for the CSP has charged me to find one. Prompt reply, please. Fraternal salutations.[16]

However nothing came of this, Robespierre's colleagues probably insisting on Fouquier's retention.

Accordingly Robespierre got Payan to investigate the CSG's own investigation into the Théot case, via the municipal police. Robespierre wrote that Payan was 'reprimanded and threatened by the CSG' for arresting 'several agents' of the CSG 'in accordance with the wishes [*voeu*] of the CSP' (10, 562). The curious use of the word '*voeu*' rather than '*arrête*' of the CSP suggests that Payan was acting under Robespierre's personal instructions rather than under those of the CSP as a whole.

Payan, stung by the CSG's 'reprimand' but undaunted by its 'menace', urged a speedy counter-attack. In an important letter to Robespierre of 9 messidor/27 June Payan argued that Vadier had presented his report to deflect attention from the conduct of the parliamentary rebels who were seeking to hide behind a 'silence hypocrite' at a time when Robespierre was seeking the consent of his colleagues on the CSP for their execution (II, 359–66). He urges Robespierre to reply with a 'grand report' and quickly:

> Beware lest in placing a long interval between the session where they raised themselves against the government (22 prairial) and the moment that is chosen to denounce them, the report produce less effect and have fewer supporters. (II, 364)

Robespierre's report must be of such scope as to obliterate all remembrance of Vadier's. It would demote the CSG: since its members possessed 'neither creative genius nor the modesty to shut up and allow themselves to be directed. In future they must be well guided and in charge of nothing' (II, 361). Robespierre took Payan's advice on delivering a 'grand report' but he took over a month to do it, ignoring Payan's advice that speed was of the essence. Whilst Robespierre dithered, Payan drew up plans to ensure that Robespierre's speech would have adequate military backing.

.   .   .

## SAINT-JUST'S RETURN TO PARIS FROM THE FRONT

At the very height of this drama behind closed doors, during the night of 10–11 messidor/28–29 June, Saint-Just entered the CSP with tidings of the great French victory at Fleurus, at which he had been present. He castigated Carnot for attempting to detach 18,000 men from Jourdan's army before and after the battle. A spell away from the hot-house atmosphere of the Pavillon de Flore enabled Saint-Just to put things into perspective. In particular he realized just how far the situation had deteriorated for the Robespierristes. He now found 'the government not so much divided as scattered'. Robespierre had been frozen out by his colleagues,

> Couthon was constantly absent [through illness]; Prieur (de la Marne) had been away for eight months; Saint-André was at [Brest]; Lindet was buried in his bureaux; Prieur (de la Côte d'Or) in his; I had been with the army; and the rest, who exercised the authority of all, seemed to me to have profited from their absence.

Saint-Just's remedy would have been to require a quorum of six members for valid decisions.[17] But together with Barère, who was not yet sure Robespierre would lose the struggle because he did not yet know what form it would take, Saint-Just sought to work out a compromise with the CSP.

This was thrashed out on 4 thermidor/22 July at a joint session of the CSP and CSG including Saint-Just but not Robespierre.[18] Saint-Just gained the promise to implement his ventôse decrees fully. The decrees had provided for six 'popular commissions' to effect a summary classification of suspects into those who had been wrongfully arrested and those who hadn't. The property of the latter was to be confiscated in favour of needy patriots, a list of whom would be drawn up by provincial officials. In fact only two commissions had been set up and they had only just begun their work. It was now agreed that the remaining four commissions would be set up immediately. In return Saint-Just agreed to send the artillery companies from four further *sections* to the artillery park Carnot had set up at Givet. Saint-Just may have further agreed to hand over running of the police bureau to the CSG, after the CSP had refused to ratify his directives. The CSP commissioned Saint-Just to make a report on the general situation to the Convention and he was asked not to mention the state religion.

The next day Robespierre attended a continuation of the joint session. He railed at Billaud and Collot and at the members of the CSG and won a further concession: four 'revolutionary commissions' were set up to judge those whom the 'popular commissions' had classified as suspects. This would have led to a vast increase in the killings because the ventôse laws had provided only for deportation (albeit to Guyana). Fortunately for them, however, Robespierre soon repudiated this compromise, feeling no doubt that Saint-Just had sacrificed Robespierre's priorities to his own.

.   .   .

## RECAPTURE OF THE JACOBINS

To compensate for his absence from the CSP and the National Convention, Robespierre increased his attendance at the Jacobins, the cradle of his power, which gave him emotional nourishment. The Jacobins was not the power-house it had been in earlier times. Saint-Just lamented: 'Last year what constituted the strength of the people' was that legislation was discussed first in the Jacobins before being introduced into the Convention. Now all the Jacobins were interested in was denunciation and the Convention with giving and taking offence. There was no constructive legislation.[19] What had really happened to the Jacobins was what had happened to many revolutionary institutions: it had passed from being a ginger group to a source, the main source, for government employees. But it was still a force to be reckoned with and Billaud and Collot were in two minds on whether to engage or disengage from the Club, in the hope of weakening it – the same dilemma as confronted Robespierre with the CSP. Billaud boycotted the Jacobins between 4 ventôse/ 14 March and 8 thermidor. Collot, on the other hand, had taken advantage of the lapses of Robespierre's attendance at the Club, notably on 7 July when he had used the occasion of 'the unveiling of a bust of William Tell to make some pointed remarks in defence of tyrannicide'.[20]

Robespierre himself had only addressed the club three times in prairial (on the 6th, 8th and 23rd) and this negligence had been rewarded by the election of Fouché to the presidency. Fouché had been succeeded as president by Barère, who was neutral towards Robespierre but Barère had been succeeded by an enemy, Elie Lacoste of the CSG. On 6 thermidor/24 July another enemy, Léonard Bourdon, was temporarily in the presidential chair and an ugly if bizarre incident occurred. Robespierre intervened to stop the reading of a letter from a soldier who had had a bone from his amputated arm made into a handle for his knife. Such conduct, Robespierre argued, was proper to excite 'horror rather than admiration'. Though Robespierre's comments found favour, Bourdon, in Robespierre's words, 'in a tone of contempt, ordered that the reading should continue' (10, 538).

Robespierre addressed the Jacobins eight times in messidor and four times during the first *décade* of thermidor. The most interesting topics for our story were Lyon politics and the denunciation we have already noted of Carnot and Pille for sending the gunners to the front. In the sessions of 23 and 26 messidor/11 and 14 July Dubois-Crancé and Fouché were attacked, the one accused of being too soft, the other too hard on the rebel city. Dubois-Crancé (or Dubois de Crancé as Robespierre insisted on calling him) it will be remembered had been recalled from Lyon by Robespierre the previous October but Crancé had successfully appealed to the Convention to have the decree against him repealed. The report, however, which eventually cleared Crancé's name, was not produced until the year III, so that Robespierre could revive his attack on him at any time. Recently Robespierre had accused him of 'intriguing' to get the Jacobins to make public functionaries ineligible for membership of the Club, which, if the Club had been so foolish as to accept such a measure, would have immobilized Robespierre's political machine since members of the Jacobins were by this time nearly all public functionaries.

On 23 messidor/11 July after denunciations by Robespierre and Dumas, Couthon successfully proposed that Dubois-Crancé be expelled. Crancé was then on mission at Rennes but on 26 messidor/14 July the CSP recalled him in disgrace: the decree was drafted by Barère, still hoping for a reconciliation with Robespierre and aware that a quarrel within the CSP could bring down the whole *gouvernement révolutionnaire*.[21] At the end of the session, Robespierre invited the absent Fouché to show good cause why he also should not be expelled and on the 26th/14 July called him 'the conspirator-in-chief' (10, 524–6).

Robespierre had many reasons of his own to break Fouché, the atheist proconsul who had proclaimed: 'death is an eternal sleep'. But he was also spurred on by the 'friends of Chalier' who formed Robespierre's habitual society in his last months. The 'friends' planned to follow up their success in having Fouché recalled from Lyon by bringing him before the Revolutionary Tribunal. The guiding spirit was again Achard, now back in Lyon and president of the Jacobins. He wrote to Gravier, juror on the Revolutionary Tribunal and Robespierre's neighbour and confidant, saying that he and the 'friends' had been gathering evidence for an indictment of Fouché for 'Caesarism' and plotting to 'replace the *gouvernement révolutionnaire*'.

However, despite having sent an indictment 'comprising 19 articles', it had been judged insufficient. 'Once again', he complains, 'what more is needed?' But he expects to send decisive evidence 'tomorrow or the day after'. But Achard would have preferred to base Fouché's prosecution 'on asking him why he had illegally formed an *armée révolutionnaire* in the *départements* of l'Allier and Nievre? What was his aim, his intentions?' He concluded, 'point de Pitié! du sang! du sang!' (II, 225–6). We don't know who found the evidence against Fouché insufficient. The CSP? Herman? Fouquier-Tinville? Robespierre? Did Achard know that Robespierre no longer attended the committee? But Achard's queries turned out to be academic: his letter is dated 10 thermidor, the date Robespierre was guillotined.

The lobbying of Paris by rival provincial factions reached epidemic proportions by July. Robespierre was in the thick of it since rival factions from the areas with which he had most contact, Arras, the Jura, Lyon and the Midi, lobbied the most intensely. On 2 thermidor/20 July in the Convention Barère denounced provincial lobbying and Paris was declared a closed city: all provincial officials had to return home within a fixed period.[22] Fouché had his own Lyon faction in Paris, composed of former members of the Temporary Commission and of the disbanded *armée révolutionnaire* which had done duty at Lyon. Robespierre believed it was this faction which had carried Fouché to the presidency of the Jacobins.[23] On 23 messidor/ 10 July Robespierre attacked the commission for becoming too soft on the accused through the intercession of women. A police report by Guérin for Robespierre dated 29 messidor/ 17 July gives details of the struggle between the 'friends of Chalier' and Fouché's group. One of the latter tells the police-man that,

> a heap of scoundrels forming Robespierre's entourage, who call themselves the friends of Chalier want to ruin his friend Fouché and the Temporary Commission. For the rest they must show themselves as there is not a moment to lose.

The police 'mouche' observing that a demonstration would be put down by the government, Fouché's man replied that the action was to take place in the Jacobins and at the bar of the Convention (II, 378–81).

These two *loci* were where the action did take place. But Fouché declined to answer the charges against him in person because, as he told his sister, the Jacobins 'had become [Robespierre's] forum'. Instead he asked the Club to postpone a decision until the report which he had asked the CSP to make on his mission had been presented to the Convention.[24] Fouché was expelled from the Jacobins on the 26th/14 July at the insistence of Robespierre, who was angered that he should appeal from the Club to the Convention where Fouché had spoken, after a long absence the day before. But Fouché having appealed to the Convention, Robespierre would have to appeal to it as well. And these successive appeals to its arbitration in themselves revivified it. Fouché had been patiently trying to sew together the disparate strands of the anti-Robespierre conspiracies and he must have thought he was nearing port for on 5 thermidor/23 July he wrote to his brother-in-law: 'Just a few more days . . . Even today perhaps, we shall see the traitors unmasked'.[25] This letter suggests that the timing of Robespierre's attack on 8 thermidor was not entirely of his choosing – even that he was acting out of self-defence.

On 3 thermidor/21 July Couthon had turned his attention to the parliamentary opposition, denouncing 'four or five' scoundrels in the Convention. On the 6th, he raised the number to 'five or six', mentioning this higher figure twice. Although he named no names he made it clear that he was referring to the corrupt representatives-on-mission: 'five or six human pygmies whose hands are full of the riches of the Republic and dripping with the blood of their innocent victims'.[26] On the 6th Robespierre said that 'the moment had come to strike the last heads of the hydra' (10, 539). In view of this the deputy Gouly, then secretary to the Jacobins, could have been forgiven for proposing an extraordinary session of the Club for the 7th to allow Robespierre and Couthon to develop their accusations with greater 'precision'. Robespierre, however, 'looked daggers' at him and his motion was not carried.[27]

.  .  .

## RECOURSE TO THE CONVENTION

Robespierre had decided to stake all on transferring the field of battle from the Jacobins to the Convention. Next day, 7 thermidor/ 25 July, the Club sent a deputation to the Convention. The Jacobin deputation denounced the ridiculing of the state religion and also denounced Pille. This thinly disguised attack on Carnot must have been made at Robespierre's instigation and really marks the start of his offensive in the Convention.

On 7 thermidor also Dubois-Crancé, who had arrived back in Paris the day before, addressed the Convention. He had not gone to the Jacobins; had not even gone home. Instead he went to the CSP. In the Convention he justified himself against Robespierre's attack and asked that the CSP and CSG report on his case 'tomorrow if possible'. The Convention ordered that the report should be made within three days. Crancé's appeal was over Robespierre's head to his governmental colleagues.[28] It may have accelerated the production of Robespierre's speech the next day.

.  .  .

## NOTES

1. J. Guilaire, *Billaud-Varenne* (1969), p. 271.
2. P.J.B. Buchez and P.C. Roux, *Histoire parlementaire de la Révolution française*, 40 vols, (1834–38), XXXIII, pp. 199–202.

3. *Moniteur Universel ou Gazette Nationale*, 70 vols (1789–1859), XX, pp. 697–700.

4. *Moniteur*, XX, debate of 24 prairial.

5. R. Levasseur, *Mémoires*, 3 vols (1829–31), III, p. 188.

6. M. Lyons, 'The 9 Thermidor: motives and effects', *European Studies Review* (1975), pp. 123–46, at p. 128.

7. Fouché, *Memoirs of Joseph Fouché, Duke of Otranto* (1892), p. 15.

8. F.-A. Aulard, *La Société des Jacobins*, 6 vols (1897), VI, p. 239, session of 6 thermidor.

9. L.-A. Pille, *Réponse de L-A Pille*, Paris, 5 thermidor.

10. A. Ording, *Le bureau de police du Comité de Salut Public* (1930), p. 99.

11. J.-N. Billaud-Varenne, *Mémoire inédit*, ed. Ch. Vellay, *Revue historique de la Révolution française* (1910), pp. 7–44, 161–75 and 321–36, 166–7.

12. Billaud-Varenne, *Mémoire*, p. 174.

13. Saint-Just, *Oeuvres complètes*, ed. Ch. Vellay, 2 vols (1908), II, p. 490.

14. G. Lefebvre, 'Sur la loi du 22 prairial an II', *Annales historiques de la Révolution française* 23 (1951), pp. 225–56, at pp. 252–3.

15. G. Walter, *Robespierre* (1946), p. 416.

16. Archives Nationales BB 3022, cited in A. Mathiez, *The Fall of Robespierre* (1927), p. 130.

17. Undelivered speech, Saint-Just, *Oeuvres complètes*, II, p. 478.

18. On this joint meeting see A. Mathiez, 'Les séances des 4 et 5 thermidor aux deux comités de salut public et de sûreté générale', in *Girondins et Montagnards* (1930), pp. 139–69.

19. Saint Just, *Oeuvres*, II, p. 508.

20. N. Hampson, *The Life and Opinions of Maximilien Robespierre* (1974), p. 288.

21. Th. Yung, *Dubois-Crancé*, 2 vols (1884), II, p. 139.

22. F. Brunel, *Thermidor: La Chute de Robespierre* (1989), pp. 78–9.

23. Aulard, *Jacobins*, VI, pp. 219 et seq.

24. J.M. Roberts and J. Hardman, eds, *French Revolution Documents*, 2 vols (1966–67), II, p. 252.

25. Roberts and Hardman, *French Revolution Documents*.

26. Aulard, *Jacobins*, VI, pp. 235 and 238.

27. G. Walter, *Robespierre* (1946), pp. 423–4.

28. Yung, *Dubois-Crancé*, II, p. 143.

*Chapter 11*

# THE FALL OF ROBESPIERRE

There is no portion of Robespierre's life so well known as his last two days. *J.W. Croker*

.   .   .

## ROBESPIERRE'S TWO-HOUR SPEECH TO
## THE CONVENTION

On 8 thermidor/26 July Robespierre returned to the National Convention after six weeks' absence and delivered himself of a long speech. Michelet marvelled that he should have chosen to issue his challenge in the form of a speech and explained it by 'his invincible respect for the law'.[1] He was in fact forced onto this unfavourable terrain because his governmental colleagues had blocked his action. Robespierre himself confessed to the forlornness of his task: 'Strange project for a man to get the National Convention to cut its collective throat with its own hands' (10, 549). Yet, as it had been with the prairial law, that was precisely his objective. Time also was running out as the sending of artillery units to the front was accelerated, with the permission if not the approval of Saint-Just.

The speech combined elements of a political testament with a practical attack: the first two-thirds is a self-indulgent lament about the calumnies and persecutions to which he has been subjected; the closing section makes certain precise proposals. As Croker wrote, 'This tirade was not a mere rhetorical de-clamation, whatever we think of its good taste; it was artfully calculated'.[2] Nevertheless, as the *Gazette française* observed at the time, 'this work does not lend itself easily to analysis' (10, 580).

186

It is allusive and Robespierre employs the same categories of reproach as his opponents. As Croker observed:

> Robespierre's speech might almost have been spoken by Bourdon [de l'Oise] and Bourdon's by Robespierre. They rang the changes on *calumny, corruption, crime, terror, cowards, traitors, tyrants, despots* – *Sylla, Verres, Clodius* and *Catilline* – with mutual rancour and indisputable truth.[3]

Indeed Robespierre himself complains that everyone was using the same rhetoric: 'All the conspirators have even outbid each other to adopt all the formulae, all the watchwords of patriotism' (10, 545).

The speech Robespierre delivered was less specific than a draft, in which Amar, Jagot and Vadier of the CSG are denounced by name (10, 552 and 562 note). Nevertheless in the speech actually delivered, apart from denouncing Cambon, Mallarmé and Ramel of the finance committee by name (10, 570), Robespierre makes unmistakeable coded references to Billaud-Varenne, Carnot and Barère of the CSP, Vadier of the CSG, Lecointre, Ruamps and Thuriot among the 'Dantonistes', as well as references to the recalled proconsuls, including Fouché whom he may have named. All would have recognized themselves and did recognize themselves, witness their frantic interventions after Robespierre had sat down (10, 546, 565 and 567).

After he had 'poured out his heart', Robespierre analysed the crisis and made concrete proposals. For him the rot started when deputies mocked him at the Festival of the Supreme Being which, he tells us, was almost cancelled at the last minute. Of this mockery he said, 'this one phenomenon explains everything which has happened since' (10, 562). 'Nothing was omitted', he continues in some lines he erased,

> to obliterate the salutary impression which the Festival of the Supreme Being had produced. The first move was Vadier's report, in which a profound political conspiracy was disguised by the recital of a mystical farce and misplaced merriment. (10, 562 note)

He then relates the war of the CSG against the CSP; the fact that his advice to the latter committee was systematically ignored so that he had not attended that body for six weeks; that nevertheless he was blamed for the increase of the Terror on the grounds that he ran the police bureau, whereas he had only run it for a short period during Saint-Just's absence and issued only 30 decrees.

It would however, he observed, be a funny sort of dictator who didn't control the army and the finances. Yet, 'In whose hands today are the armies, the finances and the internal administration of the Republic: In those of the coalition which pursues me' (10, 566). This was only part of the story. For though the armies of the line were directed by his enemy, Carnot, Robespierre, through Hanriot, controlled the armed forces of the capital. Similarly the CSG's control of internal administration was shadowed by Herman's commission and by the police bureau. At issue was a jurisdictional conflict.

Robespierre takes the CSP to task for not addressing Saint-Just's hobbyhorse of 'republican institutions', but instead of calling them 'republican' he calls them 'révolutionnaire' which suggests that the inauguration of the new institutions will not mark the end of emergency government and the Terror: 'Everything will proceed towards the true goal of revolutionary institutions; and the Terror imparted to crime will be the best guarantee of innocence' (10, 569). The Revolution will be permanent.

At the end of his speech Robespierre makes a series of concrete proposals which are directly inspired by Payan's letter of 9 messidor:

> Punish the traitors [in the Convention], renew the bureaux of the CSG,[4] purge the CSG itself and subordinate it to the CSP; purge the CSP itself and constitute unity of government under the supreme authority of the National Convention. (10, 576)

In other words Robespierre was asking for a further centralization of power in the hands of a CSP purged of his enemies. A formal dictatorship.

What did Robespierre expect to happen next? Presumably that loyalists would denounce by name those whom he had denounced in code and that the Convention would vote for their arrest: 'I have done my duty let others do theirs'. Robespierre generally left it to others to embody his suggestions. This time, however, it happened rather differently. Lecointre, whom Robespierre had twice denounced in his speech, proposed that it be published. There are several possible interpretations of his move: that, as Barère suggested, publication would bring Robespierre into contempt; that he sought to propitiate Robespierre or suddenly saw in him an ally for his primary purpose of defeating the committees. The most likely version has him saying to Rovère, who wanted him to launch his denunciation, 'No, he is attacking the Committees. They are going to destroy each other.'[5]

Next Bourdon asked for the opposite: that the question of publication should be decided by the two committees. Barère, then, to add to the confusion, backed Lecointre (later claiming a perfidious motive).[6] Couthon then raised the stakes by asking not just for the publication of the speech but that it be distributed to the communes throughout the Republic. The debate then turned on this matter rather than any immediate arrests. When the Convention finally decided that the speech should be printed for the benefit of deputies only but that it, like the report on Dubois-Crancé, should be referred to the two committees, Robespierre broke cover by saying that that was to have his speech judged by the very men he was denouncing. He also refused to hand over his speech and implied that he would distribute it himself through the national Jacobin network, as in his oppositional days.[7]

The tide turned against Robespierre when Cambon not only vigorously defended his administration of the finances but concluded with the fatal accusation: 'It is time to tell the whole truth: one man is paralysing the National Convention; that man is the one who has just made the speech; it is Robespierre; so decide.' Robespierre made a feeble half-retraction and the spell was broken. If Barère had not made a diversionary speech about recent victories, Robespierre might well have been arrested there and then.[8]

One thing, however, the debate had revealed. Although no one but Couthon supported Robespierre, with Barère at best neutral, there was no coordination between those who were supposed to have conspired against him. Those who had been directly attacked (or imagined they had) replied in kind but any traces of a conspiracy showed that it had not deviated from its primary purpose of breaking the power of the committees. Witness the most likely explanation of Lecointre's intervention and Fréron's demand that the law of 22 prairial be repealed, which was promptly quashed by Billaud.[9]

It was left to Bréard to conclude with the sententious but accurate words: 'This is a great cause which must be judged by the Convention itself; I ask that the Convention repeal its decree sending [Robespierre's speech to the provinces]'.[10] Publication was the oxygen which had supported Robespierre's public career; that career may be said to have begun when he used the prize money for an essay to pay for its publication and ended when the Convention declined to disseminate his last speech.

.   .   .

## THE BARRA AND VIALA FESTIVAL

Whilst Robespierre was making his speech, Payan and Fleuriot-Lescot were preparing for a festival, but one with a military flavour. The occasion was the transference of the bodies of Barra and Viala to the Panthéon which was due to take place on 10 thermidor. Barra was a 13-year-old volunteer who had been killed in the Vendée after performing heroic exploits for the Republic. Robespierre took his cause to heart and made a speech in the Convention which embellished the official account. Viala, another juvenile martyr, was the nephew of Agricola Moureau, a prominent Robespierriste from the Rhône valley and correspondent of Payan and Robespierre. In the notes he made for his report on Robespierre's papers, Courtois jotted down: 'Fête of Viala, the day chosen to immolate the Convention' but he does not elaborate.[11] Let us start with what is known about the projected festival.

On the 8 thermidor/26 July Lubin, Payan's deputy, wrote to the 48 *sections* to the effect that 'the National Convention has decreed that on the day of the fête of Barra and Viala it would be surrounded by soldiers wounded in the defence of the country'. Accordingly he invited each *section* to find 'either in the national hospices or families within your Section, all the soldiers of liberty who having some wound qualify to take part in this festival'. Lubin informed them that 'the rendez-vous was nine o'clock in the Tuileries Gardens'.[12]

On 7 thermidor/25 July the Commune had obtained permission from the CSP to convoke the general assemblies of the *sections* to rehearse for the festival. The permission was a spin-off from the compromise reached in the joint session of the CSP and CSG of 4–5 thermidor which Robespierre had not yet repudiated. The programme, which the general assemblies were convoked to rehearse on the 8th, was devised by Joseph Payan's commission for public instruction, with sets by another

Robespierriste, David. The convocation of the assemblies had been sanctioned by the CSP on the express condition that the *sections* confined themselves to the dress rehearsal for the festival. In transmitting their instructions to the clerk of the Commune for despatch to the *sections*, both Fleuriot-Lescot and Payan are obsessed with recording both the CSP's authorization and its restrictions. Thus Lescot:

> You will find enclosed the minute of the General Council of the Commune's decree of yesterday charging me and [Payan] with asking the CSP for authorization for the convocation of the Sectional assemblies for today. The authorization of the CSP being at the bottom of this minute, you will lose no time in sending the letter of convocation to the *sections*, indicating the precise purpose of this convocation. In the course of the day you will send me a copy of the decree, including the Committee's authorization.

Payan's letter to the clerk is even more punctilious:

> I invite you, citizen and dear friend, in the letter which you write to the *sections*, to be so good as to warn them expressly that they must only deliberate on objects relative to the fête. Before ten o'clock you should have David's reports and the other material necessary to make up the programme.

Though he was always castigating people for their respect for legal scruples, as national agent of the Commune he had shown himself to be infected with a similar disease. On numerous occasions, Payan wrote to the Convention's legislative committee to establish the legal position. Thus on 4 April to ascertain whether the *sections* had the right to assemble, apart from the fifth and last day of the *décade*, for the purpose of nominations. When he cut down the number of sessions of the Commune's general council to five per *décade*, he covered himself by sending the Convention's legislation committee a copy of the minutes. On 25 May he worried that purges in many surveillance committees left them below the quorum necessary to validate their acts.[13]

By 6.00 p.m. on the 8th nothing had arrived from Joseph Payan and David and a distraught Lescot wrote to the clerk:

> It is now past six o'clock and already several *sections* have come to ask me for the programme and David's report on account of which they have been convoked. Whether Citizen David or the commission

for public instruction have sent this material or whether it has not reached you, either way tell me why you have not informed me. There is not a moment to lose.

I interpret these facts as follows. The hierarchy of the Commune, with Robespierre's tacit consent, planned to make at least a moral demonstration outside the Convention on 10 thermidor: all the wounded in Paris would be an imposing sight and of course though the participants had been wounded their wounds were not actually bleeding. One *section* was denounced to the Convention on the 9th for atttempting to arm its youth to escort its 'invalids' to the festival.[14] The festival would mark the climax to the movement launched by Robespierre's speech on the 8th. After all the *journée* of 31 May was not completed until 2 June. The CSP, thinking it had done a deal with Robespierre on the 5th and not wishing to risk an open rupture which could entail the fall of the government, unaware that he was going to make a big speech, agreed both to the demonstration and to a dress rehearsal by the *sections* on the understanding that they confined themselves to these matters.

The CSP's condition was utterly unenforceable and that is why perhaps Payan and Lescot went to such elaborate lengths to be seen to be trying to enforce it. They wanted to do everything by the book, even an insurrection. This prefigures their caution on the morrow. The 'dress rehearsals' were meant to start at about 10.00 a.m. and the *sections* assembled. However, by 6.00 p.m. the programme had not arrived from Joseph Payan's Commission nor the choreography from David, and Lescot was anxious. Remember that by this time Robespierre had delivered his big speech and its mixed reception was known; the Jacobins were about to start their session. In the circumstances the importance Lescot pays to the sectional meetings suggests strongly that they were not just about revolutionary theatre. Yet without the choreography Lescot did not have the legal pretext to let the meetings continue. The failure of Joseph Payan and David to send their material also suggested that they were getting cold feet, and prefigured a larger betrayal.

Fleuriot-Lescot was worried that industrial unrest would mar the Barra and Viala festival and on the morning of the 9th he ordered troops for the morrow. We have noted the harsh attitude of the Commune and of Payan in particular towards strikes in favour of wage increases but on 17 messidor the Commune approved a *maximum des salaires* for Paris which would have *reduced* wages by about 20 per cent. On 5 thermidor this new schedule was published and there were widespread strikes. Hanriot noted on the 7th that 'several workers doubtless misled by the enemies of the people had left their workshops'. And in his order of the 9th Fleuriot noted that 'malcontents could profit from the proclamation of the maximum des salaires to mislead some citizens'.[15]

·  ·  ·

## AT THE JACOBINS

In the evening Robespierre repeated his speech to the Jacobins, but this time to critical acclaim (hats were thrown in the air at the climaxes). He also told the Club that the reception given to his speech in the Convention had enabled him to know 'his enemies and those of the patrie' – the two had become synonymous. Billaud and Collot, aware that Robespierre would turn to the Club, arrived first and Collot tried to address the meeting. Accounts differ as to whether he was supported by a 'small' or a 'substantial minority' (10, 586–7) but in any case it was insufficient and he descended from the tribune with 'the most profound despair' written on his face. Billaud could not even obtain a hearing and he and Collot were driven from the Club. The treatment of Billaud and Collot at the Jacobins ruined any chance of a truce between Robespierre and his colleagues in the CSP.[16] Dubarran, of the CSG, was also threatened by Robespierre's supporters.[17]

Couthon then proposed that those deputies who had opposed the dissemination of Robespierre's speech should be forced to justify themselves before the Club. This was to take place at an 'extraordinary session' on the following evening, the 9th, as a letter from Legracieux, whom Joseph Payan had brought from Valence to the commission of public instruction, makes clear. Sent on official notepaper, on the morning of the 9th, this letter informs the Payans' local club of Paul-les-Fontaines,

> This evening [the ninth] the great order of the day in the extraordinary meeting of the Jacobins is the present conspiracy. This evening *and the following days* it is war to the death to the conspirators ...[18]

This is further evidence that the Robespierristes were planning an operation extending over several days, with no particular priority attached to the 9th, less perhaps than to the 10th, the day of the fête.

Payan could not see the point of all the speechifying. He told the Jacobins: 'You have not a moment to lose! Whilst you sit here deliberating the conspirators are active, their rallying point is in the two culpable Committees'.[19]

.  .  .

## AT THE CSP

After the session at the Jacobins, Robespierre returned to his lodgings. He had been having early nights since his secession from the CSP. But his friends and enemies passed the night in manoeuvres designed to frustrate the plans and waste the time of the adverse faction. Having escaped from the Jacobins, Billaud and Collot returned to the CSP and vented their spleen on Saint-Just, who had not been to the Jacobins, had not spoken up for Robespierre in the Convention and had probably not been informed by Robespierre that he was going to make a speech. Saint-Just was very hurt by this treatment which may have included physical abuse and decided in consequence to break his promise to let the CSP vet the report on 'republican institutions' he was due to give the Convention on the 9th. He may well have altered his speech in the light of Billaud and Collot's unjustified attack, since they are the only ones denounced – and denounced by name – in his speech. Collot believed that Saint-Just's report would centre on information Robespierre's spies had gleaned about a conspiracy against Robespierre between members of the CSP and Fouché.[20]

The quarrel with Saint-Just and a separate quarrel with Couthon, who demanded the arrest of Dubois-Crancé,[21] hampered the rest of the CSP from taking counter-measures, but by 6.00 a.m. Barère had drafted a number of decrees ready for the Convention's approval next day, including a proclamation and an immediate return to the 1792 organization of the National Guard, thereby depriving Hanriot of his command. Payan and Lescot were summoned to the CSP to keep them out of mischief so that they were not able to return to their own counter-plans until 9.00 a.m. This delay, however, was probably not crucial since the ground had already been laid. According to one account the Commune authorized Hanriot to have selected officers order the National Guard to take arms at 7.00 a.m. on the 9th.[22]

Collot told the Convention on the 9th that Saint-Just's speech, 'this second volume of Robespierre's', as Collot characterized it, 'would have been [repeated] in the evening to the Jacobins and heaven knows what would have happened at the festival tomorrow'. The answer to Collot's rhetorical questions was that on the 10th the Convention, surrounded by the National Guard and the 'wounded' patriots, would purge itself yet again of those deputies who had failed the Jacobins' purge. Collot emphasizes the Robespierrist nature of the festival by telling the Convention that Maximilien had never cared for the pantheonization of Marat and had not mentioned his name once during his funeral oration for him.[23]

.　.　.

## THE ARREST OF ROBESPIERRE

The struggle in the Convention on 8 thermidor had been an internal one within the Mountain, and it had ended in stalemate. Everone knew that the remaining right-wing deputies were the key to resolving the stalemate and behind them were the 73 imprisoned Girondin backbenchers. Robespierre had saved their lives and now hoped to redeem the pledge. But on 5 thermidor/24 July Amar (who had wanted to put them on trial) and Voulland had paid the 73 an official visit on behalf of the CSG in the Madelonettes prison to which they had recently been transferred. The prison visitors asked the inmates if they had any complaints, had their mail been intercepted, 'had they been denied any of life's comforts, like coffee, cordials, chocolate or fruit'? The account they were given brought tears to the eyes of the hardened men of the police committee. In their turn the prisoners said 'how touched they were' at the committee's solicitude. Drying their eyes, Amar and Voulland departed, with one final complaint lingering in the air: the state of the beds. Payan was given a police report of this scene, which caused him to exclaim: 'Prisoners in the Madelonettes have witnessed *Amar weep*!' (II, 367–70). Nevertheless the right deputies resisted the blandishments of Robespierre's montagnard enemies until the night of the 8th or even the morning of the 9th. Why, they asked themselves, not let Robespierre keep on killing montagnards until there were none left?

The tactic adopted by the conspirators was to prevent the Robespierristes from speaking in the Convention on the 9th. It was an exact reversal of the roles in the Jacobins the night before. So when at noon Saint-Just got up to deliver the report which he had promised to show his colleagues, Collot, in the president's chair, allowed him to ascend the rostrum but did not prevent the conspirators from shouting him down after he had delivered some ten lines, probably ending with 'someone [Billaud] last night rent my heart'.[24] On the propositions of Tallien, Billaud and Delmas the Convention decreed the arrests of Dumas, president of the Revolutionary Tribunal, and of Hanriot and his entire general staff but then paused for breath as if alarmed by its own audacity. At about one o'clock Barère arrived and made a long speech culminating in the decrees he had drafted in the night.

The crisis seemed to be diffusing, resolving into farce as Vadier succeeded Barère. Vadier was the only one whose sense of humour triumphed over his sense of danger during the Terror. But he made this deadly point which no one had dared to make before:

> He [Robespierre] says: 'so and so conspires against me; I am the friend par excellence of the Republic; therefore he conspires against the Republic'. This logic is new.[25]

The night before, in the Jacobins, had not Robespierre denounced 'the enemies of myself and of the Republic' as if they were one?

Nevertheless Tallien, feeling that Vadier's jokes were lightening the atmosphere, observed that 'the discussion had strayed from the point', which gave Robespierre a chance of repartee: 'I could tell you how to bring it back'. His wit, however, was rewarded by shouts of abuse. Robespierre's voice seemed to fail him and either Garnier or Danton's close friend Legendre shouted, 'Danton's blood is choking him', to which Robespierre replied, 'So, you want to avenge Danton! Why then you wretched cowards did you not defend him?'.[26] Croker comments: 'There was spirit, truth and even dignity in this bitter retort – the last words that Robespierre ever spoke in public'. This disturbing counter-accusation released a spring and was immediately followed by the demand from an obscure montagnard deputy, Louchet, for a decree ordering Robespierre's arrest. This was

voted and was quickly followed by ones for the arrest of Couthon, Saint-Just, who had remained impassive at the rostrum
throughout the proceedings, together with that of Augustin
Robespierre. Lebas, who had married a Duplay girl and been
on missions together with Saint-Just, asked to be included in
the proscription. This was at about two o'clock. For two hours
the five refused to comply but at four o'clock they were taken
under guard to the adjoining Hôtel de Brionne, the seat of the
CSG.

. . .

## AT THE COMMUNE

The central institutions of the Revolution – the Convention,
the two committees, the Commune, the Jacobins, Robespierre's
lodgings – were all within a stone's throw of each other and
news spread quickly. Dumas had been arrested at the seat
of judgement at two; printed copies of the decree ordering
Hanriot's arrest were placarded all over Paris by five. There
was a scheduled meeting of the general council of the Commune and ordinary business was transacted between 1.30 p.m.
and 3.00 p.m. Then Fleuriot and Payan conferred with Hanriot
whose office was adjoining and who had no intention of
submitting tamely to the decree for his arrest. They told the
departing members of the council to stir up their respective
*sections*, ring the tocsin and beat the alarm drum known as the
'general'. Hanriot then signed a number of hasty orders which
combined civilian with military matters in a way that some
'formalists' found offensive. Thus Hanriot ordered each surveillance committee to send a delegate to the Commune.[27]

This distinction between the military and the civilian has
a bearing on the outcome of the day. The Commune's call
elicited a military response greater than it had asked for and
more than sufficient to defeat its adversaries: this gives the lie
to Robespierre's claim on the 8th that he was without military
strength. On the other hand, the civilian response from the
*sections* was so tepid that it was hard to argue that the Commune possessed a popular mandate. These observations can be
quantified. Hanriot ordered each of the six commanders of
legions to send 400 men to the Commune. Each legion grouped
eight *sections*, so each was supposed to supply 50 men. Fontaine,
the adjutant-general of the artillery units, was to send *all* his

men to the same rendez-vous. The response to Hanriot's order was mixed. Four legions, representing 32 *sections*, sent no troops to the Commune. On the other hand, partly because there was some confusion about whether Hanriot required 400 men per legion or per *section*, the other two legions sent far more men than Hanriot required. So by 7.00 p.m. there were 3,400 troops assembled on the Place de Grève in front of the Hôtel de Ville, a thousand more than Hanriot had ordered. They were mostly armed with pikes.

Hanriot's success with the artillery units was more complete, though the CSP had specifically ordered Fontaine, their commandant, to obey its decrees. Of the 48 companies stationed in Paris at the beginning of the summer, Carnot had by 9 thermidor sent 18 to the front. Of the remaining 30, 16 heeded Hanriot's order and 11 ignored it.

So, although morally the Commune did not receive a ringing endorsement from the Parisian armed forces, militarily they had all that they reckoned on or knew how to use. Until well on into the night, when the Convention began to assemble forces loyal to it, the Commune had the overwhelming military advantage both in numbers and in quality, since the artillery units were far more effective than the pikes. From 7.00 p.m. onwards the Commune had at its disposal 17 artillery companies and 32 cannon. The Convention had only the one company on duty; not until 11.00 did loyal units begin to assemble. The Commune's failure was to make effective use of the troops at its disposal.

Hanriot attempted to rescue Robespierre with insufficient troops and was himself arrested. At 5.30 Payan despatched Coffinhal with substantial troops to occupy the offices of the CSG. This was where Robespierre's colleagues had been taken but the CSG was independently of this the prime target of Payan's. The CSG had revenged many disputes over the summer by having Payan arrested at 3.30 though he was soon rescued by Robespierrist forces. At this stage the Convention had not ordered the arrest of Payan and Fleuriot, merely made them responsible for the safety of the Convention. This may explain the caution of Coffinhal who at 8.30 approached the Convention with 2,200 men, including 17 artillery companies. He confined himself to occupying the offices of the CSG and rescuing Hanriot who had been put there. The members of the CSG (Payan's target) had fled to the Convention and

Robespierre and his colleagues had been dispersed to different prisons. Hanriot, who according to Coffinhal was drunk, ordered a return to the Place de Grève. Thereby he missed the Robespierristes' only chance, which was to surround the Convention before its forces had assembled.

The Commune's failure to press home its advantage was partly because of the poor civilian response from the *sections*. Only 12 *sections* out of 48 sent delegates to the Commune and some of these only because the Convention had ordered Fleuriot and Payan to concert measures for its safety! Many also were observers rather than adherents. It was therefore difficult to argue that the people was entirely *debout*. Since the civilian element (which would have been available for the Barra and Viala fête on the 10th) was lacking, a purge of the Convention would have had more of the appearance of a *coup d'état* than a revolutionary *journée*. Michelet said that Robespierre and France were not yet ready for an 18 brumaire, for a Napoleonic *coup d'état*, but that Payan and Fleuriot-Lescot were.[28] This is not true. In the final analysis they were restrained by legalistic scruples.

How should the people have expressed solidarity with the Commune? There were venerable precedents, though as an immigrant to Paris Payan had not witnessed them at first hand. The first thing was to summon the general assemblies of the *sections* by tolling the bell of Notre-Dame. However, the surveillance committee of the Cité *section*, where the cathedral was situated, refused Payan's written order on the grounds that it was illegal to sound the tocsin without written authorization from the Convention. The Commune had to make do with its own more feeble instrument. Only nine of the 48 general assemblies opted unequivocally for the Commune.[29] The general assemblies customarily drafted petitions to the Convention demanding purges; a draft-petition in Payan's hand was among the papers seized at the Commune:

> The people wants to save the *patrie*; it wants to save the Convention which can do anything with the people and nothing without them. They know that the Convention has been deceived by traitors, by conspirators. The people accuses them, demands their arrest and will obtain it. This measure will save the Republic.
> Here are the names of the conspirators: Collot d'Herbois, Barère, Amar, Leonard Bourdon . . .[30]

The general assemblies and/or the surveillance and civil committees traditionally also sent delegates to the Commune to liaise and give a sense of unity. Section III article 16 of the law of frimaire, however, forebade the 'constituted authorities' from communicating with each other by delegations and so preparing another 31 May. By that same law of frimaire, the surveillance committees of the *sections* were supposed to communicate directly with the CSP and not as heretofore with the Commune. Thus a group of functionaries from the Quinze-Vingts *section* in the Faubourg Saint-Antoine, hitherto the motor of revolutionary *journées*, replied to the Commune's appeal:

> The citizens of the Faubourg Antoine have not yet lost that energy which characterizes republicans, but in the present circumstances, *under a gouvernement révolutionnaire*, they need to be guided in their actions, lest they fall into the traps constantly being set for them by the enemies of the Republic.[31]

As salaried public officials, the sectional personnel had been carefully purged by Payan and Robespierre throughout the summer. However, by making his adherents officials Robespierre thereby diminished the element of personal loyalty, at least if he should lose his own official character. This principle, as we shall see, operated at every level, from the humble member of a surveillance committee to the heads of the executive commissions, heirs to the ministries which Robespierre had staffed in germinal. Officials are hierarchical creatures, especially French ones. Robespierre himself stressed hierarchy and centralization and his concluding appeal on 8 thermidor had been precisely for an increase in this.

Another reason why the Commune delayed taking action against the Convention was because until 9.00 it had no deputies in its midst. Robespierre had been taken to the Luxembourg but the authorities there, belonging to the Commune's police and fervent Robespierristes, refused to admit him and he was taken instead to the Mairie. The Mairie served as the headquarters both of Fleuriot and of the Paris police. The administration of the latter had in recent months been expanded from four to 20, all hand-picked Robespierristes. So he was among friends though technically still under arrest, a situation with which he was more comfortable than one of leading an insurrection. Mathiez argued that by not breaking his

technical arrest he was hoping for a fair trial by the Revolutionary Tribunal but we have seen that he knew the committees would
purge it first.[32] Robespierre was invited to come to the Commune but only acceded at the second time of asking, at about
11.00, when urged by the nine-man executive committee which
had been formed to include Payan, Fleuriot and Lerebours,
the commissioner for public assistance.

Whatever his doubts, Robespierre's arrival at the Commune
at about 11.00 did mark a shift from its essentially defensive
stance and led it to direct its fire directly at the Convention
rather than merely at the CSG. Minutes after he had heard
that Robespierre had been rescued, Payan felt emboldened to
tell the Convention's usher, handing him the order summoning the municipality: 'Yes the Council will go to the Convention
but with the whole people in arms'.[33] The executive committee
resolved 'that the commander of the armed force will direct the
people against the conspirators who are oppressing the patriots
and will deliver the National Convention from the oppression
of the counter-revolutionaries'.[34]

The two Robespierres and Saint-Just then sent an urgent
message to Couthon, still held back by legal scruples, to come
and join them. They told him that 'all patriots were proscribed,
the whole people has arisen'. Those who had arisen were drift-
ing away, frightened by a decree of the Convention outlawing
the Robespierristes. In an attempt to stem defections the Hôtel
de Ville was illuminated and its exits blocked. By 1.00 a.m. the
Commune's troops had melted away from the Place de Grève
and the Convention's troops were massing for the attack.

When Couthon finally arrived, his first words were: 'We must
write to the armies'. But this proposal once again presented
Robespierre with a legal conundrum: in whose name should
the proclamation be issued? Quick as a flash Couthon replied:
'Why in the name of the Convention; is it not always where we
are? The rest are only a handful of factious persons who will
be scattered and have justice meted out to them by the armed
forces at our disposal.' Robespierre was still not satisfied; he
conferred with his brother and finally came up with the formula: 'It is my opinion that we should write in the name of the
French people'.[35] Five outlawed deputies were the Convention;
five outlawed deputies were the people!

Minutes later, as the Gods' commentary on such presump-
tion, Lebas was dead; Robespierre's jaw was smashed with a

bullet; Couthon's wheelchair had descended a stone flight of stairs, wounding his head; Augustin had jumped out of the window and broken his thigh; and Coffinhal had pushed Hanriot out of another window for missing his chances. The controversy concerning Robespierre continued to the end, with two contemporary versions of these events each championed by subsequent historians cutting across party lines. One version has Robespierre committing suicide, the other has him 'assassinated' by the invading troops of the Convention, to whom the password had been betrayed. Though it would be more elegant to have Robespierre, having denounced so many false attempts to assassinate him, finally succumbing to a real one, I prefer the suicide explanation and take the increasingly belligerent measures discussed at the end by the Robespierristes as evidence not of confidence but of despair.

Robespierre was laid out on a table in the ante-chamber to the CSP, his jaw bleeding copiously. Most of the bystanders mocked him but someone gave him a bit of tissue to wipe off the blood. Robespierre said, 'merci, monsieur' – not 'citoyen', for as Saint-Just had realized the manners of the *ancien régime* were ingrained in people of his generation. At 10.00 a.m. a passing surgeon extracted Robespierre's broken teeth and bound his jaw. The Robespierristes having been outlawed, the Revolutionary Tribunal was required simply to identify them, no trial being necessary for their execution. However, Fouquier-Tinville was quick to point out that this identification had to be performed by two municipal officers – a difficult task since they were themselves outlawed. After much debate, the Convention removed the impediment and at about 6.00 p.m. three tumbrils carrying Robespierre, Augustin, Couthon, Saint-Just, Payan and Hanriot set off for the Place de la Révolution, to which the guillotine had been returned for the occasion.

At the foot of the scaffold Saint-Just was defiant; shortly before he had written:

> I despise the dust of which I am made and you may persecute him who is addressing you and kill this dust, but I defy anyone to snatch from me the free life which I have for myself for ages to come and in heaven.[36]

Payan was cast down; the insurrection had been his and it had failed. He, together with that 'base slave' Herman who had not turned out, had been the repositories of Robespierre's power. All were silent because there was no more to say. The Revolution was over. There was none of Danton's friendly banter with the executioner or the Girondins' singing of the Marseillaise. In any case Robespierre and his brother, Couthon and Hanriot were more dead than alive. Robespierre, the last but one to be executed, was semi-conscious until the executioner ripped off his bandage to bare his neck. Then he let out a scream which has echoed down the centuries.

.  .  .

## THE JACOBINS ON 9 THERMIDOR

The Commune was the rallying point for the Robespierristes. Two other Robespierrist institutions, the Jacobin Club and the executive commissions, played lesser but revealing roles.

The Jacobins assembled at about 7.30 p.m. and declared its session to be 'permanent'.[37] The deputy Chasles then gave an objective account of the day's proceedings in the Convention, which account was booed. It was then decided that those deputies present (apparently a fair number) should be invited to say how they had voted on the decrees against the Robespierrist deputies. The acting president asked the first deputy, Brival, how he had voted, to which Brival replied that as Chasles had said the decrees were passed without dissent. The Society then expelled Brival, who handed in his card and reported back to the Convention. The Society then decided that there was indeed no point asking the deputies how they had voted and later sent a messenger to the Convention to return Brival his card.

Matters swung the Robespierristes' way on a false report that substantial artillery units, preceded by the municipal officers and followed by 'un nombreux peuple', had marched on the CSP and demanded the release of the arrested deputies. Upon this the Club decided to send missionaries to harangue the *sections* and to send a delegation to the Commune. During the course of the evening four deputations were sent, to the last of which the Commune replied that there was no point sending further deputations, what was wanted was for the whole Club, together with the 'assistance', to come bodily to the Commune to give moral support. It has been said that there was little point in having one talking shop joining another when action was needed.[38] However, whilst it is true that the Club, as a whole, had not played a part on 10 August or 31 May, on 9 thermidor it was precisely civilian weight that the insurrection lacked.

A contemporary analysis gives the most likely explanation of the Jacobins' conduct:

> On the one hand the principal agents of [the Robespierristes] found themselves at the general council of the Commune, with the staff of the Parisian army and in the key *sections*, leaving an irreparable gap in the mother society. On the other hand, Robespierre's enemies were gathered there at maximum strength.[39]

This is what we would expect, given the over-stretched resources in personnel of Robespierre's faction which, moreover, never quite managed to control the Jacobins in the summer of 1794.

In the event the Club responded to the Commune's fourth summons by sending what membership remained in the building at 1.30 a.m. But by the time they arrived at the Commune it had fallen to the Convention's troops, which at least gave the Jacobins the chance to melt into the warm thermidorian night and, most of them, save their skins. Shortly afterwards Legendre arrived at the Club with ten men; finding it almost deserted he locked the doors of the once mighty engine of the Revolution as if it had been no more than a garage and handed the keys to the new masters, the National Convention.

.   .   .

## THE COMMISSIONERS

If the Robespierristes had won the day, Joseph Payan's commission for public instruction and Herman's for 'civil administration' would have had a busy time of it, what with propaganda, executions and appointments and dismissals. Herman in particular would have had his work cut out because there were simply not enough Robespierristes to fill all the vacancies that would have been created. Possibly Bouchotte and Pache would have been released from prison and, to swell the rank and file, some more of the 3,000 'friends of Chalier' imported from Lyon. On the 9th all that was asked of the commissioners was that they turn up at the Commune; but only Lerrebours, the commissioner for public assistance, answered the summons and became a member of the executive committee. Nevertheless, he slipped away before the end, managed to escape abroad and returned to France under the amnesty of 3 brumaire year IV.

Joseph Payan, having failed to supply the programme for the festival on the 8th, refused the call to the Commune on the 9th and on the 10th managed to escape from Paris, ending up in Switzerland. In compensation the Payans' father was arrested at Paule-les-fontaines and died en route for the Revolutionary Tribunal in Paris. On 11 thermidor Joseph Payan was outlawed but he returned to France under the amnesty of 3 brumaire and from 1798 served the Directory, Bonaparte and Louis XVIII continuously as head of direct taxation. Retiring in 1816 he lived on until 1852, longer than any of the principal players in the Revolutionary drama.[40]

No more than Joseph Payan did Herman and his deputy Lanne turn out for Robespierre on the 9th and, for that reason, they were not arrested until 14 thermidor (with Fouquier-Tinville) and were not put on trial until the following year. Though Herman and Fouquier were convicted of 'seeking to provoke the dissolution of the national assembly and the overthrow of the republican regime',[41] the same charges with which they themselves had sent hundreds to their deaths, the trial was not in fact conducted in terms of this rhetoric but rather of what we would call 'crimes against humanity'.

Though in general there was little role for the commissioners to play on the 9th, one portion of Herman's portfolio, the Agence de l'envoie des lois, did have a small but vital role, for the Convention's decrees on 9/10 thermidor played an important part in Robespierre's defeat. The revolutionary authorities ceded nothing to their *ancien régime* predecessors in veneration for due procedure in law-making. As soon as a decree had been voted scribes made authentic copies and had them covered with the signatures and seals of the president and secretaries of the Convention and the visa of the inspector of the chamber. Then they were taken under guard to the Agence in the Place des Victoires where Herman had identical copies made. Having checked these he signed them and sent them to the Agence's printing press. The finished product was placarded, delivered personally or placed in the Bulletin des lois for distribution throughout the country. Given the all-pervasive legalism it was, for example, insufficient to say that the decree ordering Hanriot's arrest was a notorious fact; it was necessary to point to the decree placarded everywhere from five o'clock onwards. Herman, then, had it in his power to help or hinder the Convention's cause by ensuring or denying the seal of authenticity for its measures and their widespread and above all speedy dissemination.

Dumont told the Convention on 10 thermidor that

> Herman, commissaire, and Lahne [sic] his adjoint were sold to the usurper Robespierre; that Bernard, one of the commissaires de l'envoi, was the henchman of the execrable Couthon; that all three had been opposed to the decrees passed against the tyrant. He demanded that the administrative bodies should be purged of all the people Robespierre had place in them ...[42]

The evidence, however, suggests that Herman and his team did their best to promulgate the decrees. The dissemination of the decree ordering Hanriot's arrest (the whole process taking about four hours) has been noted. We also know that a mounted gendarme delivered to Payan from Herman the Convention's decrees concerning them together with a receipt for them which Payan was to sign and return to Herman via the gendarme. Payan crumpled it up, calling Herman a 'base slave'.[43] Herman's enclosing letter, with his and Lanne's signature, is dated 9 thermidor, 5.30 p.m.[44] This was quick work indeed, even if it was only the first decree, making Fleuriot and Payan personally responsible for the safety of the Convention. If later decrees were involved, one has to assume that Herman sent authenticated manuscript copies.

Herman disavowed Robespierre, claiming that the decree 'ordering the arrest of Robespierre lifted a great weight from his mind'.[45] He also claimed that Robespierre, even as he appointed him to the 'commission civil' in germinal, distrusted him and placed Lanne there as his deputy to keep an eye on him.[46] Herman claimed that whereas he only entered Robespierre's house three times whilst he was civil commissioner, 'at his request and not for public affairs' (and never invited him back), Lanne (who also lived round the corner in the Place des Piques) was a frequent visitor to the Duplays'. According to Herman,

> he [Lanne] knew that I blamed Robespierre's conduct, his way of doing things, the conclaves he held at his place. He knows that on more than one occasion I gave him to understand that those who

went to Robespierre's were wrong; that public functionaries ought to preserve their absolute independence; that we were the men of the Republic; that government business should not be transacted in coteries.

To this Lanne replied, 'I see clearly that you are not au courant'. I conclude this section on Herman with Mathiez's epitaph, which needs no commentary:

> Among the Robespierristes, who included so many honourable men devoted to duty and with a passionate attachment to the public weal, the figure of Herman shines out with a particular brightness.[47]

. . .

## THE FATE OF OTHER ROBESPIERRISTES

Meanwhile in Lyon Achard was still gathering his evidence against Fouché when news arrived of Robespierre's fall. Like the good public servant that he was, he hastened, as president of the Jacobins, to congratulate the Convention on once again saving the country, in a letter dated 14 thermidor/1 August.[48] Jean Boullay, Sijas's fellow deputy at the commission for army movements, was on his honeymoon. This saved him from sharing the fate of Sijas, guillotined on the 11th, though when he got back he was dismissed. Pille and Carnot purged the commission of the 20 dissident Robespierristes who had prevented it from functioning properly.[49]

. . .

## CONCLUSION: A MACHINE TESTED TO DESTRUCTION

Croker said that after the germinal trials, 'Robespierre now stood alone, *more dreaded* and *less powerful* than ever'.[50] This is only partially true, for the fall of the Hébertistes brought Robespierre a vast increase in patronage and power, adding the Commune, the National Guard and most of the executive commissions to his existing power base in the government and in the Jacobins. Nevertheless Robespierre's power was qualified. In the first place, the regime itself was brittle, and made more so by its very victories at home and abroad. The main danger came from parliament: Danton's surviving friends sought not just to avenge him but to implement his twin goals of peace and the end of *gouvernement révolutionnaire*. That is why

Robespierre's fall marked not just a palace coup, not just a change of government (the CSP was renewed on 13 thermidor), but a change of regime, in token of which within months seven former members of the CSP and CSG were impeached.

Even within the regime, Robespierre's own position was not as strong as it appeared. One has to distinguish between the power that the Robespierristes exercised on a day-to-day basis – arresting people, propagating their ideas – and how it would fare in a crisis, a proposition which was not tested until the end. Then it was discovered that Robespierre's was not an independent power, that is one that could be used independently of the CSP, still less against it. The conclusion of Robespierre's last speech was unequivocally for a strengthening of the powers of the CSP and yet his conclusion, also, as his replies made clear, was principally directed against its current personnel. Since, however, they were still in possession, they could hamper his deploying of his levers of power against them. Once the rupture had become formal, the secession open, functionaries like Herman and Joseph Payan could no longer support him as they had whilst it remained clandestine.

For the same reason most of the civil elements of the popular movement and a portion of the military did not turn out for the Commune, quite apart from any resentment they may have felt about the marginalization of their political role (a resentment which presumably would have been felt towards the government as well). Thus the Quinze-Vingts *section*, as we have seen, pleaded the hierarchy of *gouverement révolutionnaire*, that is the law of 14 frimaire, as its excuse for inaction. Such considerations also prevented the Commune from directing its forces directly against the Convention, falling back instead on the more limited objective of rescuing the five deputies and capturing the members of the CSG (in both of which endeavours they failed).

For Robespierre's post-germinal accretions of power were essentially institutional, if revolutionary ones, the men on his list of patriots became bureaucrats, if again revolutionary ones. The Revolution in any case had become institutionalized, to the regret of Saint-Just, but under the inspiration of Billaud and of Robespierre himself. Even the Jacobins, especially the Jacobins, became institutionalized, a *nomenklatura*, whilst a dynamic if anarchic organism like the *armée révolutionnaire*, in a sense Robespierre's brain-child, was disbanded. Robespierre's power during the 'first terror' (exchanged for a seat in the Convention and exercised through the insurrectionary Commune) was 'illegal' but accordingly more flexible and more personal. True there was a physical tangible basis to it, and a grisly one at that, but it was flexible and it was also based on his popularity, something intangible which, according to Billaud, made him already the most powerful man in France before he entered the CSP in July 1793. In entering the government Robespierre arguably sold his birth-right for a mess of potage for, the history of the Revolution suggested, entry into government was bound to undermine the very popularity which forced his entry.

. . .

## NOTES

1. J. Michelet, *Histoire de la Révolution française*, ed. G. Walter, 2 vols (1952), 11, p. 937.
2. J.W. Croker, *Essays on the Early Period of the French Revolution* (1857), p. 409.
3. Croker, *Essays*, pp. 405 and 407–8.
4. Notably of Senart who had 'masterminded the arrest of Catherine Théot', M. Lyons, 'The 9 thermidor: motives and effects', *European Studies Review* (1975), pp. 123–46, at p. 136.
5. Michelet, *Histoire*, II, p. 944.
6. Barère, *Memoirs of Bertrand Barère*, 4 vols (1896), II, p. 176.
7. P.J.B. Buchez and P.C. Roux, *Histoire parlementaire de la Révolution française*, 40 vols (1834–38), XXXIII, pp. 450–7; Croker, *Essays*, p. 413.
8. Croker, *Essays*, p. 413.
9. Michelet, *Histoire*, pp. 944–5; G. Lefebvre, 'Sur la loi du 22 prairial an II', *Annales historiques de la Révolution française* 23 (1951), pp. 225–56, at p. 252.
10. Buchez and Roux, *Histoire parlementaire*, XXXIII, p. 457.
11. Courtois, *Notes relatives au 9 thermidor*, in *La Révolution française*, 1887, 931.
12. The following information on the planned fête is taken from E. Chavaray, 'La Fête de Barra et Viala', in *La Révolution française* (1881), pp. 420–8.
13. M. Eude, 'La Commune Robespierriste', *Annales historiques de la Révolution française*, XII (1936), pp. 132–61, 158–9.
14. Buchez and Roux, *Histoire parlementaire*, XXXIV, pp. 38–40.
15. A. Soboul, *Les Sans-culottes Parisiens en l'an II* (1958), pp. 994–5.
16. F. Brunel, *Thermidor: La Chute de Robespierre* (1989), pp. 94–5.

17. Speech of Collot in the Convention on 9 thermidor, Buchez and Roux, *Histoire parlementaire*, XXXIV, p. 39.
18. Letter of Legracieux, Archives Nationales W. 79 no. 5, cited by P. Saint-Claire Deville, *La Commune de l'an II* (1946), pp. 195–6.
19. Lacretelle, *Histoire de France pendant le XVIIIe siècle*, cited in Buchez and Roux, *Histoire parlementaire*, XXXIV, p. 2.
20. A. Ollivier, *Saint-Just et la force des choses* (1954), pp. 509–10.
21. Lyons, '9 thermidor', p. 140.
22. Michelet, *Histoire*, II, p. 948.
23. Buchez and Roux, *Histoire parlementaire*, XXXIV, pp. 38–40.
24. Brunel, *Thermidor*, p. 97.
25. Buchez and Roux, *Histoire parlementaire*, XXXIV, p. 32.
26. Duval's version, cited by J. Croker, review article in the *Quarterly Review* (1835), pp. 517–80, at p. 577.
27. Unless otherwise stated the factual information contained in this chapter is taken from Deville, *Commune*, pp. 201–314.
28. Michelet, *Histoire*, II, p. 948.
29. Soboul, *Les Sans-culottes*, p. 1019.
30. Archives Nationales F7 4432, cited in A. Mathiez, *The Fall of Robespierre* (1968), p. 213 n. 1; Deville, *Commune*, p. 225.
31. Buchez and Roux, *Histoire parlementaire*, XXXIV, p. 58 (my italics).
32. Mathiez, *Fall*, pp. 204–5.
33. Deville, *Commune*, p. 228.
34. Deville, *Commune*, p. 283.
35. Mathiez, *Fall*, pp. 214–15.
36. F. Feher, *The Frozen Revolution: An Essay on Jacobinism* (1987), p. 126.
37. The following account is based on G. Michon, 'Les séances des 8 et 9 thermidor au Club des Jacobins', in *Annales historiques de la Révolution française* 1 (1924), pp. 495–506.
38. Deville, *Commune*, p. 294.
39. Account of Fantin-Desodoards, cited in G. Walter, *Histoire des Jacobins* (1946), pp. 337–8.
40. M. Eude, 'La Commune Robespierriste', *Annales historiques de la Révolution française* XIII (1936), pp. 289–316, at p. 311.
41. E. Campardon, *Histoire du Tribunal Révolutionnaire de Paris*, 2 vols (1975), II, pp. 332–50.
42. Buchez and Roux, *Histoire parlementaire*, XXXIV, p. 86.
43. Campardon, *Tribunal*, 334–5.
44. Archives Nationales F7 4433, pl. 1, cited in Deville, *Commune*, p. 222 note.
45. Campardon, *Tribunal*, II, pp. 332–50.
46. Evidence of the commission's concierge, Gravier, Buchez and Roux, *Histoire parlementaire*, XXXV, p. 90.
47. Mathiez, *Fall*, p. 133.

48. E. Herriot, *Lyon n'est plus*, 4 vols (1939), IV, p. 355.
49. H. Brown, *War, Revolution and the Bureaucratic State: Politics and Army Administration in France, 1791–1799* (1995), p. 136.
50. Croker, *Essays*, p. 383.

# EPILOGUE

At first it seemed that Robespierre's fall had only served to intensify the Terror: if his 'secession' had made it worse, his death had made it even worse as dozens of his adherents – 71 on 11 thermidor alone, a Parisian record – mounted the scaffold. On the 12th another 12 followed them. The utter meaninglessness of it all was vividly expressed by Michelet: 'Fouquier and his judges, his trusty jury' were 'no less convinced of Robespierre's guilt than they would have been of the guilt of his enemies, had he won'.[1] Then suddenly the blade fell silent. And yet between 11 and 14 thermidor a further 39 members of the Commune's general council had been arrested who were, in Deville's phrase, 'neither more nor less guilty than those of their colleagues who had been handed over to Sanson', the public executioner.[2]

On the 14th sittings of the tribunal were suspended pending reorganization and renewal of its personnel. And Fouquier and Herman were arrested, having performed their task of executing their own. Later they were put on trial and guillotined but there were two important differences between their trials and those they had conducted. First their trials occupied entire months and they were allowed to deploy all the legal niceties which Herman and the other Robespierristes so deplored. Indeed there were 419 witnesses, where those prosecuted under the prairial law had benefited from none. Secondly although the charges against them were still couched in the jargon of the year II, nevertheless the trial was conducted, on both sides, in terms of 'crimes against humanity' and the accused invented the defence of superior orders later employed in the Nuremburg trials. Thus Fouquier pleaded: 'I had orders, I

212

obeyed'. But there was no repentance here, no bathing the crucifix with their tears. Instead, Fouquier mouthed obscenities at the president, whilst Herman threw a book at him! His deputy Lanne wrote to his wife that he was dying 'because what had been considered virtue a year ago is a crime today'. They mounted the scaffold, on 18 floréal year III, in the company of other Robespierristes who had survived the thermidor killings: Garnier-Launay, Châtelet, Girard, Benoît and Renaudin.[3]

There had been straws in the wind even before the death of Robespierre of a change in climate, most obviously on 9 thermidor when Panis, once an intimate of Robespierre's, and Fréron called for the repeal of the prairial law. This move had been imperiously quashed by Billaud but the law was repealed on the 14th.[4] Another indicator had been that Achard's 19-article indictment of Fouché had been considered insufficient. It is just possible that Robespierre would have been acquitted by the tribunal, but for the insurrection. Milestones in the creation of this new climate had been the calls during the discussion of the prairial law for a greater precision in the use of language and Vadier's attack on Robespierre's syllogism:

> He [Robespierre] says: 'so and so conspires against me; I am the friend par excellence of the Republic; therefore he conspires against the Republic'. This logic is new.[5]

Such a change in the linguistic climate made non-sense accusations, ones that could neither be proved nor disproved, such as that against Louis of 'conspiring against liberty', difficult to sustain. Such accusations had been even more morally debilitating for the regime than those of cannibalism which may have been framed to cater for the jaded popular palate.

Baczko has shown how the 'wooden language' of the year II, that 'copious reciprocity of reproaches' which makes political analysis so difficult, survived into the year III.[6] It would be interesting to know when it disappeared – it scarcely survives in the memoirs of its practitioners.

. . .

## ROBESPIERRE'S LEGACY

Robespierre had an impact beyond the grave because he had his imitators. In his own country the regimes in which such men served were as short as his own: the Second Republic of 1848 and the Commune of 1871, which took its name from its Revolutionary predecessor. Alone of the Revolutionary leaders, no statue has been raised to him, though he lives on in a Robespierrist historiographical tradition, until recently dominant.

Outside France, Robespierre's impact has been greater through Marxism. Marx himself thought that the 'bourgeois' regime Robespierre represented was harsher than the 'feudal' one which preceded it, because *noblesse oblige* lords were kinder than market-orientated manufacturers. Nevertheless it was to be welcomed as representing a further stage towards the dictatorship of the proletariat. But the real legacies of Robespierre to Marxist politicians were his tactics, his perversion of the democratic ideal and his sense of moral superiority.

Learning from the Jansenists in the *parlement*, Robespierre invented militant politics, that is the mechanism by which a minority of activists can impose its will on a lazy majority. Its fullest flowering was in the Jacobin network, his most original creation. Its characteristics are present in the militant tendency all over the world: mastery of procedures, invention of a pompous jargon concerning them, late-night votes when all the moderates have gone home – or reversing 'bad' decisions in the morning before they have got up.

Most of these people believe that though they are a minority, they stand for all the people. The device which enables them to make this claim is the one derived by Robespierre from Rousseau's *Du contrat social* which replaces a quantitative evaluation of popular support with a qualitative one. So, Robespierre argued, the activists who stormed the king's palace on 10 August 1792 'stood proxy for the whole people'. So those who had signed monarchical petitions were excluded from elections because they were not the real people only a load of counter-revolutionaries. This perhaps is what Robespierre meant when he said that he didn't just 'represent the people but was the people'.

However, Rousseau had an even darker thought. It was that when your views do not prevail, it is because you were wrong in the first place. This led to the notion that the people should be given not what they actually want but what they would want if properly informed and motivated; what, in the vernacular, 'is good for them' – the basis of every dictatorship of the Left. It is interesting that Rousseau did not develop this doctrine in response to a crisis but *in abstracto*. Robespierre began to speak like this as soon as he had been converted to Rousseau (early 1789) and before there was any crisis. The conspirators came before the conspiracy. Such a system is easier to copy than one which evolves from critical circumstances which will never be precisely replicated at another time and in another country.

Whatever the intellectual justification of minority rule, the practitioner has to believe that his policies are morally superior to those of his opponents. Robespierre never doubted this, never could have said with Payan that Orléans was innocent but that it was expedient that he should die. He had that characteristic quality of the fanatic of never consciously doing wrong. It gave him a certain strength but also a certain detachment from reality. If hypocrisy is an inner quality, he was not burdened with it. He was not being hypocritical in so often denouncing hypocrisy in others – after 'intriguer' 'hypocrite' is his commonest term of abuse – because he was not aware of being hypocritical. A sense of moral superiority is characteristic of many of his successors.

.  .  .

## NOTES

1.  J. Michelet, *Histoire de la Révolution française*, ed. G. Walter, 2 vols (1952), II, pp. 987–98.
2.  P. Saint-Claire Deville. *La Commune de l'an II* (1946), p. 338.
3.  H. Wallon, *Histoire du Tribunal révolutionnaire de Paris*, 8 vols (1880–82), IV, p. 119.
4.  F. Brunel, *Thermidor: La Chute de Robespierre* (1989), p. 94.
5.  P.J.B. Buchez and P.C. Roux, *Histoire parlementaire de la Révolution française*, 40 vols (1834–38), XXXIV, p. 32.
6.  B. Baczko, *Comment sortir de la Terreur: Thermidor et la Révolution* (1989).

# BIBLIOGRAPHY

## MANUSCRIPT SOURCE

Nearly every surviving piece that Robespierre wrote has been published, with the exception of his directives to the police bureau, which are in the Archives Nationales, F7 4437.

## PRINTED SOURCES

F.-A. Aulard, ed., *Recueil des actes du Comité de Salut Public*, 1889–1911, 21 vols.

F.-A. Aulard, *La Société des Jacobins*, 1897, 6 vols.

Barère. *Memoirs of Bertrand Barère*, 1896, 4 vols.

J.-N. Billaud-Varenne, *Mémoire inédit*, ed. Ch. Vellay, *Revue historique de la Révolution française*, 1910, pp. 7–44, 161–75 and 321–36.

P.J.B. Buchez and P.C. Roux, *Histoire parlementaire de la Révolution française*, 40 vols (1834–38).

E. Chavaray, 'La Fête de Barra et Viala', in *La Révolution française*, 1881, pp. 420 –8.

E.B. Courtois, *Notes relatives au 9 thermidor*, in *La Révolution française*, 1887(1), 922 and 988.

C. Desmoulins, *Le Vieux Cordelier*, ed. H. Calvet, 1926.

Fouché, *Memoirs of Joseph Fouché, Duke of Otranto*, 1892.

D.-J. Garat, *Mémoires*, 1862.

J. Hardman, *The French Revolution*, 1981.

L. Jacob, *Robespierre vu par ses contemporains*, 1938.

Le Blond de Neuveglise, *La vie et les crimes de Maximilien Robespierre*, 1795.

L. Lecointre, *Les Crimes des sept membres, des anciens comités de salut public et de sécurité générale*, year III, 1795.

L. Lecointre, *Robespierre peint par lui-même*, year II, 1794.

R. Levasseur, *Mémoires*, 1829–31, 3 vols.

C. Lucas, *The Structure of the Terror: The Example of Javogues and the Loire*, 1970.

*Moniteur*, Réimpression de l'ancien *Moniteur*, 1863–70.

L.-A. Pille, *Réponse de L.-A. Pille*, Paris, 5 *thermidor*, year II, 1794.

M. Robespierre, *Oeuvres*, 1912–67, 10 vols.

M. Robespierre, *Papiers inédits trouvés chez Robespierre, Saint-Just, Payan etc.*, 1828, 3 vols.

J.-J. Rousseau, *Du contrat social*, ed. C.E. Vaughan, 1918.

Saint-Just, *Oeuvres complètes*, ed. Ch. Vellay, 1908, 2 vols.

J. Saladin, *Rapport au nom de la commission des 21*, year III, 1795.

J. Vilate, *Les mystères de la Mère de Dieu dévoilés*, year III, 1795.

· · ·

## SECONDARY SOURCES

B. Baczko, *Comment sortir de la Terreur: Thermidor et la Révolution*, 1989.

F. Bluche, *Septembre 1792: Logiques d'un Massacre*, 1986.

F. Bluche, *Danton*, 1984.

S. Bonnel, *Les 332 victimes de la Commission populaire d'Orange en 1794*, 1888.

G. Bouchard, *Un organizateur de la victoire: Prieur de la Côte-d'Or*, 1946.

F. Braesch, *La Commune de Dix Août, 1792*, 1911.

H. Brown, *War, Revolution and the Bureaucratic State: Politics and Army Administration in France, 1791–1799*, 1995.

F. Brunel, *Thermidor: La Chute de Robespierre*, 1989.

H. Calvet, 'Une interprétation nouvelle de la loi de prairial', *Annales historiques de la Révolution française*, 22 (1950), pp. 306–19.

H. Campardon, *Histoire du tribunal Révolutionnaire de Paris*, 1975 (Slatkine reprint), 2 vols.

R. Cobb, *The People's Armies*, trans. M. Elliot, 1987.

R. Cobb, *Terreur et Subsistances 1793–1795*, 1965.

J.W. Croker, *Essays on the Early Period of the French Revolution*, 1856.

J.W. Croker, 'Robespierre', *Quarterly Review* (September 1835), pp. 517–80.

M. Crook, *Elections in the French Revolution: An Apprenticeship in Democracy, 1789–1799*, 1996.

P. Saint-Claire Deville, *La Commune de l'an II*, 1946.

A.M. Duport, 'Les Congrès de sociétés populaires de Valence en juin et septembre 1793', *Annales historiques de la Révolution française*, 58 (1986), pp. 529–33.

E.W. Edmonds, *Jacobinism and the Revolt of Lyon, 1789–1793*, 1988.

M. Eude, 'La Commune Robespierriste', *Annales historiques de la Révolution française* XII (1936), pp. 146–7.

F. Ferer, *The Frozen Revolution: An Essay on Jacobinism*, 1987.

J. Guilhaumou, 'Les Congrès républicains des sociétés populaires de Marseilles', *Annales historiques de la Révolution française*, 58 (1986), pp. 533–57.

J. Guilhaumou, 'A discourse on denunciation' in *The French Revolution and the Creation of Modern Political Culture*, vol. IV, *The Terror*, ed. K. Baker, 1994, pp. 139–55.

E. Hamel, *Histoire de Robespierre*, 1865–67, 3 vols.

N. Hampson, *Danton*, 1978.

N. Hampson, *The Life and Opinions of Maximilien Robespierre*, 1974.

J. Hardman, *Louis XVI*, 1993.

E. Herriot, *Lyon n'est plus*, 1939, 4 vols.

H. Johnson, *The Midi in Revolution, 1789–1793*, 1986.

M. Kennedy, *The Jacobin Clubs in the French Revolution: The First Years*, 1982.

M. Kennedy, *The Jacobin Clubs in the French Revolution: The Middle Years*, 1988.

G. Lefebvre, 'Sur la loi du 22 prairial an II', *Annales historiques de la Révolution française* 23 (1951), pp. 225–56.

G. Lefebvre, 'Sur Danton', *Annales historiques de la Révolution française*, (1952), pp. 419–22.

C. Lucas, *The Structure of the Terror: The Example of Javogues and the Loire*, 1970.

M. Lyons, 'The 9 thermidor: motives and effects', *European Studies Review* (1975), pp. 123–46.

C. McNamara, 'The Hébertists: study of a French revolutionary faction in the reign of Terror', Fordham University, Ph. D., 1974.

G. Michon, 'Les séances des 8 et 9 thermidor au Club des Jacobins', in *Annales historiques de la Révolution française*, 1 (1924), pp. 495–506.

C.J. Mitchell, *The French Legislative Assembly of 1791*, 1988.

P. Mansfield, 'The repression of Lyon, 1793–4: origins, responsibility and significance', *French History*, 2 (1988), 74–101.

A. Mathiez, *Études sur Robespierre*, 1958.

A. Mathiez, *The Fall of Robespierre*, 1927.

J. Michelet, *Histoire de la Révolution française*, ed. G. Walter, 1952, 2 vols.

M. Mortimer-Ternaux, *Histoire de la Terreur, 1792–1794*, 1863, 8 vols.

A. Ording, *Le bureau de police du Comité de Salut Public*, 1930.

A. Ollivier, *Saint-Just et la force des choses*, 1954.

J.-A. Paris, *La jeunesse de Robespierre et la convocation des Etats-Généraux en Artois*, 1870.

A. Patrick, *The Men of the First French Republic*, 1972.

R.M. Reinhard, *Lazare Carnot*, 1952, 2 vols.

A. Soboul, *Les Sans-culottes Parisiens en l'an II*, 1958.

M. Sydenham, *The French Revolution*, 1965.

M. Sydenham, 'The Republican revolt of 1793: a plea for less localized studies', *French Historical Studies*, 12 (1981), pp. 120–38.

J.M. Thompson, *Robespierre*, 1988.

D. Van Kley, *The Religious Origins of the French Revolution, 1560–1791*, 1996.

Ch. Vellay, 'Un ami de Saint-Just: Pierre-Germain Gatteau', *Annales Révolutionnaires*, I, pp. 64–79 and 265–75.

H. Wallon, *Histoire du Tribunal révolutionnaire de Paris*, 1880–82, 8 vols.

G. Walter, *Robespierre*, 1946.

G. Walter, *Histoire des Jacobins*, 1946.

Th. Yung, *Dubois-Crancé*, 1884, 2 vols.

# CHRONOLOGY

1758   Birth of Robespierre at Arras. Publication of Voltaire's *Candide*

1762   Publication of Rousseau's *Du contrat social*

1763   Peace of Paris: France cedes Canada and control of India to England

1769   Robespierre enters the prestigious Collège Louis-le-Grand at Paris

1771   Maupeou *coup d'état* against the Parlement

1774   Death of Louis XV; accession of his grandson as Louis XVI; recall of the Parlement

1778   France enters war of American independence

1781   Robespierre leaves Louis-le-Grand and returns to Arras to practice as a barrister

1783   Peace of Paris; small French gains; the war costs France a billion livres

1787   Louis XVI summons Assembly of Notables, which refuses to endorse his reform programme. Fall of Calonne and appointment of Brienne and Lamoigon

1788   May: Lamoignon's coup against the Parlement; Robespierre praises the Parlement

       August: convocation of the Estates-General, recall of Necker

       December: *résultat du conseil* accords double representation to third estate

1789   January–April: electoral campaign

       February: publication of Sieyès's *Qu'est ce que le tiers état*

       April: Robespierre elected deputy for the third estate of Artois; Réveillon riots

       May: (5th) king opens Estates-General at Versailles; Robespierre joins the Breton (later Jacobin) Club

17 June: third estate declare themselves the National Assembly

20 June: Tennis Court Oath

23 June: *Séance royale*

12–14 July: dismissal of Necker, Paris revolt culminates in storming of Bastille

17 July: Robespierre in deputation accompanying king to Paris

July–August: peasant disturbances

4–11 August: decrees abolishing feudal rights and personal and provincial privilege

25 August: Declaration of Rights

5–6 October: October Days, king and Assembly installed in Paris; king in the Tuileries, Robespierre at 30 Rue Saintonge

November: Church lands nationalized and issue of *assignats* decreed

December: property qualifications decreed for voters and deputies: Robespierre opposes as infringement of Declaration

1790 Spread of Jacobin network

June: abolition of nobility

July: Civil Constitution of Clergy

August: mutiny at Nancy – Robespierre defends mutineers

1791 April: death of Mirabeau; Pope condemns Civil Constitution of Clergy

May: self-denying ordinance

10 June: Robespierre elected public prosecutor of Paris criminal tribunal

20/21 June: flight to Varennes

July: Champ de Mars 'massacre'; feuillant schism; Robespierre moves to 366 Rue Saint-Honoré

September: king accepts new constitution; National Assembly replaced by Legislative Assembly; Robespierre holidays in Arras

November: Pétion elected mayor of Paris; Robespierre returns from Arras and attacks war-mongering

1792 March: king appoints a Girondin ministry

April: declaration of war on Austria

June: dismissal of Girondin ministry and occupation of the Tuileries

11 July: '*patrie en danger*' declaration

27 July: *sections* declared in permanent session

29 July: Robespierre calls for king's deposition

1 August: Robespierre calls for election of National Convention

10 August: fall of the monarchy

12 August: Robespierre elected to Commune

2 September: fall of Verdun

2–6 September: prison massacres

5 September: Robespierre elected to National Convention

20 September: Prussian defeat at Valmy

21 September: Convention meets

22 September: declaration of the Republic

October: Louvet denounces Robespierre's 'dictatorship'

November: French victory at Jemappes and occupation of Belgium; decree of 'fraternité et secours'

December: trial of Louis XVI

1793 21 January: execution of the king

February: declaration of war on England and Holland; food riots in Paris condemned by Robespierre

March: declaration of war on Spain; revolt in the Vendée; defeat of Dumouriez at Neerwinden; creation of Revolutionary Tribunal

9–10 March: abortive popular rising

April: defection of Dumouriez; creation of the CSP

May: revolt at Lyon

31 May: popular rising

2 June: expulsion of Girondin deputies

24 June: adoption of Jacobin constitution

25 June: Robespierre denounces Jacques Roux

10 July: Danton voted off CSP

13 July: assassination of Marat

27 July: Robespierre enters CSP

8 August: siege of Lyon begins

14 August: Carnot enters CSP

29 August: Toulon calls in an English fleet

4–5 September: popular insurrection; entry of Collot and Billaud to CSP

17 September: law of suspects

29 September: law of the general maximum

5 October: republican calendar decreed, backdated to 22 September 1792

The year I (1793)

Vendémiaire

18/9 October: fall of Lyon

19/10 October: official suspension of the constitution for the duration

25/16 October: execution of Marie-Antoinette

26/17 October: Vendéens crushed at Cholet

Brumaire

10/31 October: execution of the Girondins

20/10 November: dechristianizing campaign culminates in the festival of reason in Notre-Dame

Frimaire

14/4 December: 'constitution' of *gouvernement révolutionnaire*

15/5 December: Desmoulins inaugurates the clemency campaign with no. 1 of *Le Vieux Cordelier*

29/19 December: recapture of Toulon

Nivôse

2/22 December: last Vendéen army defeated at Savenay: henceforth the royalists reduced to guerrilla warfare

The year II (1794)

Ventôse

8/27 February: laws of ventôse

10 February/22 pluviôse – 12 March/22 ventôse: Robespierre ill

Germinal

4/24 March: execution of the Hébertistes

7/27 March: recall of Fouché from Lyon

12/1 April: replacement of ministries by 12 executive commissions

16/5 April: execution of the Dantonistes

Floréal

9/28 April: Robespierre takes over the police bureau from Saint-Just

18/7 May: Robespierre's speech on the Supreme Being

Prairial

3/22 May: assassination attempt against Collot

4/23 May: Cecile Renault's attempted 'assassination' of Robespierre

8/27 May: decree that British and Hannoverian prisoners would be given no quarter

14/2 June: artillery companies from the Homme-armé *section* ordered to Alençon

16/4 June: Robespierre elected speaker of the National Convention

18/6 June: Fouché elected president of the Jacobin Club

20/8 June: Festival of the Supreme Being

22/10 June: law of 22 prairial reorganizing the Revolutionary Tribunal

23/11 June: row between Robespierre and his colleagues in the CSP over aspects of the prairial law; Robespierre withdraws from the collegiate life of the CSP and concentrates on running his police bureau

27/15 June Vadier (of the CSG)'s report on the Catherine Théot affair

29/17 June: execution of Admiral and Renault and their 52 'accomplices' dressed in the red-shirts of the Roman parricide

Messidor

1/19 June: the Montagne *section* opens a register for those who had voted for the 1793 constitution; this is considered a Left–Right alliance aimed at ending the *gouvernement révolutionnaire*

2/20 June: the secretariat of Robespierre's police bureau is expanded

7/25 June: Robespierre orders the arrest of the comité révolutionnaire of the Indivisibilité *section*, which included two agents of the CSG, for 'immorality'

8/26 June: decisive victory of Fleurus

9/27 June: Payan urges Robespierre to restrict the role of the CSG and unify 'moral as well as physical government'

10/28 June: the CSG closes the Montagne *section*'s register which has attracted 10,000 signatures

10/11, night of: Saint-Just arrives at the CSP with news of Fleurus

11/29 June: Hanriot ordered to send the gunners from the Poissonière *section* to Brest

12 or 13/30 June or 1 July: Carnot calls Robespierre a dictator and criticizes his running of the police bureau. Finding his directives in the police bureau increasingly blocked, Robespierre secretly secedes from the CSP. He has already ceased attending the Convention

13/1 July: Robespierre hints to the Jacobins that he may resign from the CSP. Freed from Robespierre's surveillance, Carnot establishes artillery parks at Givet and Douai as a pretext to move larger numbers of 'gunners'.

21/9 July: The CSG orders the release of the Indivisibilité *section*'s officials. Robespierre starts attending the Jacobins assiduously from now until 8 thermidor

23/11 July: Dubois-Crancé expelled from the Jacobins at the instigation of Couthon and Robespierre

24/12 July: artillery companies from the Temple and Muséum *sections* ordered to the artillery camp at Givet. Payan tells the Commune that *gouvernement révolutionnaire* must continue until all *internal* enemies have been destroyed

26/14 July: Fouché is expelled from the Jacobin Club. Widespread 'fraternal banquets' held in Paris to mark the fifth anniversary of the storming of the Bastille and the recent victories

28/16 July: in the Jacobins Robespierre attacks the '*repas fraternels*'. Robespierre denounces Carnot's ally, Pille, of the commission for troops movements, in the Jacobins

Thermidor

2/20 July: Barère denounces provincial lobbying and Paris is declared a 'ville close'. Carnot launches the *Soirée du camp*

5/23 July: Robespierre attends a continuation of the joint session of the CSP and the CSG. His colleagues erroneously believe a deal has been done. The Commune publishes a 'maximum des salaires'

7/25 July: a Jacobin deputation to the Convention denounces ridiculing of the state religion and sending gunners to the front. The Commune gets permission from the CSP to convoke the general assemblies of the *sections* to rehearse arrangements for Barra and Viala festival

8/26 July: Robespierre addresses the Convention and repeats his speech to the Jacobins; dress rehearsal for the Barra and Viala festival scheduled

9/27 July: arrest of Robespierre; insurrection organized by the Commune

10/28 July: capture of the Commune; execution of the Robespierristes

# MAPS

Map 1. The departmental framework, 1790–94
After Jones, Colin, *The Longman Companion to the French Revolution* (Longman, 1988)

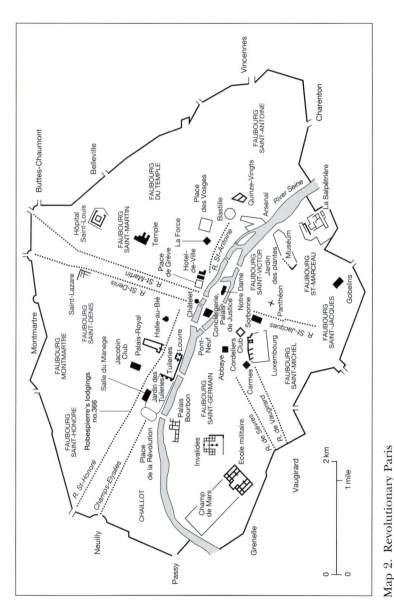

Map 2. Revolutionary Paris
After Jones, Colin, *The Longman Companion to the French Revolution* (Longman, 1988)

# INDEX

**Viot**, François, judge 142, 145
Voulland, Jean Henri, member
   of CSG 158, 195

Washington, George 9

York, Frederick Augustus, Duke
   of 93, 105, 121
Ysabeau, Claude Alexandre,
   deputy 125, 126, 151,
   153